The Modern Supernatural and the Beginnings
of Cinema

Murray Leeder

The Modern Supernatural and the Beginnings of Cinema

Murray Leeder
Calgary, Alberta, Canada

ISBN 978-1-349-84456-2   ISBN 978-1-137-58371-0 (eBook)
DOI 10.1057/978-1-137-58371-0

Library of Congress Control Number: 2016959382

© The Editor(s) (if applicable) and The Author(s) 2017
Softcover reprint of the hardcover 1st edition 2017 978-1-137-58370-3
The author(s) has/have asserted their right(s) to be identified as the author(s) of this work in accordance with the Copyright, Designs and Patents Act 1988.
This work is subject to copyright. All rights are solely and exclusively licensed by the Publisher, whether the whole or part of the material is concerned, specifically the rights of translation, reprinting, reuse of illustrations, recitation, broadcasting, reproduction on microfilms or in any other physical way, and transmission or information storage and retrieval, electronic adaptation, computer software, or by similar or dissimilar methodology now known or hereafter developed.
The use of general descriptive names, registered names, trademarks, service marks, etc. in this publication does not imply, even in the absence of a specific statement, that such names are exempt from the relevant protective laws and regulations and therefore free for general use.
The publisher, the authors and the editors are safe to assume that the advice and information in this book are believed to be true and accurate at the date of publication. Neither the publisher nor the authors or the editors give a warranty, express or implied, with respect to the material contained herein or for any errors or omissions that may have been made.

Cover image © Granger Historical Picture Archive/Alamy Stock Photo

Printed on acid-free paper

This Palgrave Macmillan imprint is published by Springer Nature
The registered company is Macmillan Publishers Ltd.
The registered company address is: The Campus, 4 Crinan Street, London, N1 9XW, United Kingdom

Dedicated to Alana and Julian

Acknowledgements

This book builds on my dissertation, "Early Cinema and the Supernatural," defended at Carleton University in 2011. Many thanks first of all to my supervisor, Charles O'Brien, and my other committee members: Marc Furstenau, Franny Nudelman, Aboubakar Sanogo and Rob King.

I would like to give special thanks to various professors from Carleton University's Film Studies programme and from the Institute for Comparative Studies in Literature, Arts and Culture, including André Loiselle, Mitchell Frank, Barbara Leckie, Barbara Gabriel, Mitsuyo Wada-Marciano, Paul Théberge, George McKnight, Mark Langer, Zuzana Pick and Chris Faulkner for their help and support over the years, as well my fellow students, including Owen Lyons, David Richler, Margaret Rose, Steve Rifkin, Jessica Aldred, Marc Raymond, Ben Wright, Dan Sheridan, Sylvie and Paul Jasen, Heather Igloliorte, Matt Croombs, Jeremy Maron, Stacey Loyer, Anne de Stecher, Danielle Wiley, Tom Everett and Kyle Devine.

I would also like to thank my colleagues from the University of Manitoba (including George Toles, Brenda Austin-Smith and David Annandale) and the University of Calgary (including Lee Carruthers, Charles Tepperman and Ryan Pierson).

Many other scholars have kindly helped this project along the way with useful advice. I would like especially to thank Simone Natale, James Cahill, Matthew Solomon, Frank Gray, Esther Peeren, Pamela Thurschwell, Jeffrey Sconce, Adam Hart, Colin Williamson, Brian Jacobson, John Warne Monroe and Tom Gunning.

My work has benefited from the recent explosion in archival material from early cinema on DVD. Special credit must go to the Flicker Alley's wonderful boxed set *Georges Méliès: First Wizard of the Cinema (1896–1913)* (2008) and its follow-up *Georges Méliès: Encore* (2010) with newer discoveries—may there be many more "encores" to follow. Other films, especially those of George Albert Smith, I viewed at the British Film Institute in London, largely on 35 mm with a few on VHS. My research into print documents and rare books and periodicals took me to the archives of the Society for Psychical Research, housed in the Cambridge University library, the Harry Price Collection at the University of London, the reading room of the Magic Circle in London and the American Society for Psychical Research in Manhattan. Many thanks to the archivists and librarians at these venues for their support and enthusiasm. I would also like to thank Donna Yates for generously hosting me during the Cambridge leg of my research.

Portions of Chaps. 5 and 6 expand upon writing previously published as "Eroticism and Death: The Skeleton in the Trick Film" in *Beyond the Screen: Institutions, Networks and Publics of Early Cinema* (2012) and Chap. 7 is an edited version of "'Visualizing the Phantoms of the Imagination': Projecting the Haunted Minds of Modernity," published in *Cinematic Ghosts: Haunting and Spectrality from Silent Cinema to the Digital Era* (2015). My thanks to John Libbey and to Bloomsbury Academic USA for permission to reprint.

Contents

1 Introduction   1

2 The Haunting of Film Theory   21

3 Light and Lies: Screen Practice and (Super-) Natural Magic   45

4 The Strange Case of George Albert Smith: Mesmerism, Psychical Research and Cinema   67

5 Aesthetics of Co-registration: Spirit Photography, X-rays and Cinema   97

6 Méliès's Skeleton: Gender, Cinema's *Danse Macabre* and the Erotics of Bone   135

7 "Living Pictures at Will": Projecting Haunted Minds   173

8 Conclusion: Lost Worlds, Ghost Worlds   191

Index   201

List of Figures

Image 3.1	A depiction of Robertson's Phantasmagoria that appeared in *L'Optique* by "Fulgence Marion"—actually Camille Flammarion (1869)	51
Image 3.2	A depiction of Pepper's Ghost that appeared in *L'Optique* by "Fulgence Marion"—actually Camille Flammarion (1869)	54
Image 5.1	The alleged New Zealand ghost horses, reprinted in *Borderland* in 1896	101
Image 5.2	Illustrations of the magic trick called "The Neoöccultism," 1897	110
Image 5.3	Illustrations of the magic trick called "The Neoöccultism," 1897	111
Image 5.4	An advertisement for "Les Rayons Röntgen" stage act, 1897	112
Image 5.5	Promotional postcard from the Paris *Cabaret du Néant*, c. 1895	113
Image 5.6	Promotional postcard from the Paris *Cabaret du Néant*, c. 1895	113
Image 5.7	Depiction of the Paris *Cabaret du Néant* from W.C. Morrow's *Bohemian Paris of To-day* (1896)	114
Image 5.8	Depiction of transformation trick from New York *Cabaret du Néant* from *Scientific American*, 1896	115
Image 5.9	Depiction of transformation trick from New York *Cabaret du Néant* from *Scientific American*, 1896	116
Image 5.10	An apparent reference to the *Cabaret du Néant* in Bram Stoker's *Dracula* (1992)	118
Image 5.11	George Albert Smith's *The X-ray Fiend* (1896)	121

Image 6.1	Georges Méliès's *The Vanishing Lady* (1896)	136
Image 6.2	Georges Méliès's *The Vanishing Lady* (1896)	137
Image 6.3	Georges Méliès's *The Vanishing Lady* (1896)	138
Image 6.4	Georges Méliès's *The Vanishing Lady* (1896)	139
Image 6.5	William Crookes with "Katie King" in 1874	151
Image 6.6	Promotional postcard from the Paris *Cabaret du Néant*, c. 1895	154
Image 6.7	"Miss November" from the EIZO's pin-up skeletons calendar (2010)	163
Image 7.1	David Starr Jordan's "Sympsychograph" (1896)	178
Image 8.1	The face of loss: from *The Lost World of Mitchell and Kenyon* (BBC, Episode 1, 2005)	194

CHAPTER 1

Introduction

In the October 1896 issue of his quarterly journal *Borderland*, W.T. Stead, the well-known British spiritualist and "new journalist," offered a dozen pages worth of "Suggestions from Science for Psychic Students: Useful Analogies from Recent Discoveries and Inventions." The "Borderland" to which the periodical's name referred straddles the realms of science and the supernatural, and "Suggestions from Science for Psychic Students" was meant to arm the faithful with analogies to convince people of the validity of spiritualist concepts about life and death, time and space. Stead's analogies come from electricity, the phonograph, the telephone, the photograph and the camera obscura, but also from the X-ray and the kinetoscope, the early motion picture exhibition device that the Edison Manufacturing Company had debuted in 1894. The article begins:

> The discovery of the Röntgen rays has compelled many a hardened sceptic to admit, when discussing Borderland, that "there may be something in it after all." In like manner many of the latest inventions and scientific discoveries make psychic phenomena thinkable, even by those who have no personal experience of their own to compel conviction. I string together a few of these helpful analogies, claiming only that they at least supply stepping stones that may lead to a rational understanding of much that is now incomprehensible. (1896, 400)

This is an excellent example of how clearly and consciously the spiritualist movement of the nineteenth century recognized its own peculiar relationship with new technologies and drew consciously on scientific rhetoric.[1] Spiritualists like Stead argued that psychic powers and contact with the dead did not seem so far removed from the modern wonders of science and technology, cinema included.[2]

We will return to Stead's "Suggestions from Science for Psychic Students" in Chap. 7, but for the moment will observe that it illustrates how new technologies, including those of recording and projection, helped make the spiritualists' ghost worlds that much more tangible and plausible. In Stead's article we see one case where cinema's first observers were inclined characterize it as a supernatural medium. The most famous instance of this, which I will discuss at length in Chap. 2, is Maxim Gorky's declaration that the Lumière brothers' films represented "the kingdom of shadows," a sort of storehouse for the unhappy dead: "Noiselessly, the ashen-grey foliage of the trees sways in the wind, and the grey silhouettes of the people, as though condemned to eternal silence and cruelly punished by being deprived of all the colours of life, glide noiselessly along the grey ground" (1960, 407). Gorky's gloomy reaction stands in contrast with that of the French reporter who asserted in 1895 that "when these cameras are made available to the public, when everyone can photograph their dear ones, no longer in a motionless form but in their movements, their activity, their familiar gestures, with words on their lips, death will have ceased to be absolute" (quoted in Burch 1990, 21),[3] but in a way they stand as complementary opposites, one promising immortality and the other a gloomy netherworld between life and death.

This book, *The Modern Supernatural and the Beginnings of Cinema*, locates late Victorian interest in supernatural phenomena as an important context for early cinema,[4] but one that is often misunderstood. The overarching question explored here is a broadly cultural one: why did such a compulsive desire to link the cinema with the supernatural exist in the late 1800s? This was not only the case for outsiders like Gorky, struck by the first encounter with the apparatus. Such metaphors also served people within the nascent film industry. In fact, the kinetoscope's inventor, W.K.L. Dickson, used séance metaphors to describe cinema in his book *The History of the Kinetograph, Kinetoscope and Kinetophonograph* (1895),[5] and one early projector, premiered by Francis Jenkins and Thomas Armat at the Cotton States Exposition in Atlanta, in October 1895, bore a name that would seem to promise ghost-viewing, or perhaps seeing through ghostly means: "Phantoscope" (Rossell 1998, 120–6). These were natural analogies to use in the supernatural-obsessed late nineteenth century.

Supernatural scenarios allowed pioneering trick filmmakers like Georges Méliès in France and George Albert Smith in England, and the whole marvellous body of trick films that followed (including the stock "haunted hotel" scenario of a traveller entering a haunted space and being beset by creepy phenomena), to show off the capacity of the medium for wonderful appearances and disappearances, animations and transformations. It can fairly be said, to quote Pamela Thurschwell, that "early cinematic ghosts were created in part because the technology available motivated their production" (2003, 26), but also that audience demand motivated supernatural-themed material. Nuanced attention to the Victorian understanding of the supernatural allows us to better understand the reception of cinema's apparent capacity to both arrest and reanimate life, its ghostly status as a half-present medium of projected light or its capacity to dematerialize and transform the human body through trick effects.

In addition to excavating early cinema's links with the late Victorian supernatural, *The Modern Supernatural and the Beginnings of Cinema* both contributes to and examines what has come to be called the "spectral turn": the concerted interest in questions of the supernatural, ghostliness and haunting within cultural and critical theory during the last two decades, the most influential work of which is Jacques Derrida's *Specters of Marx* (2006; first published in French 1992, English translation 1993). I am indebted to this body of scholarship and the freedom it has promoted to engage with issues of ghosts and magic, but at the same time I express scepticism and caution about its claims, and especially the way it has tended to look to early cinema to prove claims about cinema as a "ghostly" or "supernatural" medium. The association of early cinema with the supernatural is an important subject, but the trope of cinema in general and early cinema in particular as a haunted, spectral or magical space has been deployed in scholarship with too little attention to historical specifics—often relying on generalized and ahistorical invocations of the supernatural. While the vogue for looking back to early cinema to understand media culture today often produces valuable insights, it can also produce misconceptions about early cinema, particularly where early cinema's links to the supernatural are concerned. In particular, there is a tendency to overstate cinema's novelty and efface its continuities with prior media, and I argue that, where its links with the supernatural are concerned, early cinema's place on a lineage of haunted and haunting media is at least as important as its newness.

The Modern Supernatural

What can we mean by a "modern supernatural"? Both of these terms require some clarification. Throughout this book, I use the term "supernatural" broadly enough to encompass practices and discourses as far ranging as spiritualism, occultism,[6] psychical research and stage magic.[7] However, I am using it advisedly, aware of its controversial potential. In 2003, *Anthropological Forum* devoted a special issue to the question of whether "supernatural" is a viable term, in the process debating its relationship to such categories as "sacred," "holy," "divine," "spiritual," "mystical," "mysterious," "paranormal," "extrasensory," "miraculous," "transcendent," "religious," "magical" and "superstition," to borrow the lexicon assembled by Susan Sered in her afterword (2003, 216–17)—we can add terms like "sorcery" and "occult." I find this journal's discussion of terminology and its implications quite useful; anthropologists seem to be among the only scholars concerned with defining the "supernatural" at all. Various scholars in this special issue come out for or against the continued value of "supernatural" as a term, and I am tentatively borrowing my working definition from one of the "pro" camp: "The term 'supernatural' defines an order of existence beyond what is pragmatically visible and observable, an order of existence that is paranormal in the sense that it supposedly defies the laws of nature" (Anderson 2003, 125). I would place particular emphasis on the word "supposedly," and note that the definition uses "paranormal"—a word of twentieth-century coinage—to define the older term "supernatural." One of the reasons for the contentiousness of the term "supernatural" within anthropology is its implicit validation of western superiority. Morton Klass writes of the:

> remorseless unavoidable ethnocentric judgment of *supernatural*: that there is on the one hand a natural—real—universe and on the other hand there are notions about aspects of the universe that are situated outside the natural and the real and are therefore labeled supernatural by the person who *knows* what belongs in which category. (1995, 25, original emphasis)

The idea and the terminology of the supernatural can indeed be imperialistic and reductive, with belief in the supernatural often consigned to those on the margins: women, children, "savages," the superstitious lower classes, the rural and so on. Further complicating the terminology, advocates of supernatural concepts such as telepathy or the existence of ghosts or the human soul believe that these things are in fact not supernatural at all, but natural; for this reason, spiritualists frequently denounced the very word "supernatural" (Connor 1999, 204). The word itself is thus problematic, but I believe still the best available.

Significantly, the word itself undergoes a transformation closely linked with the modern era. The word derives from the Latin *supernaturalis*, meaning "above or beyond nature," and was usually associated with religion before the beginning of the nineteenth century, when a more secular usage, associated with ghosts and the like, began to predominate. This shift in the meaning roughly corresponds to Terry Castle's (1995) constellation of the late eighteenth century as the period of the "invention of the uncanny." Castle locates the invention of the uncanny with the internalization of the supernatural into the mind, where once external forces were turned into phantasmic "inner pictures" (1995, 132). The modern experience of the supernatural, then, often involves layers of intellectual hesitation, so often framed in optical terms—is what I am seeing "real" or is it all in my head?—which are in turn linked to a set of issues about illusionism in cinema and the centuries of screen practice before it.

So what is the "modern supernatural"? The hundred years prior to cinema's debut saw a major reconfiguration of the supernatural. It was modernized and scientificized,[8] and by 1895, the year of cinema's public debut, that process was complete. Magicians reframed their tricks as "experiments," spiritualism (often pointedly calling itself "Modern Spiritualism," simultaneously suggesting an ancient lineage and promoting its own currency) promoted itself as a scientific religion for a new rational era, and psychical researchers saw their grandest project as finding scientific evidence for the human soul and thus protecting religion from the agnostic likes of John Tyndall and T.H. Huxley (Blum 2006, 263–4).[9] Amid these blurring boundaries of faith and science, the new wave of Gothic literature, including famous novels and short fiction by H. Rider Haggard, H.G. Wells, Robert Louis Stevenson, Oscar Wilde, Henry James and Bram Stoker, was itself heavily indebted to the new science of psychical research; in these works we often find that "science is Gothicized, and gothicity is rendered scientifically plausible" (Hurley 1996, 20).[10]

This intimate relationship between science and the supernatural is clearly attested to by some of the earliest writings on cinema. One excellent example is V.E. Johnson's December 1896 article "The Kinematograph from a Scientific Point of View." Johnston writes:

> The Kinematograph having literally at its birth been dragged into the service of the omnipotent music hall ... its scientific value is likely to be obscured, if not temporarily lost—a misfortune which every earnest worker in science should, I think, do his utmost to avert ... In meteorology, isolated photographs of a storm or storm clouds, or the results of a whirlwind, are held in high esteem, but how much more valuable would be a series showing such a storm of whirlwind in action? ... Photographs of machinery at rest in all its diversified branches are of the greatest value both in business and in the education of students—how much more valuable will be photographs—faithfully representing its wonderful and oftentimes complicated movements? (1996, 25)

Johnson endorses cinema's value as a mechanical tool for science's benefit in place of its status as a means of public entertainment, but nevertheless closes his article with a magical analogy:

> When King Roderick first visited the necromantic tower of Toledo—or at least so runs legendary history—he beheld on the linen cloth taken by him from the coffer the painted figures of men on horseback of fierce demeanor; anon the picture became animated, and there at length appeared a depiction upon its magic surface a great field of battle with Christians and Moslems engaged in deadly conflict, accompanied with the clash of arms, the braying of trumpets, the neighing of horses. Can the imagination conceive that which the mind of science cannot execute? (1996, 25)

The identification of cinema as a valuable new technology and the understanding of it as the heir apparent to supernatural traditions coexist easily for commentators like Johnson. We might do well to recall Arthur C. Clarke's Third Law: "any sufficiently advanced technology is indistinguishable from magic" (1962, 36), or the corollary often attributed to Larry Niven: "any sufficiently advanced magic is indistinguishable from technology."[11] For the Victorians, cinema was one of the best feats of magic (or supernatural conjurations) to have ever come along.

Scholars of recent decades have explored the significance of magical and spiritualist practices to media history more broadly. Jeffrey Sconce's *Haunted Media: Electronic Presence from Telegraphy to Television* (2000) examines how supernatural, metaphysical and otherwise *outré* metaphors have served to help make new media technologies legible to their first users. More than this, Sconce argues that our very ideas about what constitutes the supernatural at a given historical moment have everything to do with the media of the time; he persuasively interprets, for instance, the spiritualist movement as originating in the 1840s as an unexpected outgrowth of the invention of the telegraph. Sconce focuses on such media of transmission as the telegraph, the radio, television and the internet, but cinema too is a "haunted" medium, a fact recognized both by some of its first commentators and by a body of literature in film studies. Cinema is surely not the only supernatural technology, nor even the *most* supernatural, but if, as John Durham Peters provocatively puts it, "[e]very new medium is a machine for the production of ghosts" (1999, 139), it must have supernatural particularities of its own. Of course, early cinema overlapped in fundamental ways with other media, and this book attends to some of these connections as well, most notably in relation to cinema's near-twin, the X-ray. Simon During's *Modern Enchantments: The Cultural Power of Secular Magic* (2002) rests on the simple but profound premise that "magic has helped shape modern culture" (2002, 1).[12] During proposes that, "once we fully recognize magic's role as a cultural agent, our sensitivity to the play of puzzlement, fictiveness and contingency in modernity will be heightened" (2002, 2). Just as our understanding of modernity is transformed by attention to the supernatural, so too will our understanding of cinema—so often understood as one of the emblematic technologies of modernity.[13]

What role does the supernatural play in modernity? Alan Swingewood writes that modernity "is imbricated in Enlightenment reason, the belief in progress, empirical science and positivism. Modernity signifies a culture of innovation, a rational ethos challenging traditions and rituals in the name of critical thought, empirical knowledge and humanism" (1998, 138). But the face of modernity Swingewood (1998) describes is merely one aspect of the complex, contradictory character of modernity that other scholars have emphasized (Calinescu 1987; Pels 2003). Writing about the "second phase" of modernity that encompasses the nineteenth century, Marshall Berman emphasizes both ordering and chaotic facets:

> This is a new landscape of steam engines, automatic factories, railroads, vast new industrial zones; of teeming cities that have grown overnight, often with dreadful human consequences; of daily newspapers, telegraphs, telephones and other mass media; of increasingly strong national states and multinational aggregations of capital; of mass social movements fighting these modernizations from above with their own modes of modernization from below; of an ever-expanding world market embracing all, capable of

the most spectacular growth, capable of appalling waste and devastation, capable of everything except solidity and stability. (1983, 19)

We should not be surprised that such a tumultuous and contradictory time proved a fertile environment for speculations about the supernatural to flourish. As Marina Warner has written:

> modernity did not by any means put an end to the quest for spirit and the desire to explain its mystery: curiosity about spirits of every sort ... and the ideas and imagery that communicate their nature have flourished more vigorously than ever, when the modern fusion of scientific inquiry, psychology, and metaphysics began. (2006, 10)

Mladen Dolar similarly asserts that, "Ghosts, vampires, monsters, the undead dead, etc., flourish in an era when you might expect them to be dead and buried, without a place. They are something brought about by modernity itself" (1991, 7). If "modernity and enchantment have been perceived to be dichotomous in much of Western theory" (McEwan 2008, 31), the counter-tradition described by During, Warner and others argues for more of a dialectical relationship, in which modernity is not so much the "disenchantment of the world" described by Max Weber but, on the contrary, part of the world's re-enchantment (see Chap. 3).

The view of modernity as multifaceted and dialectical has recently been taken up by thinkers on early cinema, an area where the debates on the value of modernity have raged perhaps to the point of an impasse.[14] In "Modernity and Cinema: A Culture of Shocks and Flows" (2006), Tom Gunning offers a significant revision of the formulation he first popularized in his "Cinema of Attractions" essay (1990). Gunning writes that his previous work tended to "[emphasize] what Marshall Berman might have called the 'dissolving' aspects of modernity: its discontinuity, its sense of confrontation and shock, its explosive nature, its speed and disorientation" (2006, 309). But such an emphasis, Gunning argues, marginalizes another dimension of modernity that emphasizes standardization, organization and rationalization. With both aspects under consideration, modernity emerges as Janus-faced, looking at once towards chaos and order—the titular shock and flow. Drawing on Wolfgang Schivelbusch (1986), Gunning uses the railway as an emblematic example. Railroad travel was rapid and comfortable. It was a much smoother means of transportation than the stagecoach, with its bumpy roads and unpredictable schedules. A train could handle many more passengers at once than its competitors, and allowed passengers to ride in comfort and class. A traveller could read and socialize. In many ways, rail was the representative modern form of transportation—rational, systematic, fast and efficient. But passengers knew the ever-present danger of railroad crashes that could inflict trauma on an enormous scale. The train ride embodies the dialectic between the forces of rationalization and organization and those of dissolution and chaos. Both are modern (Gunning 2006, 310).[15]

So how can it be that magicians, spiritualists, psychical researchers and so many others made such blatant appeals to science and post-Enlightenment rationality to explain, contextualize or justify ghosts, magic, telepathy and other such phenomena? If we understand modernity in the dialectical terms Gunning proposes, this dynamic seems not only unsurprising, but also inevitable. Cinema, according to Gunning's revised formulation, is best understood as partaking of both the shock and the flow of modernity. If early cinema was dominated by displays and shocks of many kinds (Gunning's "Cinema of Attractions"), post-1910 cinema would turn towards the rationalizing face of modernity, with narrative as a stabilizing force that ushers in the factory-style industrial mode of production and thus regularizes cinema's main product. But that chaotic other face remains. Gunning (2006) ultimately argues that a nuanced conception of modernity needs to acknowledge both its dissolving and stabilizing faces. Ben Singer offers a similar revision of his understanding of modernity in the 2009 essay "The Ambimodernity of Early Cinema": "Modernity is better understood as a heterogeneous arena of modern and counter-modern impulses, yielding cultural expressions that reflected both ends of the spectrum, along with, and perhaps more frequently, ambivalent or ambiguous positions in between" (2009, 38). These multifaceted, multidirectional conceptions of modernity suggest ways of addressing the question of why the most modern and rational societies always seem to have such a fascination with the magical, the supernatural and the occult.

And what of modernism? Berman defines "modernism" as "any attempt by modern men and women to become subjects as well as objects of modernization, to get a grip on the modern world and make themselves at home in it" (1983, 5). By this definition, most of the personages dealt with herein qualify as modernists, be they magicians modernizing their acts by appealing to science, spiritualists delighted by the potential of new technologies to access invisible worlds, psychical researchers applying an experimental model to supernatural phenomena or early filmmakers drawing on the stock of supernatural concepts available to them to provide material for their new medium. They are all probably most readily allied with "popular modernism" (Daly 1999) or "vernacular modernism" (Hansen 1999), though many of the canonical figures of high modernism, from such writers as Ezra Pound, T.S. Eliot and Mina Loy, to artists like Max Ernst and Marcel Duchamp and intellectuals like Sigmund Freud and Henri Bergson, had their own dabblings (and sometimes more) with spiritualism and occultism. The cultural reach of the supernatural went well beyond those who believed in it, per se; as Helen Sword writes, "even confirmed sceptics such as [James] Joyce, D.H. Lawrence and Virginia Woolf, while shunning spiritualist practice, routinely filled their fiction, poetry and essays with mediums, ghosts, séances, disembodied voices, and other invocations of the living dead" (n, x).[16]

Taking Up the Ghost

The entanglements of early cinema with the modern supernatural can be explored from any number of angles, and this book, *The Modern Supernatural and the Beginnings of Cinema*, does not claim to be exhaustive. It does, however, attempt to provide an important backstory to current debates about cinema's "supernatural," "magical" or "ghostly" properties, testing the claims of these theoretical debates against historical evidence. The central question of *The Modern Supernatural and the Beginnings of Cinema* may be phrased as something like "What conditions made early cinema's supernatural associations possible?" Why did early cinema inspire supernatural associations by commentators like Stead, Gorky and Johnson, and by those filmmakers who gravitated towards supernatural scenarios? One way to explain any supernatural qualities that cinema was recognized as possessing in its first years is through recourse to its newness, its status as a novel and wondrous new medium. I do not discount this explanation for cinema's supernatural affinities entirely, but it does not fully satisfy me. Rather, I suggest throughout this book that we can understand cinema's supernatural qualities not only through its newness but also through its continuities with some of the innumerable technologies and practices that anticipated it.

Chapter 2, "The Haunting of Film Theory," deals with the understanding of cinema as a haunted medium by such early film theorists as Ricciotto Canudo, Antonin Artaud, Jean Epstein and Béla Balázs, and the revival of this understanding in the aforementioned "spectral turn."

This chapter argues that the spectral turn, which draws from the supernatural a set of powerful discursive metaphors, has tended to mistake historically contingent aspects of cinema for essential attributes.

Having established the theoretical contexts for the book's discussion of early cinema and the supernatural, subsequent chapters try to reclaim its original context in a variety of ways. Chapter 3, "Light and Lies: Screen Practice and (Super-) Natural Magic," examines the entanglement of the supernatural and "screen practice" in a longer history leading up to the cinema. From the magic lantern, and the Phantasmagoria's complex dynamics of demystification and mystification, through the theatrical illusions of Pepper's Ghost and the ghost show in the latter half of the nineteenth century, the fascination with the supernatural implications of the projected image has a long history before cinema's debut, which helps illuminate cinema's own supernatural affinities.

Chapter 4, "The Strange Case of George Albert Smith: Mesmerism, Psychical Research and Cinema," offers a biographical examination of the relationship of cinema and the supernatural by following the unique career trajectory of a pioneering British filmmaker. Smith started as a Brighton stage performer whose thought-transference act brought him the attention of the fledgling Society for Psychical Research (SPR). After spending more than a decade working for the SPR in a variety of capacities, he returned to Brighton and made some of the most innovative films of the time, including a variety of trick films that clearly drew on his prior professions.

Chapter 5, "Aesthetics of Co-registration: Spirit Photography, X-rays and Cinema," broadens its focus outward from cinema to examine the supernatural implications of two photographic practices adjacent to cinema: spirit photography and X-ray photography. The chapter argues that both share an aesthetic principle whereby various layers of information are collapsed onto a single plane, which they share with cinematic double-exposure techniques. This aesthetic would be central to the double-exposure techniques frequently used to represent ghosts in the silent era (and to a lesser extent, beyond it).

Chapter 6, "Méliès's Skeleton: Gender, Cinema's *Danse Macabre* and the Erotics of Bone," focuses on the prominence of the figure of the skeleton in entertainment in the 1890s. Skeletons are a particularly common sight in early cinema, especially in the trick films of Georges Méliès beginning with *The Vanishing Lady* (1896). This visibility can be explained on the one hand as a vestige of *danse macabre* traditions stretching back to the Middle Ages, and on the other as an offshoot of the X-ray's contemporaneous popularity. The chapter explains how both of these causes factored into the eroticization of the female skeleton in early cinema and the late Victorian cult of dead and dying women.

Chapter 7, "Living Pictures at Will: Projecting Haunted Minds," explores a triangular relationship between internal mental spaces, the supernatural and the trope of projection. It examines several nineteenth-century texts in which this connection is made manifest: Edward Bulwer-Lytton's 1859 novella "The Haunted and the Haunters," spiritualist/journalist W.T. Stead's 1896 writings about "The Kinetiscope of the Mind" and David Starr Jordan's 1896 sympsychography hoax.

The conclusion, "Lost Worlds, Ghost Worlds," offers some final thoughts on the current fascination with the supernatural qualities of early cinema, linking it to the narrative of the "lostness" of that era of cinema.

Notes

1. The "technological" character of modern spiritualism has been explored by numerous scholars, including Swatos (1990), Peters (1999, esp. 94–101, 137–44), Sconce (2000, esp. 21–58) and Noakes (2004). Martyn Jolly writes that, "The spiritualists were modernists. They understood the phenomena they witnessed, and believed in, to be part of the same unfolding story of progress as science and technology" (2006, 143).
2. For more on Stead's occult explorations in particular, see Luckhurst (2004) and Sausman (2012).
3. Compare the account of another 1896 French journalist, Jean Badreux: "the Lumière brothers … have found a way to revive the dead … Science has triumphed over death" (quoted in Solomon 2010, 12).
4. In the past few decades this term has largely displaced "primitive cinema" to describe cinema before roughly the mid 1910s and the standardization of the feature-length narrative films as the industry's key product.
5. The book was co-authored with his sister Antonia. Matthew Solomon (2010) explores the rhetoric of the supernatural in the Dicksons' book, arguing that it borrows from exposures of spiritualism done by stage magicians (2010, 16–20). W.K.L. Dickson's employer, Thomas Edison, was himself a point of obsession for

some spiritualists. An 1884 article in *Light* argued that Edison's feat of sending electricity through a vacuum was great evidence of "how science is tending towards the spiritualism ... Spiritualists should be in the front ranks of learning in every department of knowledge in the great school of nature" (Allen 1884, 512) and a 1896 letter in *Banner of Light* insisted that Edison was a medium whose (perhaps unconscious) grand project was contacting the spirit world (Eggleston 1896, 1).

6. The Victorian occult revival, conventionally dated to the foundation of the Hermetic Order of the Golden Dawn in 1888, plays only a background role in this text. For excellent overviews, I would refer any reader to such sources as Washington (1995), Owen (2004), Gunn (2011), Drury (2011), Butler (2011) and Wilson (2013).
7. I have ruled out "paranormal" as a viable substitute because it is of twentieth-century coinage. I confess that it does some injustice to complex terms like "magic" to subsume them under "supernatural."
8. Among important scholarship on the relationship of science and the supernatural in modern culture which is not otherwise mentioned here, is Briggs (1977), Finucane (1982), Gunning (1995a), Grove (1997), Davis (1998), Marvin (1988), Vanderbeke (2006), Morrisson (2007), Brower (2010) and Lachapelle (2011, 2015).
9. This process is related to the professionalization of science that, according to John Limon, was complete by 1860. Prior to that time, one could "drop everything and become a scientist" (1990, 5), but in time science became an occulted process inaccessible to the average man. See also Knight (1986).
10. See also Luckhurst (2005, xix). For "cinematic" imagery in Gothic literature, see Williams (2007) and Foster (2015).
11. Clarke's famous words are quoted or paraphrased in a great many places, including within fictional narratives. Lex Luthor (Kevin Spacey) quotes them in *Superman Returns* (2006) (see Evans 2010, 590), as does Jane Foster (Natalie Portman) in *Thor* (2011). A 2011 *Star Trek* tie-in novel by David A. McIntee bears the title *Indistinguishable from Magic*, and James Cameron once described the impact his special effects in *The Abyss* (1989) had on an audience by evoking Clarke's Third Law, stating that it represents "how

it's supposed to be—for the audience ... The sufficiently advanced technology had become magic to them" (1992, 262).
12. More recent and more film-oriented takes on magic include Solomon (2010) and Williamson (2015).
13. Others would include the locomotive, phonograph, telegraph, typewriter, phonograph, telephone and automobile. Important sources on modernity not otherwise cited in this introduction include Kern (1983), Clark (1984), Crary (1992) and Latour (1993). For useful overviews on thinking about cinema and modernity, see Furstenau and Hasslöcher (1994) and Murphet (2008).
14. See Gunning (1995a, 2006), Bordwell (1997), Singer (2001) and Keil (2004) for a back-and-forth between rival perspectives, a once-productive conversation giving way to a quarrel. For more accounts of modernity and cinema, see Gunning (1998), Hansen (1991, 1999), Friedberg (1993), Doane (1990, 2002), Christie (1994, 2009), Charney and Schwartz (1995), Kirby (1997), Schwartz (1998) and Singer (2009). For critical views, see Carroll (2001) and Turvey (2008).
15. The considerable significance of the train and early cinema has been explored by such scholars as Kirby (1997), Bottomore (1999), Loiperdinger (2004), Blümlinger (2006) and Elsaesser (2009).
16. See Bell (2012) and Wilson (2013) for other articulations of the role of magic and the supernatural in modern societies.

Works Cited

Allen, Milton. "Electrical Exhibition at Philadelphia." *Light* 4.205 (1884): 512.
Anderson, Robert. "Defining the Supernatural in Iceland." *Anthropological Forum* 13.2 (2003): 125–30.
Bell, Karl. *The Magical Imagination: Magic and Modernity in Urban England 1780–1914*. Cambridge: Cambridge University Press, 2012.
Berman, Marshall. *All That Is Solid Melts into Air: The Experience of Modernity*. London: Verso, 1983.
Blum, Deborah. *Ghost Hunters: William James and the Search for Scientific Proof of Life After Death*. New York: Penguin, 2006.
Blümlinger, Christa. "Lumière, the Train and the Avant-garde." *The Cinema of Attractions Reloaded*. Ed. Wanda Stauven. Amsterdam: University of Amsterdam Press, 2006. 245–64.

Bordwell, David. *On the History of Film Style*. Cambridge: Harvard University Press, 1997.
Bottomore, Stephen. "The Panicking Audience? Early Cinema and the 'Train Effect'." *Historical Journal of Film, Radio and Television* 19.2 (1999): 177–216.
Briggs, Julia. *Night Visitors: The Rise and Fall of the English Ghost Story*. London: Faber, 1977.
Brower, M. Brady. *Unruly Spirits: The Science of Psychic Phenomena in Modern France*. Urbana: University of Chicago Press, 2010.
Burch, Noël. *Life to Those Shadows*. Berkeley: University of California Press, 1990.
Butler, Alison. *Victorian Occultism and the Making of Magic*. Houndmills, Basingstoke, Hants: Palgrave Macmillan, 2011.
Calinescu, Matei. *Five Faces of Modernity: Modernism, Avant-Garde, Decadence, Kitsch, Postmodernism*. Durham, NC: Duke University Press, 1987.
Cameron, James. "Effects Scene: Technology and Magic." *Cinefex* 51 (1992): 5–7.
Carroll, Noël. "Modernity and the Plasticity of Perception." *The Journal of Aesthetics and Art Criticism* 59.1 (2001): 11–7.
Castle, Terry. *The Female Thermometer: 18th Century and the Invention of the Uncanny*. New York: Oxford University Press, 1995.
Charney, Leo and Vanessa R. Schwartz, eds. *Cinema and the Invention of Modern Life*. Berkeley: University of California Press, 1995.
Christie, Ian. *The Last Machine: Early Cinema and the Birth of the Modern World*. London: British Film Institute/BBC Educational Developments, 1994.
Christie, Ian. "Moving-Picture Media and Modernity: Taking Intermediate and Ephemeral Forms Seriously." *Comparative Critic Studies* 6.3 (2009): 299–318.
Clark, T.J. *The Painting of Modern Life: Paris in the Art of Manet and His Followers*. Princeton: Princeton University Press, 1984.
Clarke, Arthur C. *Profiles of Magic: An Inquiry into the Limits of the Possible*. London: Orion, 1962.
Connor, Steven. "The Machine in the Ghost: Spiritualism, Technology and the 'Direct Voice.'" *Ghosts: Deconstruction, Psychoanalysis, History*. Eds. Peter Buse and Andrew Stott. New York: St. Martin's Press, 1999. 203–25.
Crary, Jonathan. *Techniques of the Observer: On Vision and Modernity in the 19th Century*. Cambridge, MA: The MIT Press, 1992.
Daly, Nicholas. *Modernism, Romance and the Fin de Siècle: Popular Fiction and British Culture*. Cambridge: Cambridge University Press, 1999.
Davis, Erik. *Techgnosis: Myth, Magic and Mysticism in the Age of Information*. New York: Harmony, 1998.
Dickson, W.K.L. and Antonia Dickson. *History of the Kinematograph, Kinetoscope and Kinetophonograph*. New York: Arno, 1895.
Doane, Mary Ann. *The Emergence of Cinematic Time: Modernity, Contingency, the Archive*. Cambridge, MA: Harvard University Press, 2002.

Doane, Mary Ann. "Information, Crisis, Catastrophe." *Logic of Television: Essays in Cultural Criticism*. Ed. Patricia Mellencamp. Bloomington: Indiana University Press, 1990. 222–39.

Dolar, Mladen. "'I Shall Be with You on Your Wedding-Night': Lacan and the Uncanny." *October* 58 (1991): 5–23.

Drury, Nevill. *Stealing Fire from Heaven: The Rise of Modern Western Magic*. Oxford: Oxford University Press, 2011.

During, Simon. *Modern Enchantments: The Cultural Power of Secular Magic*. Cambridge: Harvard University Press, 2002.

Eggleston, Thomas. "Is He Not a Medium?" *Banner of Light* (May 2, 1896): 1.

Elsaesser, Thomas. "Archaeologies of Interactivity: Early Cinema, Narrative and Spectatorship." *Film 1900: Technology, Perception, Culture*. Eds. Annemone Ligensa and Klaus Kreimeier. New Barnet, Herts: John Libbey Publishing, 2009. 9–22.

Evans, Nicola Jean. "Undoing the Magic? DVD Extras and the Pleasure Behind the Scenes." *Continuum: Journal of Media & Cultural Studies* 24.4 (August 2010): 587–600.

Finucane, R.C. *Appearances of the Dead: A Cultural History of Ghosts*. London: Junction Books, 1982.

Foster, Paul. "Kingdom of Shadows: *Fin-de-siècle* Gothic and Early Cinema." *Monstrous Media/Spectral Subjects: Imaging Gothic from the Nineteenth Century to the Present*. Eds. Fred Botting and Catherine Spooner. Manchester: Manchester University Press, 2015. 29–41.

Friedberg, Anne. *Window Shopping: Cinema and the Postmodern*. Berkeley: University of California Press, 1993.

Furstenau, Marc and Kerstin Hasslöcher. "Cinema/Modernism/Modernity: Towards an Archaeology of the Cinema." *European Journal for Semiotic Studies* 6.1–2 (1994): 253–305.

Gorky, Maxim. "A review of the Lumière programme at the Nizhni-Novgorod Fair," as printed in the Nizhegorodski listok, newspaper, July 4, 1896, and signed "I.M. Pacatus." Appendix 3 to Jay Leyda, *A History of the Russian and Soviet Film*. London: Unwin House, 1960. 407–9.

Grove, Allen W. "Röntgen's Ghosts: Photography, X-rays and the Victorian Imagination." *Literature and Medicine* 16.2 (Fall 1997): 141–73.

Gunn, Joshua. *Modern Occult Rhetoric: Mass Media and the Drama of Secrecy in the Twentieth Century*. Tuscaloosa: University of Alabama Press, 2011.

Gunning, Tom. "An Aesthetic of Astonishment: Early Film and the (In)Credulous Spectator." *Viewing Positions: Ways of Seeing Film*. Ed. Linda Williams. New Brunswick, NJ: Rutgers University Press, 1995b. 114–33.

Gunning, Tom. "The Cinema of Attractions: Early Film, Its Spectator and the Avant-Garde." *Early Cinema: Space, Frame, Narrative*. Eds. Thomas Elsaesser and Adam Barker. London: British Film Institute, 1990. 56–62.

Gunning, Tom. "Modernity and Cinema: A Culture of Shocks and Flows." *Cinema and Modernity*. Ed. Murray Pomerance. New Brunswick, NJ: Rutgers University Press, 2006. 297–315.
Gunning, Tom. "Phantom Images and Modern Manifestations: Spirit Photography, Magic Theatre, Trick Films and Photography's Uncanny." *Fugitive Images: From Photography to Video*. Ed. Patrice Petro. Bloomington: Indiana University Press, 1995a. 42–71.
Hansen, Miriam. *Babel and Babylon: Spectatorship in American Silent Film*. Cambridge, MA: Harvard University Press, 1991.
Hansen, Miriam. "The Mass Production of the Senses: Classical Cinema as Vernacular Modernism." *Modernism/Modernity* 6.2 (1999): 59–77.
Hurley, Kelly. *The Gothic Body: Sexuality, Materialism, and Degeneration at the Fin de Siecle*. Cambridge: Cambridge University Press, 1996.
Johnson, V.E. "The Kinematograph from a Scientific Point of View." *In the Kingdom of Shadows: A Companion to Early Cinema*. Eds. Colin Harding and Simon Popple. London: Cygnus Press, 1996. 25.
Jolly, Martyn. *Faces of the Dead: The Belief in Spirit Photography*. London: British Library, 2006.
Keil, Charlie. "'To Here from Modernity': Style, Historiography, and Transitional Cinema." *American Cinema's Transitional Era: Audiences, Institutions, Practices*. Ed. Charlie Keil and Shelley Stamp. Berkeley: University of California Press, 2004. 51–75.
Kern, Stephen. *The Culture of Time and Space 1880–1918*. Cambridge, MA: Harvard University Press, 1983.
Kirby, Lynne. *Parallel Tracks: The Railroad and Silent Cinema*. Durham: Duke University Press, 1997.
Klass, Morton. *Ordered Universes: Approaches to the Anthropology of Religion*. Boulder: Westview Press, 1995.
Knight, David. *The Age of Science: The Scientific World-view in the Nineteenth Century*. Oxford: Blackwell, 1986.
Lachapelle, Sofie. *Conjuring Science: A History of Scientific Entertainment and Stage Magic in Modern France*. Houndmills, Basingstoke, Hants: Palgrave Macmillan, 2015.
Lachapelle, Sofie. *Investigating the Supernatural: From Spiritism and Occultism to Psychical Research and Metaphysics in France, 1853–1931*. Baltimore: The Johns Hopkins University Press, 2011.
Latour, Bruno. *We Have Never Been Modern*. Cambridge, MA: Harvard University Press, 1993.
Limon, John. *The Place of Fiction in the Time of Science: A Disciplinary History of American Writing*. New York: Cambridge University Press, 1990.
Loiperdinger, Martin. "Lumière's *Arrival of a Train*: Cinema's Founding Myth." *The Moving Image* 4.1 (Spring 2004): 89–118.

Luckhurst, Roger. "Introduction." *Late Victorian Gothic Tales*. Ed. Roger Luckhurst. Oxford: Oxford University Press, 2005. ix–xxxi.
Luckhurst, Roger. "W.T. Stead's Occult Economies." *Culture and Science in the Nineteenth-century Media*. Eds. Louise Henson, Geoffrey Cantor, Goean Dawson, Richard Noakes, Sally Shuttleworth and Jonathan R. Topham. Aldershot, Hants: Ashgate, 2004. 125–35.
Marvin, Carolyn. *When Old Technologies Were New: Thinking about Electric Communication in the Late Nineteenth Century*. New York: University of Oxford Press, 1988.
McEwan, Cheryl. "A Very Modern Ghost: Postcolonialism and the Politics of Enchantment." *Environment and Planning D: Society and Space* 26 (2008): 29–46.
Morrisson, Mark S. *Modern Alchemy: Occultism and the Emergence of Atomic Theory*. Oxford: Oxford University Press, 2007.
Murphet, Julian. "Film and (as) Modernity." *The SAGE Handbook of Film Studies*. Eds. James Donald and Michael Renov. Los Angeles: Sage, 2008. 343–60.
Noakes, Richard. "Spiritualism, Science and the Supernatural in Mid-Victorian Britain." The *Victorian Supernatural*. Eds. Nicola Brown, Carolyn Burdett and Pamela Thurschwell. Cambridge: Cambridge University Press, 2004. 23–43.
Owen, Alex. *The Place of Enchantment: British Occultism and the Culture of the Modern*. Chicago: University of Chicago Press, 2004.
Pels, Peter. "Introduction: Magic and Modernity." *Magic and Modernity: Interfaces of Revelation and Concealment*. Eds. Birgit Meyer and Peter Pels. Stanford: Stanford University Press, 2003. 1–38.
Peters, John Durham. *Speaking into the Air: A History of the Idea of Communication*. Chicago: University of Chicago Press, 1999.
Rossell, Deac. *Living Pictures: The Origins of the Movies*. Albany: SUNY Press, 1998.
Sausman, Justin. "The Democratisation of the Spook: W.T. Stead and the Invention of Public Occultism." *W.T. Stead: Newspaper Revolutionary*. Eds. Laurel Brake, Ed King, Roger Luckhurst and James Mussell. London: The British Library, 2012. 149–165.
Schivelbusch, Wolfgang. *The Railway Journey: The Industrialization of Time and Space in the 19th Century*. Berkeley: University of California Press, 1986.
Schwartz, Vanessa. *Spectacular Realities: Early Mass Culture in Fin-de-siècle Paris*. Berkeley: University of California Press, 1998.
Sconce, Jeffrey. *Haunted Media: Electronic Presence from Telegraphy to Television*. Durham: Duke University Press, 2000.
Sered, Susan. "Afterword: Lexicons of the Supernatural." *Anthropological Forum* 13.2 (2003): 213–8.
Singer, Ben. "The Ambimodernity of Early Cinema: Problems and Paradoxes in the Film-and-Modernity Discourse." *Film 1900: Technology, Perception, Culture*. Eds. Annemone Ligensa and Klaus Kreimeier. New Barnet, Herts: John Libbey, 2009. 37–52.

Singer, Ben. *Melodrama and Modernity: Early Sensational Cinema and Its Contexts.* New York: Columbia University Press, 2001.
Solomon, Matthew. *Disappearing Tricks: Silent Film, Houdini, and the New Magic of the Twentieth Century.* Iowa City: University of Iowa Press, 2010.
Stead, W.T. "Suggestions from Science for Psychic Students: Useful Analogies from Recent Discoveries and Inventions." *Borderland* 3.4 (October 1896): 400–11.
Swatos, William H. "Spiritualism as a Religion of Science." *Social Compass* 37.4 (1990): 471–82.
Swingewood, Alan. *Cultural Theory and the Problem of Modernity.* New York: St. Martin's Press, 1998.
Sword, Helen. *Ghostwriting Modernism.* Ithaca: Cornell University Press, 2002.
Thurschwell, Pamela. "Refusing to Give Up the Ghost: Some Thoughts on the Afterlife from Spirit Photography to Phantom Films." *The Disembodied Spirit.* Brunswick, Maine: The Bowdon College Museum of Art, 2003. 20–31.
Turvey, Malcolm. *Doubting Vision: Film and the Revelationist Tradition.* Oxford: Oxford University Press, 2008.
Vanderbeke, Dirk. "'Science Is Magic That Works': The Return of Magic in Literature on Science." *Magic, Science, Technology and Literature.* Eds. Jarmila Mildorf, Hans Ulrich Seeber and Martin Windisch. Berlin: LIT Verlag, 2006. 209–24.
Warner, Marina. *Phantasmagoria: Spirit Visions, Metaphors and Media into the Twenty-first Century.* Oxford: Oxford University Press, 2006.
Washington, Peter. *Madame Blavatsky's Baboon: A History of the Mystics, Mediums and Misfits Who Brought Spiritualism to America.* New York: Schocken Books, 1995.
Williams, Keith. *H.G. Wells, Modernity and the Movies.* Liverpool: Liverpool University Press, 2007.
Williamson, Colin. *Hidden in Plain Sight: An Archaeology of Magic and the Cinema.* New Brunswick, NJ: Rutgers University Press, 2015.
Wilson, Leigh. *Modernism and Magic: Experiments with Spiritualism, Theosophy and the Occult.* Edinburgh: Edinburgh University Press, 2013.

CHAPTER 2

The Haunting of Film Theory

In his essay "Reflections on the Seventh Art" (1923), film theorist Ricciotto Canudo made the fascinating and puzzling statement that the famous polymath Camille Flammarion, "having witnessed a screening of a film illustrating a soul's survival after death, has once again expressed his faith in spiritism, adding to his new enthusiasm for cinema" (1988, 300). In this context, "spiritism" refers to the principally French branch of the spiritualist movement, distinguished mainly by its emphasis on reincarnation (a subject of comparatively little interest for British and American spiritualists). It is not clear whether Canudo means a fictional film, one documenting a séance, or perhaps even some sort of film made by spiritists for polemical purposes. Canudo was a key advocate of cinema as an art form, one of a group of French film theorists of the 1910s and 1920s who tried to describe the mystical, revelatory, transformative qualities specific to cinema, which often went under the name *photogénie*. Cinema was understood as synthesizing all the other arts and yet still possessing qualities that set it apart from them, and for Canudo, that potential for depicting ghostliness was one of the most significant of those qualities.[1] This chapter will demonstrate that questions about cinema's supernatural qualities have been important for thinkers on cinema almost from the beginning, though they have enjoyed a renewed prominence in the last two decades. Within the spectral turn that emerges in the 1990s, we frequently find essential or ontological claims made about cinema as a "ghostly" medium. I will argue that the scholars of the spectral turn, in using haunting and ghostliness as powerful metaphors, risk ignoring the historical character of discourse on ghosts and the supernatural.[2] While I am obviously sympathetic to the project of establishing early cinema as a locus of cinema's "hauntedness" or "spectrality," I hope to demonstrate how a critical construction conventionally made with recourse to Maxim Gorky's "Kingdom of Shadows" essay often risks obscuring the full significance of the supernatural to cinema's beginnings.

Canudo's remarks on Flammarion appear in a section of "Reflections on the Seventh Art" called "Immateriality in Cinema." Here, Canudo proposes that cinema possesses a particular power for conveying immateriality and the dimensions of the soul or the unconscious (which are spoken of almost interchangeably). Canudo argues that cinema naturally is better at this than theatre, because:

> Theatre is confined to concrete speech, and when an unconscious image is desired, it can play with light: it can throw a white mantle around Hamlet's father. But it will always remain within the exact proportions of every reality. Cinema permits, and must further develop, the extraordinary and striking faculty of *representing immateriality*. (1988, 300–1, original emphasis)

His examples are the supernatural psychodramas *The Phantom Chariot* (1921)[3] from Sweden and *Earthbound* (1920) from the United States. He spends a paragraph describing the latter film, which presents the story of a man murdered by his mistress's husband, his ghost lingering on earth until he receives forgiveness from his wife for his infidelity; his spirit embraces her, though she cannot feel or see him, writing: "Certain shots in the film, combining the real and the immaterial, the living and the dead, are often powerful and very troubling. We are reminded of the promise that man might photograph the total life of the unconscious, whose unknown rhythm might rule over our own!" (1988, 301). Canudo was neither the first nor the last commentator to see cinema's ability to depict immateriality or ghostliness as essential to its identity as an artistic medium; his observations here link cinema to occult speculations about photography that I will discuss later.

The Camille Flammarion referenced by Canudo was known as an astronomer, publisher (founder of Groupe Flammarion), novelist and psychical researcher. At the time Canudo wrote "Reflections on the Seventh Art," Flammarion was in his late seventies, and had witnessed the history of spiritism from the beginning. A committed spiritist early in the movement's history, Flammarion had even spoken at the 1869 funeral of the movement's founder, Allen Kardec.[4] As a faith that blurred religion and science, spiritism held a strong appeal to mystical-minded scientists like Flammarion. John Warne Monroe writes, "For many, like Flammarion, who cherished the consolation and moral certainty religion could provide, but who also believed in the ultimate truth-determining power of experimental inquiry, Spiritism appeared to be a definitive solution to a deeply disturbing philosophical problem" (2002, 127).[5] Canudo states that "[Flammarion] was happily surprised to see the cinema confront the evocation (if no longer the representation) of immateriality. Mr. Flammarion's remarks confirm that the cinema, *when understood and conceived of as art by artists*, must develop in specific areas that are impossible in other arts" (1988, 300, original emphasis), including embracing its own ghostly potential.[6]

The appropriateness Canudo finds in the fact that Flammarion's return to spiritism should have happened through the medium of cinema reminds us that cinema's powers and spiritist (or spiritualist) values share something important: an interest in immateriality. Canudo was by no means unique in analogically connecting cinema's specificity, its *photogénie*, to the supernatural; in fact, in 1921, Jean Epstein wrote that, "The cinema is essentially supernatural" (1988, 246). In 1927, Antonin Artaud authored an article called "Sorcery and the Cinema," in which he describes the cinema as a magical device that bestows "a quasi-animal life" (1978, 49) to the images it animates, and exalts them into almost Platonic ideal versions of themselves. Artaud writes, "The cinema is essentially the revealer of a whole occult life with which it puts us into direct contact ... A whole imperceptible substance takes shape and tries to reach the light. The cinema is bringing us nearer to this substance" (1978, 50). Whether or not these critics believed in ghosts personally, they found that the supernatural provided a stock of metaphors and images that allowed them to characterize the ineffable world they perceived in cinema. Ben Singer has recently argued that the supernatural rhetoric embraced by these critics represents a little-acknowledged counter-strain of early film theory:

> Few people today would endorse the quasi-religious, spiritualist rhetoric of French Impressionist criticism, but it would be a mistake to dismiss it as nothing more than quaint and silly mystification ... Conceptualizing cinema in terms of the occult, the supernatural, the metaphysical realms of noumena, Impressionist criticism seems very far removed from the main dynamic thrust of the cinema-and-modernity discourse. It gravitated toward

the half-light of Romantic spiritualism rather than the materialist glare of the contemporary urban industrial milieu. (2009, 47)

Broadly speaking, these reactions can be located within what Malcolm Turvey (2008) calls the "revelationist" tradition of film theory, which locates within cinema an ability to reveal to us elements of the world that the naked eye cannot perceive. Revelationism combines scepticism about human vision and adulation of the mechanical vision for its impartiality. For Turvey, *photogénie* is a key branch of revelationism, as it reveals the inner life of human beings and the secret personality of objects.

Parallel claims come from another of Turvey's revelationists, Béla Balázs. Balázs's early book *The Visible Man* (1924) contains a segment called "Miracles and Ghosts," focusing particularly on the fairy-tale film. Balázs asserts that fairy-tale films never rouse feelings of the supernatural or the uncanny because they openly present a different, distorted version of nature. Balázs instead locates cinema's supernatural in the natural. In his view, *The Cabinet of Dr. Caligari* (1920) worked less well than *Nosferatu* (1922) in this regard, on account of the former's aesthetic otherworldly harmony and the latter's depiction of a natural world overlaid "with premonitions of the supernatural" (Balázs 2010, 58–9). He concludes that:

> [it] is certain ... that no written or oral literature is able to express the ghostly, the demonic and the supernatural as well as the cinematic. For man's language is the product of his rationality, and so the Orphic words of obscure magic spells may be at worst incomprehensible, but they are not "supernatural." That is to say, *words cannot be understood when they are incomprehensible*. This is how human intelligence defends itself. But a sight *may be clear and comprehensible even though unfathomable. And that is what makes our hair stand on end.* (2010, 59, original emphasis)

Cinema's status as a medium of images, for Balázs, clinches its reputation as the greatest medium for expressing the supernatural precisely because, as a visual medium, it is able to achieve effects that circumvent the need for rationality and legibility. Similarly, in his remarkable "Supernaturalism in the Movies" (1945), the American film critic Parker Tyler states:

> Movie-camera trickery is of a magic-carpet kind—but here this expression not only is a figure of speech but denotes an actual vision, albeit only an image recorded by one mechanism and thrown by another onto a screen— an image as insubstantial as a ghost itself. With this power to render the

human substance into mere symbolic ectoplasm, the movie camera possesses a perambulation parallel to the movements supposedly initiated in actual Ghost Land. (1945, 363)

Again, the supernatural serves as a structural model to characterize cinema on the level of medium. Even Rudolf Arnheim would praise Jacques-Yves Cousteau's *World Without Sun* (1964) with supernatural language:

> a most impressive although surely unintentional display of what the most impressive films of the last few years have been trying to do, namely, to interpret the ghostliness of the visible world by means of authentic appearances drawn directly from that world. The cinema has been making its best contribution to the general trend I have tried to describe, not by withdrawing from imagery, as other arts have, but by using imagery to describe reality as a ghostly figment. (1966, 244)

It is evident that charting a relationship between cinema and the supernatural was a very real concern in both early and classical film theory—one that has returned in force in recent decades. A significant strand of recent scholarship has sought to locate cinema as "magical" or "ghostly" or "spiritual": Gilberto Perez's "material ghost" (1998). In an article called "The Crypt, the Haunted House, of Cinema" (2004), Alan Cholodenko states:

> It is a key premise of this essay that not only is the spectre a privileged subject of film but that it would be the ur figure of cinema, if cinema could have an ur figure, a figure not only operating at every second at every level in every aspect of every film, but also at the level of the cinematic, or rather animatic, apparatus of film, hence at the level of film "as such." (2004, 100)

More casually, Peter Wollen asserts that, "The cinema, after all, is an art of ghosts, projections of light and shadow, which seem while we watch them to have the substance of real beings" (1997, 18). Some version of this claim is operative in many other works: that film has a special affinity with death or the world of the ghost, or is haunted at a basic, primal level.

The Spectral Turn

"Spectral turn" is a phrase much used at present in cultural studies, assuming a moment when philosophy fixates on questions about of ghosts, haunting and spectrality like never before. Like many of the "turns" discussed in recent decades (the pictorial turn, the sensorial turn, the spatial turn, the historical turn, turn, turn, turn…), the term is drawn from Richard Rorty's model of the history of philosophy as a series of "turns," in which "a new set of problems emerges and the old ones begin to fade away" (1979, 264). The spectral turn, it is generally agreed, was inaugurated in the early 1990s with the publication of Jacques Derrida's *Specters of Marx* (1993). Complex and controversial even by Derrida's standards, *Specters of Marx* is a meditation on the fall of the Soviet Union and on the nature of ghosts. To counter both the current neoconservative self-congratulation and theoretical declarations of "the end of history," Derrida calls for the foundation of links between deconstruction and classic Marxism and declares a "New International" to maintain Marx's spirit as a sort of ghostly half-presence between life and death, presence and absence.[7] For Derrida the ghost is an innately deconstructive figure that undermines logocentric thought with its category-bending interstitiality, particularly in terms of its ability to cut through linear histories by the simultaneity of its past, present and future. Derrida provides the neologism "hauntology": "It is necessary for us to introduce haunting into the very construction of a concept. Of every concept, beginning with the concepts of being and time. That is what we would be calling here a hauntology" (1993, 6). Christine Berthin explains that, "Hauntology is the dark double of ontology. It deconstructs and empties out ontology, being and presence. Neither alive nor dead, the Derridean spectre hovers between presence and absence, making it impossible to assign definitive meanings to things" (2010, 3). Derrida's conception of the ghost has strong implications for cinema, which received key place in his discourse on ghosts.

The reception of *Specters of Marx* for Marxist and left-leaning critics was extremely mixed (Davis 2007, 8), and the book inspired critiques from within the deconstructionist ranks (notably Spivak 1995). The considerably more friendly reception it received in literary and cultural studies, however, triggered a new academic vogue for ghosts and the supernatural. When asked, "Are you a scholar who deals with ghosts?" Derrida's translator, Peggy Kamuf, answered, "Yes … although I'm not sure I would have said so with as much conviction before *Specters of Marx*" (quoted in Luckhurst 2002, 527). She was not alone in this, and though not all participants in the spectral turn draw directly on Derrida's book, they benefit from the intellectual openness to questions of ghosts and haunting fomented by it. For their titles alone, consider Jean-Michel Rabaté's *The Ghosts of Modernity* (1996), Avery F. Gordon's *Ghostly*

Matters: Ghosts and the Sociological Imagination (1997), Ashok Kara's *The Ghosts of Justice: Heidegger, Derrida and the Fate of Deconstruction* (2001), Julian Wolfreys's *Victorian Hauntings: Spectrality, Gothic, the Uncanny and Literature* (2002), Helen Sword's *Ghostwriting Modernism* (2002), Gray Kochhar-Lindgren's *TechnoLogics: Ghosts, the Incalculable, and the Suspension of Animation* (2005), Colin Davis's *Haunted Subjects: Deconstruction, Psychoanalysis and the Return of the Dead* (2007), David Appelbaum's *Jacques Derrida's Ghost: A Conjuration* (2009), Gabriele Schwab's *Haunting Legacies: Violent Histories and Transgenerational Trauma* (2010), Christine Berthin's *Gothic Hauntings: Melancholy Crypts and Textual Ghosts* (2010), Maurizio Calbi's *Spectral Shakespeares* (2013) and Esther Peeren's *The Spectral Metaphor: Living Ghosts and the Agency of Invisibility* (2014).[8] This list could go on (including many books dealing with postcolonial and racial theory),[9] and the trend shows no signs of abating. Consider the titles of some recent collections and anthologies: Jeffrey Andrew Weinstock's *Spectral America: Phantoms and the National Imagination* (2004), Jarmila Mildorf, Hans Ulrich Seeber and Martin Windisch's *Magic, Science, Technology and Literature* (2006), John Potts and Edward Scheer's *Technologies of Magic: A Cultural Study of Ghosts, Machines and the Uncanny* (2006), Sladja Blazan's *Ghosts, Stories, Histories: Ghost Stories and Alternative Histories* (2007), Jo Collins and John Jervis's *Uncanny Modernity* (2008), Joshua Landy and Michael Saler's *The Re-enchantment of the World: Secular Magic in a Rational Age* (2009), Kate Griffiths and David Evans' *Haunting Presences: Ghosts in French Literature and Culture* (2009), María del Pilar Blanco and Esther Peeren's *Popular Ghosts: The Haunted Spaces of Everyday Culture* (2010), Lisa Kröger and Melanie Anderson *The Ghostly and the Ghosted in Literature and Film* (2013) and Blanco and Peeren's *The Spectralities Reader: Ghosts and Haunting in Contemporary Cultural Theory* (2013). The first line of the *Popular Ghosts* is "It seems that ghosts are everywhere these days" (Blanco and Peeren 2010, ix) … indeed. Numerous journals have published special issues on spectral topics: *Space and Culture* on "Spatial Hauntings" in 2001, *Art History* on photography and spiritualism in 2003, *Cultural Geographies* on "Spectro-geographies" in 2008.

The phrase "spectral turn" has also been used in a different way: both Jeffrey Andrew Weinstock (2004) and Diane E. Goldstein, Sylvia Ann Grider and Jeannie Banks Thomas (2007) have used the phrase to denote not a body of academic writing, but a cultural fascination emblematized by many supernaturally themed films and television shows at the dawn of the third millennium (perhaps "cycle of production" would suit better than "turn" in this context). Throughout the spectral turn, one finds adjectives like "haunted," "supernatural," "spectral," "ghostly" and even "uncanny"[10] used with a lack of clarification, sometimes even interchangeably, due to the uncertain semantic parameters of each term.[11] Historians of the supernatural also often regard the claims of the spectral turn theorists with scepticism. The editors of the collection *The Victorian Supernatural* (2004), Nicola Brown, Carolyn Burdett and Pamela Thurschwell, note that, "for Derrida, history is structurally and necessarily haunted, but where is the supernatural to be found in this kind of haunting? The problem is that the ghost is only one in a series of deconstructive tropes" (2004, 12). They argue that Derrida's conception of the ghost, though evocative, is necessarily an ahistorical one. It is not sensitive to how the supernatural means different things in different cultures and at different times, and is not well suited to considerations of people's actual experience of the supernatural. In the essay that coined the phrase "spectral turn," "The Contemporary London Gothic and the Limits of the 'Spectral Turn'" (2002), Roger Luckhurst made a similar case, urging that we resist using a generalized structure of spectrality or "haunted modernity" instead of a historical interpretation lodged in issues of politics and ideology. He warns against the "generalizing economy of haunting" (2002, 534) as ahistorical and limiting, producing a paradigm whereby the ghost is not a specific symptom singular to its time and place but rather is understood only within "the generalized structure of haunting [which] is symptomatically blind to its generative loci" (2002, 528). Luckhurst is among the scholars whose attitude towards the spectral turn might be described as "cautious interest," his critique not designed to disparage the spectral turn outright but to point to its limits.

I am not unsympathetic to the spectral turn or its applications within film studies, but, like some of these critics, believe that a sense of historical rigour brought to bear on the trope of "cinema as ghostly" is necessary to balance these more theoretical considerations by providing an important backstory. As we have established, the idea that cinema has a special relationship with the supernatural is by no means a new one, but I wish to suggest that it was not the case that early cinema's audiences were encountering a more essential or authentic version of cinema (as a persistent, romantic construction of early cinema's spectators would have it), but rather that the association of cinema with the supernatural is reflective of the cultural role played by the supernatural more broadly at the moment of cinema's emergence.

Phantomachia and the Kingdom of Shadows

If the understanding of cinema as troubling the binaries of life and death, presence and absence, does not begin with Derrida, he certainly played a considerable part in cementing its current vogue. As in most fields, the reception of hauntology in film studies has been a mixed one. At the 2008 Society for Cinema and Media Studies Conference in Philadelphia, Steven Shaviro served as the respondent for a panel called "Untimely Bodies: Towards a Comparative Film Theory of Human Figures, Temporalities and Visibilities," featuring presentations by Tom Gunning, Brian Wall, Chika Kinotsha and James Prakash Younger. Shaviro began with a swipe at Derrida that nevertheless reaffirmed the usefulness of his ideas about ghosts: "In his massively disappointing book *Specters of Marx*, Jacques Derrida nonetheless has one marvellous invention." Shaviro went on to state:

> Deeper than any ontology, deeper than being, deeper than what *is*, there is that which haunts being, spectrally, without being reducible to it. Derrida ... presents hauntology as an absence which underlies, and disrupts, any assertion of presence. But, of course, this formulation is reversible; it just as well designates a continuing subsistence, or insistence, at the very heart of death and absence. Something that has died, something that is in the past, nonetheless refuses to go away. Or something that is not yet born, something that is in a potential future, casts its premonitory shadow even before it has arrived. In either case, something that is invisible and impalpable fails to be simply absent, simply *not there* ...
>
> The speakers on this panel all point ... to the hauntological dimension of the movies ... But beyond this, they suggest that film is itself the hauntological art *par excellence*. It is not just that a certain practice of cinema might be described as hauntological; but more importantly that hauntology itself, in its evanescent yet more-than-real spectrality, is inherently cinematic. Film does not capture and reproduce the real, so much as it always already haunts reality ... (2009, n.p.)

I quote Shaviro's speech at some length because it illustrates the extent to which the ghostliness of cinema has become a fairly accepted theoretical concept. Where ghosts in Derrida's sense should be present in every imaginable medium (indeed, he says that we need to introduce "haunting into the very construction of a concept" [2006, 6]), for some reason cinema seems unusually prone to inspire reflections on this fact. This was true for Derrida himself. In Ken McMullan's experimental feature *Ghost Dance* (1983), Derrida appears as himself in several scenes. In the longest of these, lead actress Pascale Ogier asks Derrida if he believes in ghosts. Derrida says:

> Here the ghost is me. Since I've been asked to play myself in a film which is more or less improvised, I feel as if I'm letting a ghost speak through me. Curiously, instead of playing myself, without knowing it I let a ghost ventriloquize my words, or play my role ... Cinema is an art of phantoms (*phantomachia*), a battle of phantoms. I think that's what the cinema's about, when it's not boring. It's the art of letting ghosts come back.

Implicitly positioning himself against Max Weber's disenchantment paradigm (to be discussed in the next chapter), he goes on to say, "I believe that modern developments in technology and telecommunication, instead of diminishing the realm of ghosts ... enhances the power of ghosts and their ability to haunt us ... I say, 'Long live the ghosts.'" Ogier died a year after the film was released, the day before her twenty-sixth birthday, and Derrida later would describe the experience of watching the film again with the knowledge of her death:

> I suddenly saw Pascale's face appear on the screen, and I knew it was the face of a dead woman. She was replying to my question: "Do you believe in ghosts?" As if she were looking straight into my eyes, she was still saying to me on the big screen, "Yes, now, yes." Which now? Years afterwards in Texas, I had the overwhelming feeling of the return of her ghost, the ghost of her ghost, coming back to say to me, to me, here, now: "Now ... now ... now, that is, in this darkened room, on another continent, in another world, there, now, yes, believe me, I believe in ghosts." (quoted in Davis 2007, 20)[12]

In an essay called "Cinema and the M̶e̶a̶n̶i̶n̶g̶ of 'Life'" (2006) Louis-Georges Schwartz writes, "The cinema provides a succinct figure for hauntology as well as participating in the process of haunting which, by itself, deconstructs life/death, presence/absence and being/non-being" (2006, 13). Schwartz quotes Derrida's interview with the editors of *Cahiers du cinéma*, where he stated that, "cinematographic experience belongs to spectrality from beginning to end" (2006, 14). Schwartz provides a nuanced and thorough understanding of Derrida's hauntology and the place of cinema. It includes a discussion of Derrida's belated encounter with the cinematic "ghost" of Pascale Ogier, which links Derrida's reaction back to early cinema:

> Instead of exorcising Ogier's ghost by explaining her away as a mechanical illusion, even an absolute illusion, or as an effect of mourning whereby a mere appearance is invested with the energy the mourner had given to the lost object, Derrida writes a description of the experience in an attempt to think this haunting and hauntology in general. If in the accounts of the first Lumière projections, the moving image comes to restore life to the dead, in Derrida's writings, the cinematic ghost appears as neither living nor dead, an appearance that changes the very nature of the categories. (2006, 18)

Schwartz acknowledges Derrida as a being on a lineage with, yet not precisely duplicating, those early commentators.[13]

Among those scholars claiming a supernatural specificity for the cinema, there is a strong tendency to appeal, if selectively, to early cinema and its initial commentators. The key example is Maxim Gorky's "Kingdom of Shadows" essay (a retrospective label), written under the pseudonym "I.M. Pacatus" upon seeing an 1896 screening of the Lumière programme in Nizhni-Novgorod. Gorky viewed the films at the theatre of Charles Aumont, which doubled as a fashionable brothel, a fact to which the review makes a few coy references. Rather than emphasizing shock or excitement the way many initial accounts of cinema did, Gorky described cinema as something drab and depressing, an unnerving netherworld:

> Last night I was in the Kingdom of Shadows.
> If you only knew how strange it is to be here. It is a world without sound, without colour. Everything there—the earth, the trees, the people, the water and the air—is dipped in monotonous grey. Grey rays of the sun across the grey sky, grey eyes in grey faces, and the leaves of the trees are ashen grey. It is not life but its shadow, not motion but its soundless spectre. (Leyda 1960, 407)

The review continues for three pages in this mode of intense gothic melancholy. Of the people on the screen, Gorky states:

> the grey silhouettes of the people, as though condemned to eternal silence and cruelly punished by being deprived of all the colours of life, glide noiselessly along the grey ground.

> Their smiles are lifeless, even though their movements are full of living energy and are so swift as to be almost imperceptible. Their laughter is soundless, although you see the muscles contracting in their grey faces. Before you a life is surging, a life deprived of words and shorn of the living spectrum of colours—the grey, the soundless, the bleak and dismal life.
>
> It is terrifying to see, but it is the movement of shadows, only of shadows. Curses and ghosts, the evil spirits have cast entire cities into eternal sleep, come to mind and you feel as though Merlin's vicious trick is being enacted before you. (1960, 407–8)

Gorky paints cinema as both a kind of Hades for grey and insubstantial shades and as the grand conjuration of an evil magician. Later, he describes *Partie de cartes* (1895) in similar terms:

> Three men seated at the table, playing cards. Their faces are tense, their hands move swiftly. The cupidity of the players is betrayed by the trembling fingers and by the twitching of their facial muscles. They play ... Suddenly, they break into laughter, and the waiter who has stopped at their table with bear, laughs too. They laugh until their sides split but not a sound is heard. It seems as if these people have died and their shadows have been condemned to play card in silence unto eternity. (408)[14]

Gorky's words have an evocative power and are cited in a great many places. In general, critical deployments of Gorky's essay fall into two (somewhat overlapping) categories. One uses it to speak about how European intellectuals rejected cinema as lacking, as Noël Burch puts it, "the requirements of the naturalistic ideology of representation" (1990, 23), invoking the metaphor of the shadow to describe cinema as insubstantial and incomplete. Gorky's article is thus understood as embodying an early scepticism towards cinema's grey, silent world, and also as anticipating later iconophobic theoretical formations that object to cinema's purported illusionism. The other category focuses on the fact that Gorky's intellectual scepticism does little to obscure the visceral impact cinema obviously has on him, and finds suggestive potential in his characterization of cinema as a haunted space, "an encounter with the living dead" (Lowenstein 2010, 124).

Gorky's essay has given a title to Colin Harding and Simon Popple's excellent collection of early writings on cinema, *In the Kingdom of Shadows: A Companion to Early Cinema* (1996), as well as the documentary *Kingdom of Shadows: The Rise of the Horror Film* (1998) about silent "horror" films, now available as part of Kino International's *American*

Silent Horror collection. Gorky's is indeed an important essay, considerations of which have helped scholars develop a more nuanced and balanced understanding of early audiences' reactions to cinema than once prevailed; it is also the epigraph to Gemma Files's novel *Experimental Film* (2015), in which the works of an obscure early Canadian filmmaker reveal a gateway to conjuring the Slavic demon Lady Midday. Gorky's gloomy response to the Lumière films certainly helped scholars to complicate the simplistic "Lumière = Realism, Méliès = Formalism" dichotomy that once dominated treatments of early cinema, since Gorky imagines a phantasmal world built around images that would otherwise seem to epitomize realism. Tom Gunning drew on Gorky to counter the then-prominent Metzian model of early spectators' reactions to cinema as "submitting passively to an all-dominating apparatus, hypnotised and transfixed by its illusionist power" (1995, 32) with one that emphasizes the sophistication of the audiences, and their ability to recognize cinema's illusionary qualities and reflect intelligently upon them. The early cinema spectator, for Gunning, is closer to Gorky than the credulous rube of the *Uncle Josh at the Moving Picture Show* (1902) variety.

Gorky's early writings on cinema are seldom discussed within their Russian context, with Yuri Tsivian's (2004) writings as the key exception. The fact that Gorky's article has been taken as an ahistorical, or at least transcultural, proof of cinema's ghostly qualities could be taken as evidence for the generalizing economy of the supernatural against which Luckhurst cautioned.[15] In both examples cited above, the Harding-Popple anthology and the horror film documentary of the same title, the phrase "the Kingdom of Shadows" implicitly represents a certain period of filmmaking (early cinema or even silent cinema as a locus for cinema's ghostliness, which presumably does not apply as readily beyond the introduction of sound).[16] Neither work is particularly about Gorky—the documentary never even mentions him. Take also Lee Grieveson and Peter Krämer's *The Silent Cinema Reader* (2004), the introduction of which begins by citing Gorky's famous words, even though the entire book scarcely references Gorky again. In *The Haunted Gallery: Painting, Photography, Film c. 1900* (2007), Lynda Nead, after an excellent discussion of haunted paintings as a late Victorian trend that transitioned naturally into cinema, draws on Gorky only at the last minute, and then only as a means of shifting the argument which she has been making with respect to England and France to a seemingly universal one (2007, 104); she does something similar at the end of the subsequent chapter (2007, 131). The very words

"Kingdom of Shadows" are in danger of becoming a mantra, estranged from their original context.

A similar objection can be raised with respect to Laura Mulvey's *Death 24× a Second: Stillness and the Moving Image* (2006). For Mulvey, the ghostly qualities of cinema identified in writings like Gorky's are attributable to cinema's absolute newness:

> It is impossible to see the Lumière films as simple demonstrations of a new technology; every gesture, expression, movement of wind or water is touched with mystery. This is not the mystery of the magic trick but the more disturbing, uncanny sensation of seeing movement fossilized for the first time. This uncanny effect was also vividly present for the cinema's first spectators; the images' silence and lack of colour added to the ghostly atmosphere. (2006, 36)[17]

For Mulvey, these ghostly qualities of cinema were effaced through familiarity, at least until our present moment and the disruptions created by the digital image. "But now, after more than a hundred years ... The phantom-like quality observed by Gorky and his contemporaries returns in force. The inanimate images of the filmstrip not only come alive in projection, but are the ghostly images of the now-dead resurrected into the appearance of life" (2006, 36). For Mulvey, the digital makes for a new version of the Gorkian spectator, experiencing the "technological uncanny," but in this process the historical specifics of early cinema and its relationship to the supernatural as it was understood at the time may get lost. Somewhat similarly, "In the Kingdom of Shadows: Cinematic Movement and the Digital Ghost" (2009) by Trond Lundemo, reaches to early cinema to draw comparisons to the internet's brand of spectrality, using the example of Louis Le Prince, the early cinema experimenter who mysteriously vanished in 1890 (murdered to protect rival patents, some say) and whose fragmentary films are now available on YouTube, widely distributed for the first time.[18]

Tsivian's contextual reading of Gorky's essay yields rich insights. How fascinating to read that Gorky's description of the card players in *Partie de cartes* as condemned souls playing cards for all eternity is an allusion to a line from Pushkin (2004, 5–6), or that Gorky also wrote a short story inspired by the suicide of a chorus girl/prostitute at Aumont's, which Gorky attributed to seeing a happy family on the screen and realizing her life will never be as sweet (2004, 36–7). Tsivian's inquiry into the culture of the magic lantern in Russia that pre-dated cinema helps us understand that Gorky's reaction was not (or at least, not just) a timeless and acultural reaction of cinema's supernatural implications, but a culturally contingent and historically specific reaction to *pre-existing* associations between the projected image and the supernatural.

The spectral turn's embrace of early cinema can be viewed as symptomatic of an interesting reversal in attitudes towards early cinema and its spectators in the recent decades. It was once the case that early or "primitive" cinema was understood merely as a set of way stations on the road to the classical model supposedly codified by D.W. Griffith, riddled with dead ends and wrong turns. This teleological model is also an Oedipal one, locating Griffith as the father of cinema and thereby relegating everything before him to him illegitimacy: after all, you cannot pre-date your father. Under this model, early spectators became characterized by ignorance, fear and panic. From the 1970s on, critics came along to counter this attitude, though it has scarcely been eliminated, but another notion has emerged that is almost as insidious: early cinema as Edenic and innocent, existing in a state of grace, with both filmmakers and audiences more in touch with cinema's true nature. Tom Gunning once cautioned that the term "primitive cinema" connotes "an elementary or even childish mastery of form in contrast to a later complexity," adding parenthetically, "and need we add that this viewpoint often shelters its apparent reversal in the image of a cinema of a lost purity and innocence?" (1990, 96).

When it comes to the trope of ghostliness, the latter attitude is pervasive. If cinema is and always has been ghostly or spectral, it is implicitly the case that early spectators simply knew the true nature of cinema better than we because they are presumed to have reacted to it in a direct and unmediated fashion. This fact is "proved" by commentaries like Gorky's, as well as the choice of material of some early filmmakers. For instance, Cholodenko states:

> In taking the spectre as the "ur" figure of cinema ... I take a cue from the fact that the spectre is a privileged subject of film, even giving birth to its "own" genre—the ghost film—a staple of cinema from its earliest days to the most recent times. Between 1896 and 1907, a rash of haunted hotel, castle, inn, manor and chateaux films were made ... More recent examples of this genre include *Poltergeist* (1982), *Evil Dead* (1983), *Ghostbusters* (1984), *Beetlejuice* (1988), *Ghost* (1990), *Ghost Dad* (1990), *Truly Madly Deeply* (1991), *Casper* (1995) ... Then there are those films that acknowledge that

special relation between film and the spectre by marking their titles with the sign of the ghost and the haunted house, for example, *The Phantom of the Opera*. (2004, 103)

But the cinematic ghost film is not without its roots in other media, especially literature and theatre, and so it seems excessive to claim it as a "privileged subject" for cinema. The ghost as subject matter for cinema comes in and out of favour. There are relatively few in the 1930s, for instance, and between the heyday of the comic and romantic ghost films sometimes labelled "*film blanc*" (Valenti 1978) in the 1940s and a new cycle triggered by *Heaven Can Wait* (1978) (Genelli and Genelli 1984; Fowkes 1998, 2004), ghost stories are somewhat rare in Hollywood. The mere fact that films about ghosts were and continue to be made proves nothing about cinema's ontology (or hauntology), but may tell us something about the conditions of its emergence. Mandy Merck makes a similar claim for an innate affinity between cinema and the figure of the ghost (her argument also quotes Gorky):

> As if in recognition of its own peculiar "hauntology" as the medium of exchange which transforms the pro-filmic event into an apparition, the early cinema produced scores of "phantom rides" in which cameras were mounted on gondolas, cars, balloons, funiculars, and especially trains, to provide the first eerily moving shots of the landscape; and it soon specialized in ghostly characters created by double exposure and superimposition. An entire comic genre was created to employ these effects, the "trick film" ... (1999, 168)

Again, the argument seems to be that ghosts were a common subject for early cinema (and perhaps even for cinema in general) because of an essential or ontological connection between cinema and the supernatural. In the next chapter, I suggest a reverse formulation: the introduction of cinema into the supernatural-obsessed late Victorian culture and cinema's heritage of existing practices associated with the supernatural resulted in affinities that have never entirely vanished with the familiarization of the medium.

Notes

1. For a cogent explanation of *photogénie*, see Willemen (1994, 124–33). See Dalle Vacche (2005, 95–9) for more on Canudo's life, writings and influence on early Italian cinema.

2. The difficulty of defining "ghost" in a way that is universally applicable is taken up by Potts (2006). See Finucane (1982) for a treatment of how European ghosts have changed substantially over the centuries and Collins (1996) on shifting aesthetics of the supernatural.
3. Directed by Victor Sjöström as *Körkarlen*, more commonly known in English as *The Phantom Carriage*.
4. Flammarion would later distance himself from spiritism, so Canudo's remarks may allude to a late-life reaffirmation of his spiritist faith.
5. For more on Flammarion's spiritism, see Canguilhem (2004).
6. See Cooper (2013, 43–4) for another discussion of Canudo, within a discussion of film theory's construction of the related topic of the soul.
7. For other Marxist treatments of the ghost, see Clery (1995), Wayne (2004) and Smith (2010).
8. Consult Auerbach (2004), Gunn (2006) and Lincoln and Lincoln (2015) for surveys of much of the central material of this turn. For a take more focused on the study of horror, see Hills (2005, 154–8).
9. Key examples include Brogan (1998), Bergland (2000), Del Villano (2007), Khair (2009), Lim (2009), Parham (2009) and Blanco (2012).
10. Freud's 1919 essay on the uncanny received no special focus in scholarship until the 1970s and subsequently rose to the status of a founding text in the 1990s (see Jay 1998; Collins and Jervis 2008; Masschelein 2011).
11. Colin Davis laudably delineates his use of "spectre," "phantom" and "ghost," using the first for Derrida's sense, the second for that of Nicholas Abraham and Maria Torok and the third for more general uses. He confesses, however, that he is imposing stricter terminological consistency than the original authors (2007, 160).
12. Derrida's conversations in the *Cahiers du cinéma* in 1998 and 2000 with Antoine de Baecque and Thierry Jousse were recently translated by Peggy Kamuf in *Discourse*.
13. See Simmons (2011) for another discussion of *Ghost Dance* and its relationship to Derrida's hauntology.
14. The words of Gorky quoted here and in virtually all citations' accounts of Gorky's review(s) come from a translation of the essay appearing in Jay Leyda's *Kino: A History of the Russian and Soviet*

Film (1960), credited to "Leda Swan." Gorky also wrote a piece for an Odessa paper on the same events, which was translated to English by Leonard Mins for the anthology *New Theatre and Film 1934 to 1937*. Even though the translation appeared significantly earlier (Leyda himself cited it in an 1946 article in *Hollywood Quarterly* 37), it is far less cited in scholarship than the essay translated in Leyda's book. While it contains references to shadows and ghosts akin to those found in the more familiar essay, the overall tone is less gloomy and poetic but comes somewhat closer to straightforward reportage. It has been suggested that the supernatural implications are created or at least amplified by the translation in the Leyda book (Ruffles 2010, 238), but to the best of my knowledge no alternative translation has emerged.

15. Gorky's essay can also be put into the service of cases made about cinema's nature, essence or ontology in terms slightly different from (though perhaps parallel to) the trope of ghostliness. For example, Daniel Frampton (2006) places a quote from Gorky alongside an anecdote from the DVD of *Contact* (1997) where Jodie Foster expresses an uncanny feeling about having her face manipulated (2006, 1). Both examples, from a century apart, combine to paint cinema as an artificial otherworld.

16. Davies (2007) has a chapter called "Projecting Ghosts," which follows the creation of ghostly images from the sixteenth century on to a discussion of ghosts in cinema, but stops in the late silent period; it thus reflects an understanding that silent cinema (or frequently, only early cinema) is to be understood as ghostly, haunted, uncanny—and the rest of cinema is not, or at least not as pointedly so. This is particularly shortsighted when one considers the ghostly implications that were *produced* by the coming of sound. Indeed, the practice of voice faking was referred to as "ghosting" (Durovicová 2003, 88). See Spadoni for an exploration of the uncanny properties of early film sound (2007, 8–30), and Donnelly (2010) for more on the occult properties of film sound.

17. Compare Žižek (2007, 88).

18. If there is one mode of filmmaking with reference to which the film-as-ghostly motif is deployed nearly as frequently as early cinema, it is surely the German Expressionist cinema. We need think only of the title of Lotte Eisner's foundational text of German Expressionism, *The Haunted Screen* (1969). Anton Kaes cites

Gorky in his discussion of *Nosferatu* (1922), stating: "For Murnau, film is 'not life but its shadow,' just as it was for Gorky ... Nosferatu, a purely cinematic creature ... rules in the kingdom of shadows, which is none other than the kingdom of film" (2009, 125).

Works Cited

Appelbaum, David. *Jacques Derrida's Ghost: A Conjuration*. Albany: SUNY Press, 2009.
Arnheim, Rudolf. "Art Today and the Film." *Art Journal* 24.3 (Spring 1966): 242–44.
Artaud, Antonin. "Sorcery and the Cinema." *The Avant-Garde Film: A Reader of Theory and Criticism*. Ed. P. Adams Sitney. New York: New York University Press, 1978. 49–50.
Auerbach, Nina. "Ghosts of Ghosts." *Victorian Literature and Culture* 32.1 (March 2004): 277–284.
Balázs, Béla. *Béla Balázs: Early Film Theory: Visible Man and the Spirit of Film*. New York: Berghahn Books, 2010.
Bergland, Renée L. *The National Uncanny: Indian Ghosts and American Subjects*. Hanover, NH: University Press of New England, 2000.
Berthin, Christine. *Gothic Hauntings: Melancholy Crypts and Textual Ghosts*. Houndmills, Basingstoke, Hants: Palgrave Macmillan, 2010.
Blanco, María del Pilar. *Ghost-Watching American Modernity: Haunting, Landscape and the Hemispheric Imagination*. New York: Fordham University Press, 2012.
Blanco, María del Pilar and Esther Peeren. "Introduction." *Popular Ghosts: The Haunted Spaces of Everyday Culture*. Eds. María del Pilar Blanco and Esther Peeren. New York: Continuum, 2010. ix–xxiv.
Blanco, María del Pilar and Esther Peeren, eds. *The Spectralities Reader: Ghosts and Haunting in Contemporary Cultural Theory*. London: Bloomsbury Academic, 2013.
Blazan, Sladja, ed. *Ghost, Stories, Histories: Ghost Stories and Alternate Histories*. Newcastle: Cambridge Scholars Publishing, 2007.
Brogan, Kathleen. *Cultural Haunting: Ghosts and Ethnicity in Recent American Literature*. Charlottesville, VA: University Press of Virginia, 1998.
Brown, Nicola, Carolyn Burdett and Pamela Thurschwell. "Introduction." *The Victorian Supernatural*. Eds. Nicola Brown, Carolyn Burdett and Pamela Thurschwell. Cambridge: Cambridge University Press, 2004. 1–22.
Burch, Noël. *Life to Those Shadows*. Berkeley: University of California Press, 1990.
Calbi, Maurizio. *Spectral Shakespeares: Media Adaptations in the Twenty-First Century*. Houndmills, Basingstoke, Hants: Palgrave Macmillan, 2013.

Canguilhem, Denis. "Flammarion and Eusapia Palladino." *The Perfect Medium: Photography and the Occult*. Eds. Clément Chéroux, Andreas Fischer, Pierre Apraxine, Denis Canguilhem and Sophie Schmit. New Haven: Yale University Press, 2004. 235–7.
Canudo, Ricciotto. "Reflections on the Seventh Art." *French Film Theory and Criticism: A History/Anthology, 1907–1939*. Volume 1. Ed. Richard Abel. Princeton: Princeton University Press, 1988. 291–302.
Cholodenko, Alan. "The Crypt, the Haunted House, of Cinema." *Cultural Studies Review* 10.2 (September 2004): 99–113.
Clery, E.J. *The Rise of Supernatural Fiction, 1762–1800*. Cambridge: Cambridge University Press, 1995.
Collins, Christopher. "Writing and the Nature of the Supernatural Image, or Why Ghosts Float." *Languages of Visuality: Crossings Between Science, Art, Politics, and Literature*. Detroit: Wayne State University Press, 1996. 242–62.
Collins, Jo and John Jervis. "Introduction." *Uncanny Modernity: Cultural Theories, Modern Anxieties*. Eds. Jo Collins and John Jervis. Houndmills, Basingstoke, Hants: Palgrave Macmillan, 2008. 1–10.
Cooper, Sarah. *The Soul of Film Theory*. Houndmills, Basingstoke, Hants: Palgrave Macmillan, 2013.
Dalle Vacche, Angela. *Diva: Defiance and Passion in Early Italian Cinema*. Austin: University of Texas Press, 2008.
Davies, Owen. *The Haunted: A Social History of Ghosts*. New York: Palgrave Macmillan, 2007.
Davis, Colin. *Haunted Subjects: Deconstruction, Psychoanalysis and the Return of the Dead*. Houndmills, Basingstoke, Hants: Palgrave Macmillan, 2007.
Del Villano, Bianca. *Ghostly Alterities: Spectrality and Contemporary Literatures in English*. Stuttgart: Ibidem-Verlag, 2007.
Derrida, Jacques. Interview with Antoine de Baecque and Thierry Jousse. "Cinema and Its Ghosts: An Interview with Jacques Derrida." Trans. Peggy Jamuf. *Discourse* 37.1–2 (Winter/Spring 2015): 22–39.
Derrida, Jacques. *Specters of Marx: The State of Debt, the Work of Mourning and the New International*. New York: Routledge, 2006.
Donnelly, K.J. "On the Occult Nature of Film-image Synchronisation." *Cinephile: The University of British Columbia's Film Journal* 6.1 (2010): 39–43.
Durovicová, Nataša. "Local Ghosts: Dubbing Bodies in Early Sound Cinema." *Film and Its Multiples*. Ed. Anna Antonioni. Udine, Italy: Forum, 2003. 83–98.
Eisner, Lotte. *The Haunted Screen: Expressionism in the German Cinema and the Influence of Max Reinhardt*. London: Thames & Hudson, 1969.
Epstein, Jean. "The Senses of I (b)." *French Film Theory and Criticism: A History/Anthology, 1907–1939*. Volume 1. Ed. Richard Abel. Princeton: Princeton University Press, 1988. 241–5, 291–302.
Files, Gemma. *Experimental Film*. Toronto: ChiZine Publications, 2015.

Finucane, R.C. *Appearances of the Dead: A Cultural History of Ghosts*. London: Junction Books, 1982.
Fowkes, Katherine A. *Giving Up the Ghost: Spirits, Ghosts and Angels in Mainstream Comedy Films*. Detroit: Wayne State University Press, 1998.
Fowkes, Katherine A. "Melodramatic Specters: Cinema and *The Sixth Sense*." *Spectral America: Phantoms and the National Imagination*. Ed. Jeffrey Andrew Weinstock. Madison, WI: University of Wisconsin Press, 2004. 185–206.
Frampton, Daniel. *Filmosophy*. London: Wallflower, 2006.
Freud, Sigmund. "The 'Uncanny.'" *The Standard Edition of the Complete Psychological Works of Sigmund Freud. Vol. XVII* (1917–1919). London: Hogarth, 1964. 219–56.
Genelli, Tom and Lynn Davis Genelli. *Journal of Popular Film* 12.3 (Fall 1984): 100–11.
Goldstein, Diane E., Sylvia Ann Grider and Jeannie Banks Thomas. *Haunting Experiences: Ghosts in Contemporary Folklore*. Logan, Utah: Utah State University Press, 2007.
Gordon, Avery F. *Ghostly Matters: Haunting and the Sociological Imagination*. Minneapolis: University of Minnesota Press, 1997.
Gorky, Maxim. "Gorky on the Films, 1896." *New Theatre and Film 1934 to 1937*. Ed. Herbert Kline. San Diego: Harcourt Brace Jovanovich, 1985. 227–31.
Gorky, Maxim. "A review of the Lumière programme at the Nizhni-Novgorod Fair," as printed in the Nizhegorodski listok, newspaper, July 4, 1986, and signed "I.M. Pacatus." Appendix 3 to Jay Leyda, *A History of the Russian and Soviet Film*. London: Unwin House, 1960. 407–9.
Grieveson, Lee and Peter Krämer, eds. *The Silent Cinema Reader*. New York: Routledge, 2004.
Griffiths, Kate and David Evans, eds. *Haunting Presences: Ghosts in French Literature and Culture*. Cardiff: University of Wales Press, 2009.
Gunn, Joshua. "Review Essay: Mourning Humanism, or, the Idiom of Haunting." *Quarterly Journal of Speech* 92.1 (February 2006): 77–102.
Gunning, Tom. "An Aesthetic of Astonishment: Early Film and the (In)Credulous Spectator." *Viewing Positions: Ways of Seeing Film*. Ed. Linda Williams. New Brunswick, NJ: Rutgers University Press, 1995. 114–33.
Gunning, Tom. "'Primitive' Cinema: A Frame-Up? Or, the Trick's on Us." *Early Cinema: Space, Frame, Narrative*. Eds. Thomas Elsaesser and Adam Barker. London: British Film Institute, 1990. 95–103.
Harding, Colin and Simon Popple, eds. *In the Kingdom of Shadows: A Companion to Early Cinema*. London: Cygnus Press, 1996.
Hills, Matt. *The Pleasures of Horror*. London: Continuum, 2005.
Kaes, Anton. *Shell Shock Cinema: Weimar Culture and the Wounds of War*. Princeton: Princeton University Press, 2009.

Khair, Tabish. *The Gothic, Postcolonialism and Otherness: Ghosts from Elsewhere.* Houndmills, Basingstoke, Hants: Palgrave Macmillan, 2009.

Kochhar-Lindgren, Gray. *TechnoLogics: Ghosts, the Incalculable, and the Suspension of Animation.* Albany: SUNY Press, 2005.

Jay, Martin. *Cultural Semantics: Keywords of Our Time.* Amherst: University of Massachusetts Press, 1998.

Kara, Ashok. *The Ghosts of Justice: Heidegger, Derrida and the Fate of Deconstruction.* San José: iUniversity Press, 2001.

Kröger, Lisa and Melanie Anderson, eds. *The Ghostly and the Ghosted in Literature and Film: Spectral Identities.* Lanham, MD: University of Delaware Press, 2013.

Landy, Joshua and Michael Saler. "Introduction: The Varieties of Modern Enchantment." *The Re-Enchantment of the World.* Eds. Joshua Landy and Michael Saler. Stanford: Stanford University Press, 2009. 1–14.

Leyda, Jay. "Prologue to the Russian Film." *Hollywood Quarterly* 2.1 (Oct. 1946): 35–41.

Lim, Bliss Cua. *Translating Time: Cinema, the Fantastic and Temporal Critique.* Durham: Duke University Press, 2009.

Lincoln, Martha and Bruce Lincoln. "Toward a Critical Hauntology: Bare Afterlife and the Ghosts of Ba Chúc." *Comparative Studies in Society and History* 56.1 (2015): 191–220.

Lowenstein, Adam. "Living Dead: Fearful Attractions of Film." *Representations* 110 (Spring 2010): 105–28.

Luckhurst, Roger. "The Contemporary London Gothic and the Limits of the 'Spectral Turn.'" *Textual Practice* 16.3 (2002): 527–46.

Lundemo, Trond. "In the Kingdom of Shadows: Cinematic Movement and Its Digital Ghost." *The YouTube Reader.* Eds. Pelle Snickars and Patrick Vonderau. Stockholm: National Library of Sweden, 2009. 314–29.

Masschelein, Anneleen. *The Unconcept: The Freudian Uncanny in Late-Twentieth-Century Theory.* Albany: SUNY Press, 2011.

Merck, Mandy. "The Medium of Exchange." *Ghosts: Deconstruction, Psychoanalysis, History.* Eds. Peter Buse and Andrew Stott. New York: St. Martin's Press/Macmillan Press, 1999. 163–78.

Mildorf, Jarmila, Hans Ulrich Seeber and Martin Windisch, eds. *Magic, Science, Technology and Literature.* Berlin: LIT Verlag, 2006.

Monroe, John Warne. *Laboratories of Faith: Mesmerism, Spiritism and Occultism in Modern France.* Ithaca: Cornell University Press, 2002.

Mulvey, Laura. *Death 24× a Second: Stillness and the Moving Image.* London: Reaktion, 2006.

Nead, Lynda. *The Haunted Gallery: Painting, Photography, Film c. 1900.* New Haven: Yale University Press, 2007.

Parham, Marisa. *Haunting and Displacement in African American Literature and Culture.* New York: Routledge, 2009.

Peeren, Esther. *The Spectral Metaphor: Living Ghosts and the Agency of Invisibility*. Houndmills, Basingstoke, Hants: Palgrave Macmillan, 2014.
Perez, Gilberto. *The Material Ghost: Films and Their Medium*. Baltimore: The Johns Hopkins University Press. 1998.
Potts, John. "The Idea of the Ghost." *Technologies of Magic: A Cultural Study of Ghosts, Machines and the Uncanny*. Eds. John Potts and Edward Scheer. Sydney: Power Publications, 2006. 78–91.
Potts, John and Edward Scheer, eds. *Technologies of Magic: A Cultural Study of Ghosts, Machines and the Uncanny*. Sydney: Power Publications, 2006.
Rabaté, Jean-Michel. *The Ghosts of Modernity*. Gainesville: University of Florida Press, 1996.
Rorty, Richard. *Philosophy and the Mirror of Nature*. Princeton: Princeton University Press, 1979.
Ruffles, Tom. *Ghost Images: Cinema of the Afterlife*. Jefferson, NC: McFarland, 2004.
Schwab, Gabriele. *Haunting Legacies: Violent Histories and Transgenerational Trauma*. New York: Columbia University Press, 2010.
Schwartz, Louis-Georges. "Cinema and the ~~Meaning~~ of 'Life.'" *Discourse* 28.2–3 (Spring/Fall 2006): 7–27.
Shaviro, Steven. "SCMS08Response.pdf." *Shaviro.com*. http://www.shaviro.com/Othertexts/SCMS08Response.pdf. Accessed October 16, 2009.
Simmons, Lawrence. "Jacques Derrida's Ghostface." *Angeliki: Journal of the Theoretical Humanities* 16.1 (2011): 129–44.
Singer, Ben. "The Ambimodernity of Early Cinema: Problems and Paradoxes in the Film-and-Modernity Discourse." *Film 1900: Technology, Perception, Culture*. Eds. Annemone Ligensa and Klaus Kreimeier. New Barnet, Herts: John Libbey, 2009. 37–52.
Smith, Andrew. *The Ghost Story, 1840–1920: A Cultural History*. Manchester: Manchester University Press, 2010.
Spadoni, Robert. *Uncanny Bodies: The Coming of Sound Film and the Origins of the Horror Genre*. Berkeley: University of California Press, 2007.
Spivak, Gayatri Chakravorty. "Ghostwriting." *Diacritics* 25.2 (1995): 65–84.
Sword, Helen. *Ghostwriting Modernism*. Ithaca: Cornell University Press, 2002.
Tsivian, Yuri. *Early Cinema in Russia and Its Cultural Reception*. New York: Routledge, 2004.
Turvey, Malcolm. *Doubting Vision: Film and the Revelationist Tradition*. Oxford: Oxford University Press, 2008.
Tyler, Parker. "Supernaturalism in the Movies." *Theatre Arts* 26.6 (June 1945): 362–9.
Valenti, Peter L. "The 'Film Blanc': Suggestions for a Variety of Fantasy, 1940–45." *Journal of Popular Film* 6.4 (1978): 294–304.

Wayne, Mike. "Spectres, Marx's Theory of Value and the Ghost Film." *Film International* 10 (2004): 4–13.

Weinstock, Jeffrey Andrew. "Introduction: The Spectral Turn." *Spectral America: Phantoms and the National Imagination.* Ed. Jeffrey Andrew Weinstock. Madison, WI: University of Wisconsin Press, 2004. 3–17.

Willemen, Paul. *Looks and Frictions: Essays in Cultural Studies and Film Theory.* Bloomington: Indiana University Press, 1994.

Wolfreys, Julian. *Victorian Hauntings: Spectrality, Gothic, the Uncanny and Literature.* Houndmills, Basingstoke, Hants: Palgrave Macmillan, 2002.

Wollen, Peter. "Compulsion." *Sight and Sound* 7.4 (April 1997): 14–18.

Žižek, Slavoj. *The Plague of Fantasies.* London: Verso, 2007.

CHAPTER 3

Light and Lies: Screen Practice and (Super-) Natural Magic

One attractive way scholars have attempted to explain early cinema's supernatural qualities is through an appeal to the medium's newness. The "new" (a word for which we might substitute "novel," "astonishing," "wondrous" and so on) often appears to be unsettling and otherworldly, and new media can have these qualities in spades,[1] provoking that "sense of uncertainty and disorientation which has always accompanied a new technology that is not yet fully understood" (2006, 27) that Laura Mulvey calls the "technological uncanny." I suggest in this chapter that we may actually reverse this formulation by proposing that associations of cinema with the supernatural came not (or at least not only) from its newness but rather from its continuities with older screen practices like the Phantasmagoria, Pepper's Ghost and the "ghost show." Examination of these practices will show us that the affinities of the supernatural with media of projected light existed long before cinema's debut and made the association of cinema with the supernatural not only understandable but perhaps inevitable. Perhaps one need not choose one explanation over the other (a "newness thesis" versus a "continuity thesis"),[2] but when Mulvey makes statements like "This was the cinema that (like the twentieth century itself) left behind the morbid spirit of the Victorians to become an emblem of modernity" (2006, 37), she underestimates the extent to which things supernatural do not necessarily exist in opposition to the modern, but rather *are* modern. This chapter explores the "continuity thesis" to locate cinema within a longer history of the supernatural and the projected image. It focuses on the concept of the projected image as

© The Author(s) 2017
M. Leeder, *The Modern Supernatural and the Beginnings of Cinema*, DOI 10.1057/978-1-137-58371-0_3

"natural magic," beginning in the seventeenth century, which held that illusions could be used for purposes of enlightenment and entertainment; this was a progressive idea in an iconophobic period where visual illusion was frequently associated with witchcraft and the Devil, understood in medieval Christian tradition as a master of illusion who merely imitates the true miracles reserved for God (Warner 2006, 123). But regardless of any enlightened purposes to which the projected image was put, its supernatural associations would never entirely vanish.

Visual Trickery and Illusions

Various studies of nineteenth-century ghosts—both literary and "actual"—emphasize visuality as the exemplary character of haunting phenomena (McCorristine 2010; Smajić 2010). Obviously, not every supernatural phenomenon is visual: the spiritualists' spectacular "full materializations" were preceded by a long period of predominantly auditory phenomena, and the annals of psychical research rarely contained anything as spectacular as a fully fledged visible ghost (though visible "crisis apparitions"—the *Phantasms of the Living* named in the title of Edmund Gurney, F.W.H. Myers and Frank Podmore's 1886 study—were the subject of some of the early Society for Psychical Research's most famous research). Nonetheless, ghosts loom in the cultural imagination first and foremost as things to be *seen*, although perhaps more by one's mind than by one's eyes: "Neither the advent of gaslight nor electric light could banish the ghost from the visual field for the ghost-sight had long been affirmed as being an *interior* visuality in both occultist and psychological discourses" (McCorristine 2010, 6, original emphasis). Similarly, in his discussion of the "modern optical uncanny," Tom Gunning stresses that not all uncanny experiences are optical (or sensory at all) and that the optical uncanny is not strictly modern. Nonetheless, he holds that "in modernity not only does the optical uncanny become crucial and dramatic (as evident in the development of Fantastic literature), but the modern scientific and technological exploration of vision and optics (such as the proliferation of new optical devices) multiply and articulate the possibilities of the optical uncanny" (2008, 70).[3] It is in this compulsive focus on seeing—on seeing things that may or may not be there—that we can recognize one powerful connection between the supernatural and early cinema. The advent of cinema found audiences facing images that were profoundly lifelike but which they understood as, in some way that is often difficult to characterize, mere illusions.

It seems there was a general understanding that "illusion" was resident in cinema, but less consensus about what that word meant. As the verisimilar style of filmmaking was becoming established during the Transitional Era (roughly 1908–16), its advocates in the trade press freely used the word "illusion" to describe its recreation of reality, even as that illusion they referred to was of a variety opposite to that of the fantastical illusions of in the trick film. Close-ups and other shifts in camera distance were regarded with suspicion, for their violations of cinema's sense of space were thought to disrupt cinema's all-important illusion of reality (Brewster and Jacobs 1997, 164–9; Keil 2001, 164–5). Indeed, many of the earliest works of what we now call film theory were consumed with questions about how an audience can have its attention held by and be entertained by these illusions. The 1960s and 1970s would see similar debates emerge around the apparatus theorists' conception of the interpellated spectator enthralled by cinema's dominance, a point to which I shall return at the end of this chapter.

A Longer History of Ghosts and the Projected Image

In the first chapter of *The Emergence of Cinema: The American Screen to 1907* (1990), Charles Musser argues that we should stop looking for the fraught and slippery origins of cinema in the late nineteenth century and instead consider the invention of the cinematographic apparatus within a much longer history of "screen practice." This label describes practices dating back to the birth of the catoptric lamp and its successor, the magic lantern, in the mid 1600s. Musser places particular emphasis on the Jesuit Athanasius Kircher and his 1646 text *Ars Magna Lucis et Umbrae*, "The Great Art of Light and Shadow," which urged that the lantern be used for educational purposes only and stressed that the lantern itself must be in full view of the spectators, rather than hidden away.[4] Writes Laurent Mannoni:

> [Kircher] did not want to pass himself off as a sorcerer, and denounced the quacks who used optics to take advantage of the credulous. Kircher's aim in revealing all these illuminated and shadowy optical tricks was partly to enlighten the general public ... The spectacular effects of mirrors made his object lessons on "natural magic" all the more effective. (2000, 23–4)

This term "natural magic" appears to have been coined by the Italian polymath Giambattista della Porta (or John Baptista Porta) in *Natural Magic* (*Magiae Naturalis*), first published in 1558. Porta's book condemned witchcraft but defended the "natural magic" of learning as good and godly, just as long as it is put to the service of entertainment and enlightenment. Porta's natural magic is category large enough to subsume subjects as diverse as cooking and metallurgy, optics and perfume, magnetism and poison. The goal of natural magic, upheld by Kircher through his lantern work, was to "emulate the wonders of the nature and glorify their 'wondrousness'" (Hankins and Silverman 1995, 5), promoting an understanding of the world as innately magical that conflicted with the experimental model of science that would begin to take hold in the Enlightenment.

By reaching back to Kircher and the advent of natural magic as the origin of screen practice, Musser ties cinema's roots to the demystification of magical practices: "The origins of screen practice … can be traced back to the mid-1600s and the demystification of those magical arts in which observers confused the 'lifelike' image with life itself" (1990, 16). Musser argues that the seventeenth century's scientific revolution not only resulted in the technology of the magic lantern but also created the climate in which it could be appreciated as a wondrous illusion: "As belief in ghosts declined, as witch burnings ceased, the apparent logic and effectiveness of projecting apparatus as instruments of mystical terror also diminished" (1990, 19). Musser's understanding of the origins of screen practice parallels Simon During's definition of "secular magic" as "illusions understood as illusions" (2002, 2). Importantly, Musser's word "demystification" is one of the translations of the German *Entzauberung*, more commonly rendered as "disenchantment." This term is, of course, most associated with Max Weber, who proclaimed in 1917 that "The fate of our times is characterized by rationalization and intellectualization and, above all, by the 'disenchantment of the world'" (1967, 155).[5] According to Weber, the "mysterious incalculable forces" once present in the world have been chased away by a slowly evolving "intellectualist rationalization, created by science and by scientifically oriented technology" (1967, 139). Modern rationalism and science were now understood as sufficient to explain features of the world that were once mysterious, so belief in the supernatural was no longer required: "It is no longer necessary, as it was for the savage who believed in such forces, to resort to magic in order to control or supplicate the spirits. Instead, technical devices and calculation perform that function. This means that the world is disenchanted" (1967, 139).

Many scholars have argued, however, that the disenchantment of the world has never been a total process.[6] The purported age of disenchantment actually sees a remarkable boost in interest in the supernatural, and I would likewise suggest that the demystification process described by Musser is never complete: the projected image retains supernatural implications long after Kircher and the Scientific Revolution tried to put them to rest. In *The Virtual Window* (2006), Anne Friedberg teases us with the question of whether or not, despite Kircher's enlightened goals, "[*Ars Magna Lucis et Umbrae*] trained a new legion of mystifiers" (2006, 316) who did not disenchant the world but enchanted (or re-enchanted) it with their illusions. Indeed, many of Kircher's descendants paid lip service to education and demystification while exploiting the magic lantern's occult affinities and something similar can be said for the first practitioners of cinema.

Porta's phrase "natural magic" persisted into the nineteenth century with a somewhat different inflection, less connected to the occult. In 1832, Scottish inventor David Brewster, who counted the kaleidoscope and the stereoscope among his inventions, authored *Letters on Natural Magic*.[7] A strict Calvinist who positioned himself against deceit and deception of all kinds, Brewster was a scientific popularizer and a debunker of the supernatural. He argued, in fact, that optical trickery has been responsible for all of the superstition and the false gods of history, and rallied science to prove it. The ancient priests, he suggests:

> must have been familiar with the property of lenses and mirrors to form erect and inverted images of objects ... There is reason to believe that they employed them to effect the apparitions of their gods; and in some of the descriptions of the optical displays which hallowed their ancient temples, we recognize all the transformations of the modern Phantasmagoria. (1832, 19)

Brewster sought to overhaul the idea of natural magic, hoping to see it become "a term for distinguishing between the practices of illusion and spectacular display associated with popular scientific cultural and those associated with the supernatural" (Pierson 2002, 19). Brewster was an intellectual descendant of Kircher, not only because of the technological lineage connecting the magic lantern to the stereoscope, but because they shared the conviction that optical trickery should be deployed only in service of education and never to truly deceive. In his 1856 book *The Stereoscope: Its History, Theory and Construction*, Brewster even allowed that "[f]or the purposes of amusement, the photographer might carry us even into the regions of the supernatural" (1856, 205), explaining the techniques that would shortly be used by spiritualists to create spirit photographs. For Brewster, however, such trick photographs were meant to serve rationalism by demonstrating the inadequacy of human vision in distinguishing between the supernatural and illusions created by scientific means.

Like Kircher, Brewster saw himself as fighting a war against ignorance and superstition, and the fact that he needed to argue against the supernatural implications of illusions proves that they still existed in the "age of disenchantment," and illustrates the extent to which the disenchanted "natural magic" of the nineteenth century remains haunted by the occult "natural magic" of Porta. Brewster's invocation of the Phantasmagoria in the above quote helps demonstrate this fact, for he knew as well as anyone that the projected image has been bound up with the supernatural for centuries. In this context, the term "Phantasmagoria" describes a variety of lantern performance that began in the 1790s, notable for its supernatural subject matter and its tendency to mystify the mechanism of projection.[8]

Because it required darkness to operate, the magic lantern was sometimes called "the Lantern of Fear" and naturally tended to grotesque and ghostly images even before the Phantasmagoria. Johann Schröpfer, a Leipzig coffee shop owner and freemason, flagrantly violated Kircher's precepts by using lantern technology to present himself as a necromancer. He staged séances, even one for Prince Charles of Saxony, who was trying to communicate with his deceased uncle. Schröpfer committed suicide in 1774, supposedly because he began to suffer delusions of his own illusions coming to life (Heard 2006, 48–9). Where Schröpfer passed off his lantern tricks as legitimately supernatural, the men behind the Phantasmagoria presented themselves as capable showmen even as they exploited the general association of illusions with ghosts. The most famous of these exhibitors were Étienne-Gaspard Robert (under the stage name "Robertson") and Paul de Philipstal (as "Philidor"). Beginning in the 1790s, Robertson famously staged gloomy Phantasmagorical spectacles in the crypt of an abandoned Capuchin convent near the Place Vendôme in Paris. His ingenious methods included a "fantascope": "a large magic lantern that could slide back and forth on a double track between fifteen and eighteen feet long. When this lantern was moved along its track, the images projected

LIGHT AND LIES: SCREEN PRACTICE AND (SUPER-) NATURAL MAGIC   51

Image 3.1 A depiction of Robertson's Phantasmagoria that appeared in *L'Optique* by "Fulgence Marion"—actually Camille Flammarion (1869)

on the screen from behind would grow or diminish in size, depending on the distance from the machine to the screen" (Terpak 2001, 301). Daring lanternists even conjured up the spectres of revolutionaries like Danton and Robespierre mere months after their executions (Image 3.1).

Robertson would introduce his performances with rhetoric that described the persistence of supernatural ideas in the putative Age of Enlightenment:

> This is a spectacle which man can use to instruct himself in the bizarre effects of the imagination, when it combines vigor and derangement: I speak of the terror inspired by the shadows, spirits, spells and occult work of the magician: terror that practically every man experienced in the young age of prejudice and which even a few retain in the mature age of reason. (quoted in Musser 1990, 24)

The Phantasmagoria's reliance on imagery of ghosts, skeletons and demons was in keeping with earlier lantern traditions, and the insistence of its operators that it served Enlightenment values may have constituted lip service at best. Castle notes that, "Producers of phantasmagoria often claimed, somewhat disingenuously, that the new entertainment would serve the cause of public enlightenment ... Ancient superstitions would be eradicated when everyone realized that so-called apparitions were in fact only optical illusions" (1995, 143). Like the shadowplayer (Alexander Granach) in Arthur Robison's *Warning Shadows* (1923), they manipulated people's senses with perverse glee, but did so for ostensibly moral purposes.[9] But any enlightened intentions were hampered by the illusionists' desire to conceal their techniques: "The illusion was apparently so convincing that surprised audience members sometimes tried to fend off moving 'phantoms' with their hands or fled the room in terror ... the spectral technology of the phantasmagoria mysteriously recreated the emotional aura of the supernatural" (Castle 1995, 144). The most persistent myth of early cinema is the so-called "Myth of the Grand Café"—the claim that audience members viewing the Lumière programme were traumatized by incoming train in *L'Arrivée d'un train en gare de La Ciotat* (1895), which may be as specious as it is persistent.[10] The myth itself has a considerable prehistory, including the shows of Robertson, Philidor and their ilk. The destinies of the supernatural and the technology of the projected image entwine in the Phantasmagoria, neither for the first nor the last time.

The nineteenth century saw an explosion of scientific interest in vision and the invention of many "philosophical toys" that mark the road to cinema as we generally understand it: the phenakistiscope, thaumatrope, stroboscope, tachyscope, zoetrope, viviscope, mutoscope, kineoptoscope and more.[11] Magic lantern technology continued to improve throughout the nineteenth century, and one of its offshoots marked a new chapter in projected imagery, again with ghosts and the supernatural taking on a central, emblematic role. In England in the 1860s, engineer Henry Dircks devised a new method that would allow an actor to appear to interact with a ghost onstage. It called for a huge pane of glass separating the audience and the theatre, onto which the image of a highly illuminated actor, in a space beneath the stage concealed from the audience's view, could be projected through mirrors. The effect was that the actor on stage remained fully embodied and present while the ghost appeared two-dimensional and half-present, yet both seemed to share space and time. The actor could appear to interact with the ghost, and even to pass through it. Dircks initially had difficulty selling his invention. Jim Steinmeyer writes:

> Like many inventors, Dircks saw only the advantages of his plan and ignored its inconveniences. In fact, his invention would have not only revolutionized stage productions, but it would have demanded that theatres be rebuilt.

London playhouses recognized that Dircks's proposal was for a brand new construction, with the stage lying below the audience and all the seats in a raised balcony. Dircks also called for special windows installed into the ceilings and walls, insisting that it would take sunlight—and daytime performances—to witness that effect. And yet, matinees were not in favour, and London has never been able to bank on bright sunshine. (2003, 26)

The fate of the "Dircksian Phantasmagoria"[12] would lie with Brewster's disciple John Henry Pepper, who had been the director of London's Royal Polytechnic Institution since 1854. The Polytechnic, standing at 309 Regent Street, had opened in 1838 as a venue for "Practical Science," showcasing new feats of science and engineering. It evolved into a venue where modern science and technology were presented as modern wonders. It included a lantern theatre where "dissolving views" illuminated by oxyhydrogen (limelight) illustrated lectures on subjects like geology, astronomy and microbiology, as well as views of faraway places (Weeden 2008, 43–50). In an 1843 article in the *Illustrated Polytechnic Review*, the author describes the Polytechnic as an institution designed for high-minded educational (to say nothing of nationalistic) purposes, specifically rejecting the "vile phantasmagoria" of previous lantern shows:

> We now behold them no longer administering to the vulgar and depraved appetite, alternately exciting the laughter and terror of the beholders; but, assisted by the genius of philosophy and the pencil of art, they picture forth the truthful representations of lovely and picturesque scenery, the holy temples of distant nations, and the heart-stirring scenes of our country's triumphs. (quoted in Weeden 2008, 47)[13]

Pepper, a lantern lecturer with a degree in chemistry, was just the mix of grand showman and distinguished scientist appropriate to the Polytechnic's emphasis on mass education and tasteful wonder. Pepper took Dircks's design and improved it, replacing the need for sunshine with the oxyhydrogen lamp, previously used with the projecting microscope that Pepper had used to display gigantic microbes on a 425-square foot screen (Steinmeyer 2003, 27–9). "Pepper's Ghost," as the new technique came to be known, despite Pepper's dutiful crediting of Dircks, debuted on the Christmas Eve of 1862 during a Polytechnic presentation of one of Dickens's Christmas ghost stories, "The Haunted Man"[14] (Image 3.2). The ghost, in keeping with the *danse macabre* imagery that I will discuss later, was envisioned as a glowing skeleton that seemed to slowly

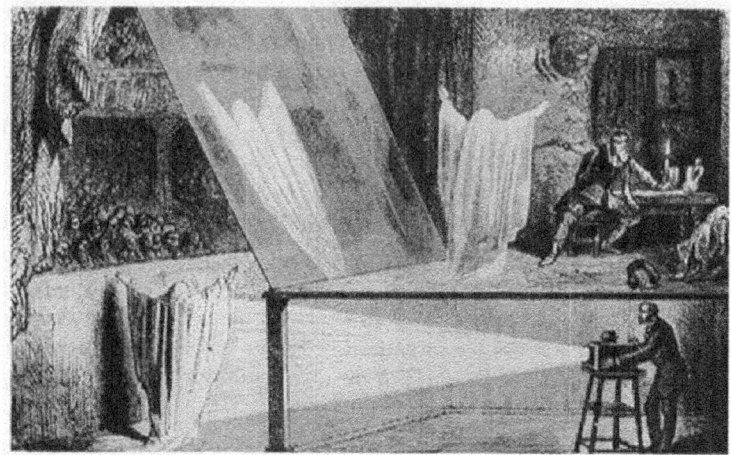

Image 3.2 A depiction of Pepper's Ghost that appeared in *L'Optique* by "Fulgence Marion"—actually Camille Flammarion (1869)

materialize out of mid air, and who would disappear and reappear to torment the play's protagonist. The presentation was intended as a spectacular showcase for developments in the field of optics, and Pepper intended to make a presentation at the end explaining how the illusion was accomplished. But on witnessing the ecstatic reaction of the audience, so amazed and so terrified by the Ghost, Pepper declined explanation (Steinmeyer 2003, 30). Pepper's impulse towards showmanship trumped sober science where the Ghost was concerned, and the legitimate social phenomenon he would soon have on his hands testified to the continued power possessed by phantasmagoric projections.

Pepper restaged "The Haunted Man" in the Polytechnic's main auditorium on 1 June 1863 and different scenarios followed to explore the Ghost's possibilities. Pepper's Ghost shows would be a mainstay on the Polytechnic stage for many years to come. It was a public sensation to the extent that a racehorse called "Pepper's Ghost" appeared at Ascot in 1864 and London cabmen adopted the name to describe customers who vanished without paying (Davies 2007, 207). If it is the case that a more general ghost craze in the 1850s that accompanied the spiritualist boom played a role in Dircks's and Pepper's interest in ghosts, as Mervyn Heard has suggested (2006, 229), then the relationship with spiritualism proved reciprocal. Pepper received numerous letters from spiritualists insisting that he conjured real ghosts on his stage, over his own protestations (Steinmeyer 2003, 21).[15] Pepper's 1890 memoir is strongly critical of spiritualism and, in the spirit of "natural magic," he asserts that the Ghost's role was to confront people with the illusionary character of haunting phenomena. This line of explanation did not endear him to spiritualists: "I vigorously denounced the traders in spirits, founding my arguments on the belief that God was too merciful to us to add to the troubles of this world the fear and trembling brought about by pretended communication with the invisible world" (1890, 28). Pepper even claims that Polytechnic employees were needed to escort him home when spiritualists threatened personal violence against him.

Despite Dircks's and Pepper's attempts to control their respective patents, copies proliferated and the Ghost would be a fixture of supernatural theatre for decades. Pepper's Ghost was staged more often in the fairground "ghost shows" than for the conventional stage, and was seized upon by numerous itinerant showmen. Ghost shows bore wonderful names like the "Captain Payne's Ghost Show," "Wallser's Ghost Illusion" and "Phantaspectra Ghostodrama" (Davies 2007, 209). Writes Vanessa Toulmin:

> the travelling showmen had a major advantage of over their static rivals (who had to install the huge glass whenever the trick was required) as the glass needed for the effect of the ghost on the travelling shows could remain fixed in place in its own purpose-built box, protected from the rigours of the journey by two hinged doors which, like those of the later bioscope show, could be pulled out to form part of the stage. By the mid-1870s many fairground exhibitors had seen the advantages of this innovation and showmen such as Randall Williams, Harry Wall and Tom Norman were exhibiting "The Ghost" at venues throughout the country. (1998, 7)

Williams, called "the King of the Showmen," brought his ghost show to more than a dozen fairs a year, the biggest being the Hull Fair in October and the London's World's Fair, which ran for six weeks beginning on Christmas Eve. Since the mid century, these fairs had been squarely focused on entertainment and exhibition, from steam-powered carousels to menageries, wax museums to illusionists, shooting salons to kinetoscopes, and they granted a prominent place to the ghost show. Between 1873 and 1896, Williams's show displayed projected ghosts and goblins, anchored by

Williams's own oration. Advertisements boasted that Williams offered "The Greatest Ghost Show in the World" and his press notices referred to him as a "next to Barnum the most successful showman" (Toulmin 1998, 15).

Near the end of the century, the ghost show seemed quaint and its illusions had lost their currency. Williams responded by unexpectedly shifting his show entirely to the exhibition of moving pictures at the 1896–7 World Fair, apparently the first fairground exhibitor to make this switch. Many would follow quickly. One press note for the World Fair said, "Randall Williams's ghost show is again located here, but they have this year abandoned the spectral business and are giving an exhibition of animated pictures, an alteration that appears to meet with approval" (Toulmin 1998, 24). Williams continued exhibiting cinema until his death from typhoid fever in 1898. The fact that one of the first exhibitions of cinema in Great Britain occurred under the label of the "Phantascopical Exposition" and replaced a ghost show that employed a version of Pepper's Ghost displays the ease with which cinema was received as the next stage in a tradition of theatricalized depictions of the supernatural. Williams's initial exhibition included Loie Fuller's serpentine dances, footage of the Russian Czar and other decidedly non-supernatural subjects, yet Pepper's Ghost's legacy of blurring entertainment, science and the supernatural, as well the longer association of the projected image with natural (and supernatural) magic, infuse the nascent cinema in so many important ways. The spectral thrills of the ghost show provided one of cinema's first exhibition venues, and many audiences first experienced it as the heir apparent to that fading practice.

Phantoscopes

The chronology of the supernatural and the projected image I have offered takes us up to the traditional beginnings of cinema. The association of projections and the supernatural has a long history, as have debates about the moral, educational and religious ramifications of displaying such illusions to the public. American inventor Charles Francis Jenkins named his projection device the "Phantoscope," a counterpart to more "lively" names like the Biograph and Vitascope (which the Phantoscope became after Thomas Edison purchased the rights). This name makes sense when we recognize cinema as the logical successor to the "ghost show" and the inheritor of the whole haunted history of projected media before it. "Phantascope" was earlier a name of the philosophical toy otherwise known as the phenakistiscope (Robinson 1996, 33–40), and may echo the Robertsonian Phantasmagoria method called the "fantascope." The name combines the Greek *skopein* (looking or inspecting) and the Latin-derived medieval French *fantosme* and the Middle English *phantom*, connoting unreality and ghostliness. There was also a "Grand Phantascope" among the English ghost shows (Davies 2007, 209). If the cinema is indeed a ghost-viewer, it was understood as being only the latest of a lineage.

The word "phantasmagoria" would also take root in Marxist theory, connoting something illusory and weightless which nonetheless masquerades as real and substantial. This fact allows us to approach the question of cinema and illusion from a slightly different angle. In the first volume of *Capital*, published in 1867, Karl Marx would refer to the commodity-form as "the phantasmagoric form of a relation between things" (1976, 165), an unreal and deceptive simulation that conceals an essential absence. Following Marx, Theodor Adorno would use phantasmagoria metaphors to describe "the occultation of production" (Adorno 2005, 74; see also Huyssen 1986, 34–42; Buck-Morss 1992, 22–7; Crary 1992, 132–3), and Walter Benjamin argued that, in Rolf Tiedemann's words, "the fate of nineteenth-century culture lay precisely in its commodity character, which Benjamin thereupon represented in 'cultural values' as *phantasmagoria* … a deceptive image designed to dazzle, is already the commodity itself, in which the exchange value of value-form hides the use value" (1988, 276, original emphasis).[16] It is therefore something more than just analogy to suggest a parallel between the advocates of natural magic, as far removed in time as Kircher and Brewster, and the apparatus theorists, the Marxist-influenced body of film theorists who tended to construct the spectator as a passive figure trapped within the ideological dominance of the apparatus.[17] The apparatus theorists (Christian Metz, Jean-Louis Baudry, Jean-Louis Commoli, Paul Narboni and others) did not believe that cinematic spectators mistook the image for reality, but rather that the illusionism of cinema gave the false impression of a transparent, ideology-free window onto reality. As Commoli puts it:

> The most analogical representation of the world is still not, is never, its reduplication. Analogic repetition is a false repetition, staggered, disphased, deferred and different; but it produces *effects* of repetition and analogy which imply the disavowal (or the repression) of these differences and which thus make of the *desire* for identification, recognition, of the desire the *same*, one of the principal driving forces of analogic figuration. (1980, 138, original emphasis)

Again, cinema is understood as being essentially deceptive and untrustworthy on account of its illusionism. But where Kircher and Brewster saw the projections of light as reformable, even useful, when presented with a sense of openness and clarity, the apparatus theorists generally did not share this optimism. They rather construct a cinematic spectator akin to Peter (Ralph Michael) in the Robert Hamer-directed segment of *Dead of Night* (1945), inexorably absorbed and possessed by the haunted (screen-) mirror. Cinema, for the apparatus theorists, is thus *phantasmagoric* in both Marx's sense and that of Robertson.

Musser's construction of demystification as central to, and indeed a precondition for, modern screen spectatorship was in no small part a rejection of the apparatus theorists' model of the spectator. For apparatus theorists, the burden of "demystification" belongs to the critic, tasked with exposing the obscured ideological workings of the apparatus. For Musser, it is rather the opposite: the defining characteristic of screen spectatorship is the ability of a spectator to construct an intellectual distance between what is present on the screen and what it signifies. In similar terms, Tom Gunning rejected the apparatus theorists' conception of:

> audiences submitting passively to an all-dominating apparatus, hypnotized and transfixed by its illusionist power. Contemporary film theorists have made careers out of underestimating the basic intelligence and reality-testing abilities of the average film viewer and have no trouble treating previous audiences with such disdain. (1995, 115)

In a later essay linking early controversies around cinema to a broader association of the image with evil in western society, Gunning added: "A suspicion of cinema, understood as a visually powerful medium rooted in an illusion of reality and exerting unconscious influences on the viewer, underlies both a conservative antimodern resistance to the new medium at the dawn of the twentieth century and a neo-Marxist ideological critique decades later" (2004a, 26).

We can see that the supernatural implications of the projected image that have come down to cinema through the Phantasmagoria, Pepper's Ghost and others not only persist but also resonate in film theory. At least one scholar explicitly links the tradition of denouncing cinema's illusionistic character to natural magic. In *The Magician and the Cinema* (1981), Erik Barnouw proposes that the art of stage magic led directly to, and was then sadly supplanted by, the cinema. In his conclusion, Barnouw frames this transition in terms of natural magic—where stage magic and the trick film were expressions of natural magic that declared themselves as illusions, the verisimilar mode of classical cinema is deceitful precisely because it naturalizes its magic.[18] Painting a narrative of paradise lost, Barnouw writes:

> It may well be that a central element in the [cinema's] power is the astonishing fact that media images are no longer seen by the public as optical illusions offered by magicians, but as something real. The unawareness is equivalent to defenselessness. The new industrialized magic may be closer to "black magic" than "natural magic." (1981, 112)

Barnouw here echoes Georges Méliès himself, who denounced the incipient classical/institutional model of cinema on a similar basis, as magic that does not acknowledge itself as such (During 2002, 170). Barnouw also, of course, strongly echoes the apparatus theorists in his distrust of cinema's illusions as dangerous and deceptive, creating a "defenseless" and thoroughly mystified audience. It is intriguing to find these familiar debates framed explicitly in the terms of "natural" versus "black" magic. Critical discussions about cinema's status as illusion and the ideological implications thereof continue to this day,[19] but they are permutations of debates that have been going on since at least the seventeenth century, when Athanasius Kircher allied the magic lantern technology with the idea of natural magic. Barnouw's remarks remind us that, just as cinema represents only one stage of a much longer history of the projected image, so too are many of the classic debates of film theory rooted in debates about natural magic stretching back centuries.

Notes

1. For discussions of the idea of newness in media, see Onians (1994) and Gunning (2003).
2. I here echo Gunning's argument that the theme of animation in early cinema can be both seen as part of cinema's modernity and a link to older traditions with no necessary contradiction (2001, 5).
3. Fantastic literature is the literary mode characterized by Tzvetan Todorov (1975) as depending on a vacillation between naturalistic and non-naturalistic explanations for the supernatural. Gunning also writes on vision and the supernatural in "To Scan a Ghost" (2007).

4. Kircher was once generally named as the inventor of the magic lantern, though he was preceded by Christiaan Huygens and other experimenters. Brian Winston notes the Eurocentric bias of most accounts of the origins of the magical lantern, as similar devices existed in China and the Arab world significantly earlier (1996, 16).
5. Weber's phrase "*die Entzauberung der Welt*" draws on a line written Friedrich Schiller over a century earlier: "*die Entgöterung der Natur*," the "dis-godding of the world" (Berman 1981, 69). See Cascardi (1992) for a useful discussion of Weber's disenchantment thesis, locating it within broader currents in continental philosophy.
6. See for instance Jenkins (2003), Owen (2004), Murdock (2008), Locke (2011) and the collection *The Re-Enchantment of the World: Secular Magic in a Rational Age* (Landy and Saler 2009).
7. See Burwick (1991) for more on Brewster.
8. The supernatural lantern spectaculars of the Phantasmagoria, in particular, have in recent decades been a productive topic of exploration for scholars like Theodore X. Barber (1989), Laurent Mannoni (2000), Tom Gunning (2004b), Mervyn Heard (2006), David J. Jones (2014) and the aforementioned Terry Castle (1995).
9. See Guerin (2005, 89–108) for a reading of *Warning Shadows*, emphasizing its play on the boundaries of realism and illusion.
10. For discussions of the "Myth of the Grand Café," see Bottomore (1999), Loiperdinger (2004), Elsaesser (2009) and Leeder (2010).
11. Most famously chronicled by Crary (1992, esp. 97–136).
12. In a surviving fragment of the Ruth Roland serial *Haunted Valley* (1923), we learn that the titular valley is actually "haunted" by hologram-like projections of ghostly human forms (cinematically realized with double exposures) that are diegetically described as the inventions of a character named "Dirks."
13. For another take on the early life of the Polytechnic and the climate of Victorian natural magic as the birthplace of cinema, see McGrath (1996).
14. For examinations of the Ghost's early life, see Brooker (2007), Groth (2007), Lightman (2007, 167–218) and Posner (2007).
15. This dynamic anticipates the later insistence on the part of numerous spiritualists, including Arthur Conan Doyle, that Harry

Houdini was using magic powers in his acts without acknowledging or perhaps even realizing it.
16. For more on Walter Benjamin's use of phantasmagoria metaphors, see Britzolakis (1999).
17. See Baudry (1974) and Metz (1982). The apparatus theorists operated within an iconophobic tradition stretching back to Plato (see Jay 1993, 329–80).
18. To quote Gunning on this transition, "In parallel editing the 'magical' switches from one line of action to another are not the product of a Méliès-like prestidigitator, nor indications of a marvellous overturning of the laws of space and time ... Griffith's 'trick work' is in the service of the drama, a narrativizing of the possibilities of filmic discourse" (1991, 190).
19. For other key contributions to debates about cinema's "illusionism," see Carroll (1988, 90–106), Allen (1993), Anderson (1996), Currie (1996), Kania (2002) and North (2008).

Works Cited

Adorno, Theodor. *In Search of Wagner*. London: Verso, 2005.
Allen, Richard. "Representation, Illusion, and the Cinema." *Cinema Journal* 32.2 (Winter 1993): 21–48.
Anderson, Joseph D. *The Reality of Illusion: An Ecological Approach to Cognitive Film Theory*. Carbondale: South Illinois University Press, 1996.
Barber, X. Theodore. "Phantasmagorical Wonders: The Magic Lantern Ghost Shows in Nineteenth-century America." *Film History* 3 (1989): 73–86.
Barnouw, Erik. *The Magician and the Cinema*. New York: Oxford University Press, 1981.
Baudry, Jean-Louis. "Ideological Effects of the Basic Cinematographic Apparatus." *Film Quarterly* 28.2 (Winter 1974–1975): 39–47.
Berman, Morris. *The Reenchantment of the World*. Ithaca: Cornell University Press, 1981.
Bottomore, Stephen. "The Panicking Audience? Early Cinema and the 'Train Effect'." *Historical Journal of Film, Radio and Television* 19.2 (1999): 177–216.
Brewster, Ben and Lea Jacobs. *Theatre to Cinema: Stage Pictorialism and the Early Feature Film*. Oxford: Oxford University Press, 1997.
Brewster, David. *Letters on Natural Magic*. New York: J & J. Harper, 1832.
Brewster, David. *The Stereoscope: Its History, Theory and Construction, with Its Application to the Fine and Useful Arts and to Education, Etc.* London: John Murray, 1856.

Britzolakis, Christina. "Phantasmagoria: Walter Benjamin and the Poetics of Urban Modernism." *Ghosts: Deconstruction, Psychoanalysis, History*. Eds. Peter Buse and Andrew Stott. New York: St. Martin's Press, 1999. 72–91.
Brooker, Jeremy. "The Polytechnic Ghost: Pepper's Ghost, Metempsychosis and the Magic Lantern at the Royal Polytechnic Institution." *Early Popular Visual Culture* 5.2 (2007): 189–206.
Buck-Morss, Susan. "Aesthetics and Anaesthetics: Walter Benjamin's Artwork Essay Reconsidered." *October* 62 (Autumn 1992): 3–41.
Burwick, Frederick. "Science and Supernaturalism: Sir David Brewster and William Scott." *Comparative Criticism* 13 (1991): 83–114.
Carroll, Noël. *Mystifying Movies: Fads & Fallacies in Contemporary Film Theory*. New York: Columbia University Press, 1988.
Cascardi, Anthony J. *The Subject of Modernity*. Cambridge: Cambridge University Press, 1992.
Castle, Terry. *The Female Thermometer: 18th Century and the Invention of the Uncanny*. New York: Oxford University Press, 1995.
Commoli, Jean-Louis. "Machines of the Visible." *The Cinematic Apparatus*. Eds. Teresa de Laurentis and Stephen Heath. London: Macmillan, 1980. 121–42.
Crary, Jonathan. *Techniques of the Observer: On Vision and Modernity in the 19th Century*. Cambridge, MA: The MIT Press, 1992.
Currie, Gregory. "Film, Reality and Illusion." *Post-Theory: Reconstructing Film Studies*. Eds. David Bordwell and Noël Carroll. Madison, WI: University of Wisconsin Press, 1996. 325–45.
Davies, Owen. *The Haunted: A Social History of Ghosts*. New York: Palgrave Macmillan, 2007.
During, Simon. *Modern Enchantments: The Cultural Power of Secular Magic*. Cambridge: Harvard University Press, 2002.
Elsaesser, Thomas. "Archaeologies of Interactivity: Early Cinema, Narrative and Spectatorship." *Film 1900: Technology, Perception, Culture*. Eds. Annemone Ligensa and Klaus Kreimeier. New Barnet, Herts: John Libbey Publishing, 2009. 9–22.
Friedberg, Anne. *The Virtual Window: From Alberti to Microsoft*. Cambridge: The MIT Press, 2006.
Groth, Helen. "Reading Victorian Illusions: Dickens's *Haunted Man* and Dr. Pepper's 'Ghost.'" *Victorian Studies* 5.10 (Autumn 2007): 43–65.
Guerin, Frances. *A Culture of Light: Cinema and Technology in 1920s Germany*. Minneapolis: University of Minnesota Press, 2005.
Gunning, Tom. "An Aesthetic of Astonishment: Early Film and the (In)Credulous Spectator." *Viewing Positions: Ways of Seeing Film*. Ed. Linda Williams. New Brunswick, NJ: Rutgers University Press, 1995. 114–33.
Gunning, Tom. *D.W. Griffith and the Origins of American Film: The Early Years at Biograph*. Urbana: University of Illinois Press, 1991.

Gunning, Tom. "Flickers: On Cinema's Power for Evil." *Bad: Infamy, Darkness, Evil and Slime on Screen*. Ed. Murray Pomerance. Albany: SUNY Press, 2004a. 21–38.
Gunning, Tom. "The Ghost in the Machine: Animated Pictures at the Haunted Hotel of Early Cinema." *Living Pictures* 1.1 (2001): 3–17.
Gunning, Tom. "Phantasmagoria and the Manufacturing of Illusions and Wonder: Towards a Cultural Optics of the Cinematic Apparatus." *The Cinema, A New Technology for the 20th Century*. Eds. André Gaudreault, Catherine Russell and Pierre Veronneau. Lausanne, Switzerland: Editions Payot Lausanne, 2004b. 31–44.
Gunning, Tom. "Re-newing Old Technologies: Astonishment, Second Nature and the Uncanny in Technology from the Previous Turn-of-the-century." *Rethinking Media Change: The Aesthetics of Transition*. Eds. David Thorburn and Henry Jenkins. Cambridge: MIT Press, 2003. 39–60.
Gunning, Tom. "To Scan a Ghost: The Ontology of Mediated Vision." *Grey Room* 26 (Winter 2007): 94–127.
Gunning, Tom. "Uncanny Reflections, Modern Illusion: Sighting the Modern Optical Uncanny." *Uncanny Modernity: Cultural Theories, Modern Anxieties*. Eds. Jo Collins and John Jervis. Houndmills, Basingstoke, Hants: Palgrave Macmillan, 2008. 68–90.
Gurney, Edmund, Frederic W.H. Myers and Frank Podmore. *Phantasms of the Living*. London: Trübner and Co., 1886. 2 vols.
Hankins, Thomas L. and Robert J. Silverman. *Instruments and the Imagination*. Princeton: Princeton University Press, 1995.
Heard, Mervyn. *Phantasmagoria: The Secret Life of the Magic Lantern*. Hastings: The Projection Box, 2006.
Huyssen, Andreas. *Across the Great Divide: Modernism, Mass Culture, Postmodernism*. Bloomington: Indiana University Press, 1986.
Jay, Martin. *Downcast Eyes: The Denigration of Vision in Twentieth-century French Thought*. Berkeley: University of California Press, 1993.
Jenkins, Richard. "Disenchantment, Enchantment and Re-Enchantment: Max Weber at the Millennium." *Max Weber Studies* 1 (2003): 11–32.
Jones, David J. *Sexuality and the Gothic Magic Lantern: Desire, Eroticism and Literary Visibilities from Byron to Bram Stoker*. Houndmills, Basingstoke, Hants: Palgrave Macmillan, 2014.
Kania, Andrew. "The Illusion of Realism in Film." *British Journal of Aesthetics* 42 (2002): 243–58.
Keil, Charlie. *Early American Cinema in Transition: Story, Style, and Filmmaking, 1907–1913*. Madison, WI: University of Wisconsin Press, 2001.
Landy, Joshua and Michael Saler. "Introduction: The Varieties of Modern Enchantment." *The Re-enchantment of the World*. Eds. Joshua Landy and Michael Saler. Stanford: Stanford University Press, 2009. 1–14.

Leeder, Murray. "M. Robert-Houdin Goes to Algeria: Spectatorship and Panic in Illusion and Early Cinema." *Early Popular Visual Culture* 8.2 (2010): 187–203.

Lightman, Bernard. *Victorian Popularizers of Science: Designing Nature for New Audiences.* Chicago: University of Chicago Press, 2007.

Locke, Simon. *Re-crafting Rationalization: Enchanted Science and Mundane Mysteries.* Farham, Surrey: Ashgate, 2011.

Loiperdinger, Martin. "Lumière's *Arrival of a Train*: Cinema's Founding Myth." *The Moving Image* 4.1 (Spring 2004): 89–118.

Mannoni, Laurent. *The Great Art of Light and Shadow: The Archaeology of Cinema.* Exeter: University of Exeter Press, 2000.

Marx, Karl. *Capital.* Volume 1. Harmondsworth: Penguin, 1976.

McCorristine, Shane. *Specters of the Self: Thinking about Ghosts and Ghost-seeing in England, 1750–1920.* Cambridge: Cambridge University Press, 2010.

McGrath, Roberta. "Natural Magic and Science Fiction: Instruction, Amusement and the Popular Show, 1795–1895." *Cinema: The Beginnings and the Future. Essays Marking the Centenary of the First Film Show Projected to a Paying Audience in Britain.* Ed. Christopher Williams. London: University of Westminster Press, 1996. 13–23.

Metz, Christian. *The Imaginary Signifier: Psychoanalysis and the Cinema.* Bloomington: Indiana University Press, 1982.

Mulvey, Laura. *Death 24× a Second: Stillness and the Moving Image.* London: Reaktion, 2006.

Murdock, Graham. "Re-enchantment and the Popular Imagination: Fate, Magic and Purity." *Northern Lights* 6 (2008): 27–44.

Musser, Charles. *The Emergence of Cinema: The American Screen to 1907.* New York: Maxwell Macmillan International, 1990.

North, Dan. *Performing Illusions: Cinema, Special Effects and the Virtual Actor.* London: Wallflower, 2008.

Onians, John. "'I Wonder...': A Short History of Amazement." *Sight & Insight: Essays on Art and Culture in Honour of E.H. Gombrich at 85.* London: Phaidon, 1994. 11–34.

Owen, Alex. *The Place of Enchantment: British Occultism and the Culture of the Modern.* Chicago: University of Chicago Press, 2004.

Pepper, John Henry. *The True History of the Ghost and All About Metempsychosis.* London: Cassell & Company, 1890.

Pierson, Michele. *Special Effects: Still in Search of Wonder.* New York: Columbia University Press, 2002.

Posner, Dassia N. "Spectres on the New York Stage: The (Pepper's) Ghost Craze of 1863." *Representations of Death in Nineteenth-century U.S. Writing and Culture.* Ed. Lucy Elizabeth Frank. Aldershot, Hants: Ashgate, 2007. 189–204.

Robinson, David. "Realising the Vision: 300 Years of Cinematography." *Cinema: The Beginnings and the Future. Essays Marking the Centenary of the First Film*

Show Projected to a Paying Audience in Britain. Ed. Christopher Williams. London: University of Westminster Press, 1996. 33–40.

Smajić, Srdjan. *Ghost-seers, Detectives and Spiritualists: Theories of Vision in Victorian Literature and Science*. New York: Cambridge University Press, 2010.

Steinmeyer, Jim. *Hiding the Elephant: How Magicians Invented the Impossible and Learned to Disappear*. New York: Carol & Graf Publishers, 2003.

Terpak, Frances. "Objects and Contexts." *Devices of Wonder: From the World in a Box to Images on a Screen*. Los Angeles: Getty Publications, 2001. 142–364.

Tiedemann, Rolf. "Dialectics at a Standstill: Approaches to the *Passagen-Werk*." *On Walter Benjamin: Critical Essays and Recollections*. Ed. Gary Smith. Cambridge, MA: The MIT Press, 1988. 260–91.

Todorov, Tzvetan. *The Fantastic: A Structural Approach to a Literary Genre*. Ithaca, NY: Cornell University Press, 1975.

Toulmin, Vanessa. *Randall Williams: King of Showmen. From Ghost Show to Bioscope*. London: The Projection Box, 1998.

Warner, Marina. *Phantasmagoria: Spirit Visions, Metaphors and Media into the Twenty-first Century*. Oxford: Oxford University Press, 2006.

Weber, Max. "Science as a Vocation." *From Max Weber: Essays in Sociology*. Eds. H.H. Gerth and C. Wright Mills. London: Routledge, 1967. 129–158.

Weeden, Brenda. *The Education of the Eye: History of the Royal Polytechnic Institution 1838–1881*. Chesterton, Cambridge: University of Westminster, 2008.

Winston, Brian. *Technologies of Seeing: Photography, Cinematography and Television*. London: BFI, 1996.

CHAPTER 4

The Strange Case of George Albert Smith: Mesmerism, Psychical Research and Cinema

Only one name has a prominent place in the histories of both Victorian investigations into the supernatural and of early cinema.[1] This is George Albert Smith, a Brighton stage mesmerist who participated in an important (and still contentious) set of early telepathy experiments and was a long-standing employee of the Society for Psychical Research (SPR) before becoming one of the loose-knit group of film pioneers known as the "Brighton School" or "Hove School." The eccentric circuits of Smith's careers help us explore industrial and cultural affinities between the supernatural and cinema on more of a biographical level, and in this chapter I will explore this one man's strange case. Film historians have described Smith as a pioneer with key contributions to editing,[2] the close-up,[3] colour[4] and the double exposure. Smith outlived virtually every other cinema pioneer and, though he lived in obscurity for decades, he did live to see his work garner new interest in the 1940s and 1950s. He gave interviews to film historians like Georges Sadoul and Rachael Low, and in 1955 he was elected a Fellow of the British Film Academy. On 16 October 1957, he attended the opening of the National Film Theatre under Waterloo Bridge in London. A group photograph taken that night shows him alongside HRH Princess Margaret, Gina Lollabrigida, Laurence Olivier, René Clair, John Ford, Vittorio de Sica and Akira Kurosawa,[5] with Smith serving as a living embodiment of Britain's proud cinematic tradition. He would die two years later at the age of 95.

Less than a decade after his death, a book would cast Smith in a rather different light, as a fraudster and cheat with a measure of responsibility

© The Author(s) 2017
M. Leeder, *The Modern Supernatural and the Beginnings of Cinema*, DOI 10.1057/978-1-137-58371-0_4

for the suicide of the prominent late Victorian psychologist and psychical researcher Edmund Gurney. *The Strange Case of Edmund Gurney* (Hall 1964) was one of several scathing books about the founders of psychical research written by a disgruntled ex-SPR member named Trevor H. Hall. The fact that the SPR of the time meticulously collected reviews of and responses to Hall's books (still present in their Cambridge archives) speaks to the depth of their interest in or embarrassment at his claims, especially those relating to the death of SPR co-founder Gurney.[6] Later historians of psychical research, such as Fraser Nicol, C.D. Broad, John Beloff, Alan Gauld, Janet Oppenheim and Gordon Epperson, would provide more sympathetic and balanced treatments of the early SPR and often disputed Hall's claims; Epperson calls *The Strange Case of Edmund Gurney* "mainly a work of fiction" in scholarly trappings (1994, 142). Hall's most sensational claim was that the death of Gurney from an overdose of chloroform in a Brighton hotel on 22 July 1888 was a suicide, inspired by learning that the Blackburn-Smith telepathy experiments he had conducted in 1882–3 had been faked by their participants: Douglas Blackburn and none other than George Albert Smith, whom Gurney had retained as a secretary and assistant in the years since. Hall further alleged that the SPR leadership of the time concealed the facts of Gurney's suicide and conspired to present it as an accidental death in order to avoid bringing unwanted scrutiny to their still-fledging organization.[7]

The matter of whether or not Gurney committed suicide is thoroughly marginal to the considerations of this chapter, except insofar as it is unfortunate that the best known source on Smith's early life (still useful for its biographical details) is also one that paints him as a hoaxer who played a part in Gurney's death. I submit that it is not most productive to understand Smith simply as a fraud but rather as a figure uniquely positioned between two (at least two) worlds, whose life and careers can tell us something about their connections. I have mentioned Smith's status as a pioneer of double exposure aesthetics, and this is a place where the connection between the supernatural and cinematic technique reveals itself tangibly; Smith was one of the first filmmakers, if not the very first, to bring the ghostly aesthetic familiar from the spirit photograph to cinema, and thus inaugurated a strategy for the visualization of the supernatural that would remain standard for many decades. His diverse output as a filmmaker includes some early trick films reflective of his former careers, many utilizing double exposures. Paul Virilio notes that the "ghost industry" of spirit photography "had a huge impact on the aesthetic and technical vocabulary of the cinema" (1989, 38), and though he is speaking particularly about the First World War era and Germany, his words probably apply even better to early cinema and the case of Smith in particular. W.K.L. and Antonia Dickson even included trick photographs borrowing the aesthetic of the spirit photograph in *History of the Kinematograph* (Solomon 2010, 18–19). In spite of these strong associations, there never was a properly cinematic equivalent of spirit photography that would display proof of the existence of ghosts on screen, though such "Spirit-Cinema" was indeed craved by various writers (2010, 24–5). But if Spirit-Cinema was not to be,[8] the use of the double exposure to envision the supernatural would be standard in cinema for decades, and at the beginning of that tradition is George Albert Smith, who reflects the entanglement of cinema and the supernatural on both personal and professional levels perhaps better than any other person.

Smith the Mesmerist

Various sources that describe Smith's early career as a theatrical performer have called him a magician, a mesmerist, a hypnotist, a spiritualist and a mentalist. In a sense, this array of labels is not unwarranted and reflects the close conjunction of these various practices in the stage entertainments of the time, but a lack of historical precision has led to several misunderstandings. This chapter brings more precision to the discussion of Smith's various careers and how they fit within the culture of the day.

Smith was born in East London in 1864 and his family moved south to Brighton during his childhood. By 1881, his father was deceased and his mother operated a seaside boarding house (Hall 1964, 92–3), while the 17-year-old Smith worked as a seaside entertainer, honing an act that blended mesmerism, thought-transference and stage spiritualism. To understand the significance of Smith's act, we must briefly examine the history of mesmerism, especially in Britain. The practice takes the name of Franz Anton Mesmer, the German physician who began his studies into what he called "animal magnetism" (from the Latin *animus*, spirit) in the 1770s; "mesmerism" may not have been said in his lifetime. Mesmer proposed that souls are electromagnetic constructions and theorized the existence of a kind of spiritual fluid that could flow from person to person, which was responsible for health and illness. Mesmer's experiments were centred on the way in which a doctor/magnetizer could place a patient *en rapport* and effect cures by manipulating animal magnetism.[9]

The "mesmeric" rapport between doctor and patient was fraught with sinister, sometime sexual, implications related to the apparent abdication of will on the patient's part. Roger Luckhurst notes that "the first wave of the Gothic in the late eighteenth century perfectly matched the advent of Mesmer's theories of animal magnetism" (2002, 204) and the exploration of dream, distraction, reverie and trance throughout Gothic art and literature was fuelled in large part by Mesmer's theories. Mesmeric themes figured significantly in the supernatural throughout the nineteenth century and beyond, as I shall discuss later in this chapter.[10]

Mesmerism reached Britain in 1837, well after its boom in popularity in continental Europe. The distinguished doctor John Elliotson began doing mesmeric experiments with patients at the University College Hospital in London and presenting public demonstrations before members of London society. Along with W.C. Engledue of Brighton, Elliotson founded *The Zoist: A Journal of Cerebral Physiology & Mesmerism*, which ran from 1843 to 1864. Elliotson's experiments and claims inspired widespread debate and ushered in an enormous vogue for mesmerism in Britain. Alison Winter writes that "Mesmerism could be seen almost everywhere and was practiced by individuals of virtually all professions and classes" (1998, 16), with mesmeric imagery commonplace in political cartoons and other similar social satires of the day. Terry Parssinen explains that while mesmerism and debates surrounding it diffused through the printed word to a degree, it was the "small army" of itinerant mesmeric performers through which mesmerism truly spread (1977, 89). Many of the mesmeric performers were of low social origins but achieved widespread audiences of mixed social standing, blurring the already hazy lines between scientist and performer, professional and amateur.

In 1842, the Scottish surgeon James Braid developed hypnosis, in part from the examination of mesmerized subjects. Even his rejection of animal magnetism in favour of psychophysiological explanations for mesmeric states did not inure Braid from criticism: "Braid's success in ridding his practice of some of mesmerism's controversial features was one factor in hypnotism's survival, although in the 1840s he was regarded as only one of many controversial practitioners, and drew his share of attacks" (Winter 1998, 184). It would take many decades of debate within the psychological establishment before hypnotism reached the status of generally accepted scientific fact. But mesmerism's story did not end with the establishment of hypnotism. It continued as a stage practice, "transformed from a doctrine which made serious medical and scientific claims into an amusement to be placed in a category with conjuring or fortune-telling, and mesmeric performers were transformed from scientific lecturers and healers into entertainers" (Parssinen 1977, 104). Further, spiritualists and occultists were far too invested in Mesmer's ideas about animal magnetism and his fluidic model of the universe to abandon them when the scientific orthodoxy did. Journals like *Light* and *Borderland* regularly printed pieces on mesmeric healing and mesmeric clairvoyance in the 1880s and 1890s, and the new field of psychical research had mesmerism in its intellectual lineage, even as it officially allied itself with hypnotism and established science.

A September 1882 review in the *Brighton Herald* emphasized how the youthful George Albert Smith's act drew rhetorically on the (by then heavily discredited) Mesmeric model of animal magnetism:

> Mr. Smith cited numerous proofs of the existence in the human body of a magnetic force, remarking that he considered it was some such force which, emanating from the brain and acting through the nerves, contracted the muscles and produced motion; and that it was through the medium of magnetism that impressions were also received. Proceeding then to consider whether the magnetism of one person could be affected by that of another, he contended that we had under the control of our will a subtle magnetic force, and that it was possible to make other people feel that force. The effect it produced corresponded very closely with that of sleep, in which, the voluntary action of the brain being suspended, the involuntary action gave rise to dreams, and sometimes to somnambulism. By means of mesmerism, it was possible to suspend the voluntary action of the brain of the subject; and then, by inducing in them certain mental impressions, to produce such phenomena as he had demonstrated upon the platform. (Anon. 1882b, 2)

As part of the act, Smith would give a mesmerized baker named Fred Wells a candle and tell him it was sponge-cake, not stopping him until he had eaten half of it (Hamilton 2009, 124–5). A July 1882 review from the *Brighton Herald* carried the following description:

> Mr. Smith professes to show how some of his subjects, whilst retaining consciousness, are, nevertheless, unable to move or to refrain from moving, as the case may be except at his bidding. At other times the audience is asked to believe that the mental as well as the physical faculties of the subjects are wholly subjugated to the mesmerist's will, when he seems able to produce any impression upon their minds, including the sensations of heat and cold. (Anon. 1882a, 3)

Smith would soon adopt a thought-reading act[11] in partnership with local journalist Douglas Blackburn. Blackburn found Smith doing a mesmerism act in a small Brighton hall and discovered that his own office-boy, Mahoney, was one of Smith's shills, pretending to be put under the influence and subject to Smith's will (Hall 1964, 93). Blackburn took to shilling Smith in another sense, writing a series of articles about him for *The Brightonian* throughout 1882, all written with unbridled enthusiasm. A 22 July article read:

> Mr. G.A. Smith's concluding appearance at the Aquarium on Saturday evening was an event in the history of the institution. The crowd was simply enormous, and the excitement and enthusiasm proportionate. Someone calling himself a doctor seized one of the subjects whilst under control and administered sundry brutal kicks and prickings, and the boy still remaining unconscious the sceptic had the audacity to denounce him as a fraud. This was too much for the audience, so they threw the interrupter out.
>
> The engagement has proved the most successful ever made by the Aquarium management, and throws Crowther, Little Louie and the Midgets far into the shade. Mr. Smith has received an offer for a re-engagement in a fortnight, but he proposes giving a series of select high-class séances for the popularizing of the science. (quoted in Hall 1964, 94)

This announcement does much to remind us how porous the worlds of magic, mesmerism and stage spiritualism were at the time.

By September 1882, Blackburn would join Smith onstage as his partner, having already been a "silent partner" stoking public interest in Smith's performances. Smith would be blindfolded on stage while the audience produced various objects, the identity of which Blackburn would "telepathically" convey to Smith, allowing him to identify them. Smith and Blackburn adapted the methods of the American mentalist Washington Irving Bishop, who had proved a success in London the year prior. Bishop was the star of "muscle reading," a technique where the mentalist grips a subject's hand and purports to read his or her thoughts through subtle and involuntary responses on his or her part. Bishop was born to spiritualist parents and became the manager of the stage medium Anna Eva Fay, but went through a remarkable reversal in 1876, publishing a book exposing Fay's methods and hawking it at his own anti-spiritualist magic show (During 2002, 161). Despite his anti-spiritualist posture, Bishop came into conflict with the important English magician John Nevil Maskelyne; Maskelyne even successfully sued Bishop over a libellous newspaper article in which Bishop had accused Maskelyne of colluding against him. To Maskelyne, people like Bishop were little better than the spiritualists, exploiting the credulity of audiences; they represented a breed of new magic that clashed with the mechanized and secularized Robert-Houdin-influenced version of magic nurtured at London's Egyptian Hall.

Bishop, Stuart Cumberland and other early mentalists played an important part in triggering the scientific investigation of thought-transference, which would shortly be redubbed "telepathy." Despite the fact that Bishop attributed his powers to muscle reading and not anything supernatural, and even published a guide to memorizing the mnemonics used by stage clairvoyants (Luckhurst 2002, 63), he and other performers like him became rallying points for those eager to promote telepathy as scientifically verifiable. Writes Luckhurst, "[Bishop] invited scientific observers to help explain his mysterious sensitivity ... and this left a space for supernatural accounts of these performances" (2002, 65). Scientific investigators looked to stage performers as subjects for study, and stage performers embraced such opportunities for free publicity. Smith and Blackburn's relationship with the SPR proved a classic example of this symbiosis. The pair solicited scrutiny for their act through a letter Blackburn had printed in the spiritualist periodical *Light* on 26 August 1882, entitled "THOUGHT-READING EXTRAORDINARY." It read:

> *To the Editor of* "LIGHT."
> Sir, The following details of the latest and most marketable development of that form of Thought-reading popularized by Mr. Irving Bishop may prove of interest to your readers. In conjunction with Mr. G.A. Smith, a Brighton mesmerist, not unknown to readers of this and other Spiritualist journals, I have had the satisfaction of experiencing some demonstrations of mind-sympathy which are, I believe, almost without precedent. The *modus* of Mr. Smith's experiment is this: He places himself *en rapport* with myself by taking my hands; and a strong concentration of will and mental vision on my part has enabled him to read my thoughts with an accuracy that approaches miraculous. Not only can he, with slight hesitation, read numbers, words, and even whole sentences which I alone have seen, but the sympathy between us has been developed to such a degree that he rarely fails to experience the taste of any liquid or solid I choose to imagine. He has named, described, or discovered small articles he has never seen, when they have been concealed by me in the most unusual places, and on two occasions he has successfully described portions of a scene which I either imagined or actually saw.

Mr. Smith has exhibited marked power as a thought-reader through the mediumship of other persons, but on no occasion has he attained to anything like the power he invariably displays when *en rapport* with myself. I may add that we have for some time been experimenting together with a view of developing one or the other, but until quite recently the results were not of a nature to call for special remark. The results at each sitting have so far shewn such a marked improvement that it may be safely assumed that ere long Mr. Smith will develop a sympathetic power equal to anything shewn by sensitives in the mesmeric or clairvoyant state. The experiments have created great interest in local scientific circles, and we propose giving a series of séances to members of the Sussex National History or other scientific associations.

We shall be happy to receive a visit from any Spiritualist or scientific inquirer who may be at Brighton during the ensuing month, especially as we are about to inaugurate a series of private séances, at which this most interesting phase of psychic force may be investigated and developed.—I am, Sir, yours obediently

Douglas Blackburn
Editor of *The Brightonian*
Brightonian Office
24 Duke Street, Brighton

This letter would shape the direction of the rest of George Albert Smith's life.

Smith and the SPR

The notice published by Blackburn in *Light* did indeed attract the attention of the fledgling Society for Psychical Research in the persons of SPR co-founders Frederic William Henry Myers and Edmund Gurney. The SPR was founded earlier in 1882 to provide scientific scrutiny of claims of mediumship, telepathy, haunted houses and the like. Its principal players were a group of well-educated, mostly Cambridge, psychologists, philosophers and scientists, largely disenchanted with mainstream Christianity but hopeful that science would yield fresh evidence in support of God and the human soul. The SPR carefully constructed a rationalist, empiricist posture, and would come to host an impressive number of Victorian intellectuals and scientists on its membership list.[12] The SPR initially formed a series of committees to investigate different psychic phenomena, among them the Committee on Mesmerism, the Committee on Haunted Houses and the Committee on Thought-Reading, swiftly renamed with less-invasive sounding "Thought-transference." Myers and Gurney were representing the latter when they came to Brighton to investigate Blackburn and Smith. Finding scientific evidence to verify the existence of telepathy was the SPR's grand project at the time, and it promoted theories that enfolded other supernatural phenomena within it. The SPR offended spiritualist sensibilities by generally offering "a retheorization of the ghost as a telepathic phantasm" (Luckhurst 2002, 182), denying the existence of the intelligent and motivated spectre representing a human being's surviving consciousness in favour of theories relating ghost phenomena to telepathic projections and psychic resonances.

In 1883, F.W.H. Myers coined the word "telepathy" from the Greek for "feeling at a distance." The adoption of such scientific (some would say pseudo-scientific) language was designed to help separate psychical research from spiritualism, theosophy, astrology and the rising interest in Eastern magic. There was a strong drive to promote the SPR as a legitimate, mainstream group of researchers, and for a time this worked well, thanks in large part to wide appeal of the idea of telepathy. The SPR's overarching project in its early existence was to turn telepathy into what Roger Luckhurst calls a "black box," borrowing language from Bruno Latour to describe a concept in science the substance of which is no longer disputed. Writes Luckhurst, "The transformation of thought-reading into telepathy shifted the locale of unaccountable transmission from the séance, the parlour, and the stage, to a site they intended to resemble a laboratory" (2002, 70). Among the prominent thinkers who quickly became interested in telepathy were physicists like William Barrett, Oliver Lodge and Balfour Stewart and Harvard psychologist/philosophers Charles Sanders Peirce[13] and William James.[14] The SPR's leadership seemed highly optimistic that telepathy would soon achieve legitimacy. Despite the empirical bearing the SPR chose for itself, the very fact that Myers and Gurney were willing to take the bait of publicity-seeking stage performers like Smith and Blackburn shows how thinly separated were the worlds of science and entertainment.

Blackburn and Smith would be the subject of the second major set of experiments in telepathy conducted by the SPR. The first was done with the Creery sisters, Mary, Alice and Maud, the teenage daughters of Reverend Creery of Buxton, Derbyshire. In June 1882, a paper jointly authored by Barrett, Gurney and Myers appeared in *Nineteenth Century*, entitled "Thought-reading." It details the results of 382 experimental trials with the Creerys, where words or playing cards were transferred from room to room. Writes Luckhurst:

The results exceeded chance, and the statistical probabilities of guessing five or even eight playing cards in a row, as the children occasionally achieved, seemed impossible without further explanation. Since the investigation was of a private middle-class family of a priest, the investigators excluded trickery, collusion, or the vulgar pursuit of notoriety. None of the children exhibited a "morbid state of mind" and they always played in a "perfectly normal" state of consciousness, unconnected to any form of mesmeric trance. Given the exclusion of these possibilities, Barrett argued that this was evidence of thought-reading "*without physical contact* or anything approaching it." (2002, 68)

The lack of physical contact distinguished these experiments from the "muscle reading" of performers like Bishop. Writes Pamela Thurschwell, "The 1881 successes with the Creery girls became the basis for a firm belief by [the SPR] that thought-transference was a proven phenomenon" (2001, 24). In the flush of this success they looked for more experimental subjects, taking them to Blackburn's letter in *Light*. Testing on the Creery sisters continued, but the results became less impressive as the test conditions tightened. In October 1887, the sisters were caught cheating during an experiment conducted in Cambridge and confessed to have been employing a set of codes all along (Oppenheim 1985, 359–60); this was one of the events that severely damaged the SPR's quest for credibility in its promotion of the scientific reality of telepathy. We shall see elements of this narrative play out again with Blackburn and Smith.

The first Blackburn-Smith experiments in thought-transference began in December 1882 in a Brighton hotel room rented by Gurney and Myers.[15] Additional experiments took place in January and April of the following year in London, at the Society's premises in Dean's Yard, Westminster (Beloff 1993, 86). The experimental set up (more or less—each source on these experiments varies slightly on minor details) had Smith under a blanket with his eyes bandaged. In a neighbouring room, Myers would show a word, number or image to Blackburn. Blackburn would pace, impressing the figure on his mind, for ten minutes or so. Blackburn would then stand behind Smith and "telepathically" impart the image to him ... whether or not they had any physical contact during this process varies depending on the account. Smith would then take up the pencil and draw whatever impressions entered his mind. The most dramatic results were a set of images published in the *Proceedings of the Society for Psychical Research* of pictures shown to Blackburn which were then reproduced by Smith under the blanket in a rough, inchoate form, but unmistakably as copies of the original images. On other occasions, Blackburn was pricked in various parts of his body and Smith was asked to recognize, via their telepathic rapport, the location of the pain.

Latter-day writers have been extremely critical of the Blackburn-Smith experiments. According to Robert Henry Thouless:

> There were various defects in the experimental design, including the fact that Blackburn and Smith were in the room together at the time of the reproduction and could, therefore, have been communicating by means of some code. ESP [extra-sensory perception] experiments in which a friend or relative of the percipient knows the right answer before the response is given can never be sound evidence of ESP. (1972, 41)

Likewise, Herman Spitz cites the experiments as an example of how "eminent, respected and highly achieving professionals can become deeply enmeshed in obvious fraud and nonsense" (Spitz 1997, 80). At the time, however, Myers and Gurney deemed the experiments a success, and according to Charles Edward Mark Hansel, the experiments "might well have gone down in the history of parapsychology as one of the conclusive investigations providing irrefutable evidence for telepathy" (1966, 32) were it not for Blackburn's claims, in a series of magazine articles between 1908 and 1911, that he and Smith had faked them.[16] Apparently Blackburn was under the mistaken impression that all the players of the events were dead; Gurney and Myers were, but Smith was not. Blackburn claimed that he and Smith took no pleasure in their prank and in fact that:

> Within three months of our acquaintance with the leading members of the Society for Psychical Research Mr. Smith and myself heartily regretted that these personally charming and scientifically distinguished men should have been victimized; but it was too late to recant. We did the next best thing. We stood aside and watched with amazement the astounding spread of the fire we had in a spirit of mischief lighted. (rpt. in Coover 1997, 484)

Later in the article, Blackburn seems to contradict himself, claiming that they saw Gurney and Myers as the same sort of credulous dupes, "spiritualistic cranks," who attended their shows. He states that he and Smith felt a moral obligation to expose them, and found that Gurney and Myers left much to be desired as impartial examiners:

too anxious to get corroboration of their theories to hold the balance impartially. Again and again they gave the benefit of the doubt to experiments that were failures ... They allowed us to impose our own conditions, accepted without demur our explanations of failure and, in short, exhibited a complaisance and confidence which, however complimentary to us, was scarcely consonant with a strict investigation on behalf of the public. (Coover 1997, 485)

Blackburn describes his and Smith's successful fraud as a mix of luck and the employment of touch-codes such as those pioneered by Bishop. Additionally, he describes them working out a method where he would secretly draw an extra copy of the image he was to "telepathically" transfer on cigarette paper and then slip it into the brass protector of the pencil he slipped to Smith.

For his part, Smith always maintained that the experiments were genuine, first when the SPR dispatched Alice Johnson to Brighton in 1908 to question him about Blackburn's confession (Wiley 2012, 200–2), then again in a piece in the *London Daily News* dated 4 September 1911, and finally towards the end of his very long life when visited by Dr E.J. Dingwall in 1954 (Hall 1964, 173; Wiley 2012, 164). In the 1911 instance, Smith told an interviewer from the *London Daily News*:

> Mr. Blackburn's story is a tissue of errors from beginning to end. In the first place, I most emphatically deny that I ever, in any degree, any way, when working with Mr. Blackburn, attempted to bamboozle Messrs. Myers, Gurney and Podmore. These gentlemen, long before they met us, had spent years in investigating psychic phenomena, and were aware of every device and dodge for making sham phenomena; they were watching not only for premeditated trickery, but for unconscious trickery as well. You could not deceive them, and the quack mediums hated them in consequence. It makes my blood boil to see them held up to ridicule ... (Anon. 1911, 1)

Smith lists a litany of errors he finds in Blackburn's account, and reaffirms that the experiments were bona fide; in particular he denies that he and Blackburn ever had any physical contact during the experiments that could have allowed a muscle code of the Bishop type. The Smith of 1911 characterizes himself as a rational, sceptical sort but stresses his belief in telepathy, having witnessed and experienced it.

Accounts of the Blackburn-Smith experiments take on a *Rashomon* (1950) quality, with so many conflicting and disputed details of what happened in those Brighton hotel rooms. The truth will never be known, and perhaps for our purposes it is less important than where these experiments took Smith. He would ultimately prove himself to be useful to the SPR in ways far beyond any supposed telepathic powers. For one, Smith's talents as a hypnotist made him a strong asset. Fraser Nicol says that, "It may well be that in the long history of psychical research Smith was the most gifted hypnotist ever known" (1966, 26). He was the usual hypnotist for the Committee on Mesmerism, and among the first experiments was one carried out with the same Brighton baker Fred Wells who was a feature of Smith's stage mesmerism act (Nicol 1966, 38), further demonstrating the continuity between the stage and laboratory.

In addition to his hypnotism, Smith had many less sensational skills that made him invaluable to the SPR. In his 2009 biography of Myers, Trevor Hamilton terms Smith the SPR's "factotum" (2009, 118), an appropriate term given the number of diverse roles he played for them. He became private secretary to Edmund Gurney, then the Honorary Secretary of the SPR in 1883, a position he held until Gurney's contentious death in 1888. Subsequently, Smith would hold the same position for Myers. Gurney assigned Smith, alongside Frank Podmore, to checking facts for his massive book compiling people's experiences of visual hallucinations, *Phantasms of the Living* (1886). Smith also interviewed subjects reporting supernatural experiences, and in 1886 he was sent as far as Florida to interview a train driver named Mr Skilton, whose life was saved by a premonition (Hamilton 2009, 249). The SPR used him as a covert investigator too; on one occasion he was tasked with investigating the medium Leonora Piper for evidence of fraud, including searching her luggage and correspondence, an assignment that led to Smith being beaten (2009, 206). So trusted was he that Gurney wrote in a letter to William James on 16 April 1886:

> Smith's *bona fides* is quite beyond all doubt to anyone who knows him. I know him, I believe, quite completely. He has been acting as my private secretary for more than a year—with me for hours a day, & I believe I know his character as well as, say, you have known that of any one of your pupils. He has been my pupil in a sense. He is blameless & acute, perfectly steady and self-respecting, devoted to the work, & excellent at tracing impostures. (Gauld 1968, 181)

Articles occasionally appeared under Smith's byline in the SPR's periodicals, and these give the impression of a Smith as a level-headed and sceptical observer. In an 1895 article in the *Journal of the Society for Psychical Research*, he recounts a performance by American stage mesmerist (or "somnomancer," a term of his own coinage) Samri Baldwin.[17] Smith's account concludes with: "The whole business was most cleverly and successfully carried out here; but careful observers agreed that there was no good proof of occult or psychic powers, whilst, on the other hand, the proofs of conjuring and trickery were abundant" (Smith 1895, 228). Earlier, the March 1885 issue of the *Journal for the Society of Psychical Research* contained an account of his visiting a reputedly haunted house on "____ Road" in Norwich at the behest of its inhabitant, a clerk and his wife whom Smith refers to only as "Mr. and Mrs. X." They claimed to have both heard strange noises (including a voice stating "Hark! the master of this house has returned; we must depart" [Smith 1885, 314]) and to also have witnessed the apparition of an old gentleman. Smith says of his time there:

> I, myself, heard strange sounds, but could account for nearly all of them. They were caused by the next door people going up and down stairs, by their fire being poked, by their voices, by passers in the street, and by the vibrations of distant carts. In addition to these there were some sounds which I could not exactly localise or account for, but they only consisted of such creaks and strains as one is almost sure to hear in a completely empty house, or, indeed, in any other house if intently listened for. (1885, 316)

He goes on to relate the opinion of friends and family of Mr and Mrs X. that the apparition was a dream image (Mr X is described by Smith as "imaginative and somewhat excitable" [1885, 316] and the wife as "a young woman, very voluble, and fond of ventilating her religious creed" [1885, 317]). Smith concludes that "self-deception was at work to a *very* considerable extent" (1885, 316, original emphasis) in this case and the tone of his report suggests he puts next to no stock in supernatural explanations for this particular haunted house.

Likely due to his experiences in Norwich or dealing with similar haunted houses, in 1888, the SPR paid Smith and his new bride to live for nearly a full year in a reputedly haunted house in Brighton. In a touch of morbid irony, Smith's benefactor Gurney visited this house to meet with the landlord about the lease during the trip to Brighton on which he died (Smith was away on his honeymoon when this happened). Writes Fraser Nicol, "[during the year of their occupancy] thirty-nine investigators slept in the house on 137 nights. Some of the researchers had mildly odd experiences, but no apparitions were seen. Once, while young Mrs. Smith was kneeling on the hearthrug saying her prayers, a guitar on the wall twanged repeatedly" (1966, 14). Hamilton wonders "just what the new Mrs. Smith thought about this as an introduction to married bliss" (1966, 249). Difficult to say, but soon enough Laura Eugenia Smith (née Bayley) would be the star of a great many of his films, including some with supernatural themes. She would even enact the role of a ghost herself, which perhaps she was equipped to do, having managed to get more "first-hand" experience with supernatural than most SPR members ever did.

Smith the Filmmaker

A picture emerges of Smith as a dependable middle-class everyman, well liked by and loyal to his employers, good at picking up new skills and equal to a diverse range of tasks. No doubt these qualities served him in good stead once he and the SPR parted ways and he took up the mantle of an enterprising businessman. In 1892, he acquired St Ann's Well and Wild Garden in Hove, which had been a park, spa and local tourist attraction for over 150 years. Under Smith's management it would expand and improve, offering a wide range of entertainments, including gypsy fortune-tellers, monkey houses, productions of Shakespeare and magic lantern presentations. Smith's lantern skills, honed through the 1890s, appear to be a key factor in his transition into filmmaking (Gray 1998, 15). In 1897, St Ann's would become a site for filming and the production of films, and Smith would join James Williamson, Esme Collings and Alfred Darling in the "Brighton School." Michael Chanan describes this loose-knit group as middle-class technicians quite removed from the fairground showmen who represented another set of British film pioneers:

> not only socially removed from working-class culture, but ... hardly any closer to the world of high culture, and certainly totally removed from the ferment which had come to grip the avant-garde in the closing years of the century, in the struggle against the restrictions of the late Victorian bourgeois mentality ... For them, artistic culture was essentially decorative and inoffensive. (1996, 157)

The extent to which this description fits Smith is debatable, but what is noteworthy here is that nowhere does Chanan's book reference Smith's showman roots, nor his tenure with the SPR. I believe that, to the contrary, Smith's background—theatrical and psychical—is of great importance in assessing his filmmaking.

A tendency exists to describe Smith as a tinkerer and technician, and his films as empty mechanical exercises, but in fact his films are frequently clever and playful, with a special interest in using cinema's resources to depict altered states of consciousness and reality. Take *Let Me Dream Again* (1900), a two-shot film where a man is flirting with an attractive young lady, only to wake up and realize that he is in bed with his fat and unattractive wife. The transition between these two shots is accomplished by allowing the camera to go out of focus and then back in, representing the transition between dream and reality. The effect is unostentatiously achieved and the scenario was innovation enough to be copied by Ferdinand Zecca the following year as *Rêve et réalité*. Also in 1900, Smith made *The House that Jack Built*. It shows a little boy and girl playing with building blocks, and the boy maliciously topples the elaborate structure the girl has created. But then the film is reversed, causing the structure to be magically rebuilt. These films and others through Smith's career display a willingness to explore the technical qualities of cinema to overturn space and time. If Smith is often discussed as a pioneer of linkages that seem proto-classical in character (of editing, close-ups and cut-ins), it seems equally possible to discuss him as a director fascinated by cinematic disruptions, especially in his trick work. This aspect of Smith's work must owe something to the extreme possibilities he was exposed to during his tenure with the SPR; as Shane McCorristine states, "the type of films he made … attest[s] to the interest which the [supernatural] still held for Smith, and also shows the extent to which such subject matter could be at home both in the S.P.R. scientific experiments on telepathy and the new mass entertainment of ghostly films" (2010, 188).

Smith has been called the "English Méliès," a label that is reductive insofar as Georges Méliès and Smith had a reciprocal influence on each other. The two were apparently in regular correspondence in the late 1890s (Salt 1982, 282), and John Barnes argues that "If Smith was influenced by Méliès, it is equally true to say that Méliès owed a little to Smith" (1983, 35), a point he demonstrates by listing a number of scenarios used by Smith before Méliès, including several based on mesmerism and spirit photography. It is documented that Smith purchased a copy of Méliès's *The Haunted Castle* (1896) in 1898 (Barnes 1983, 35), but also that Smith's use of double exposures precedes that of Méliès. We know most of Smith's trick films only from catalogue descriptions, with the odd exception like *The X-ray Fiend*, to be discussed in the following chapter, and the charming *Santa Claus* (1898). The latter film features a complex uses of stop-motion and double exposures, which Frank Gray argues constitutes an early form of crosscutting in itself (2004, 53):[18] a circle appears inserted against a black background to represent the sleeping children's dreams of the arrival of Santa Claus. It then disappears as Santa himself arrives, fills the children's stockings and vanishes. Leigh Wilson makes the point that the version of vision expressed here is, "for the spectator ... not dream but telepathy" (2013, 134).

Some of Smith's trick films draw clearly on his experiences as a stage performer and at the SPR. Perhaps the most obvious is *The Mesmerist, or, Body and Soul* (1898), displaying a fantastic version of his prior trade. Its catalogue description reads:

> "Professor Fluence" in his study is visited by old lady who wishes to see some "Mesmerism." Professor mesmerises little girl and proceeds to draw her "spirit" from her body. Little girl's spirit leaves body and walks over the furniture. "Spirit," which is quite transparent, is finally conducted back to the body, and the mesmerist awakens his subject, much to the relief of the old lady. (Barnes 1983, 33)

Smith uses cinematic means to materialize the most outlandish claims invested in mesmerism by its devotees, with the old lady as a figure of the credulous audience. Frank Gray notes that the film, though "may easily have been interpreted by contemporary spiritualists as a portrait of the possible. As such, Smith's film becomes a projection of what might happen when contact is made with the 'other side'" (2000, 173). I would add that the film also comically narrativizes of one of the SPR's central claims: telepathy as a justification for ghost phenomena. Smith's *The Mesmerist*, despite its comic tone and the fact that it features in Professor Fluence a rather more benign mesmerist than Svengali or Dracula, is perhaps the first cinematic iteration of a tradition that would ultimately include Drs Caligari and Mabuse.[19] Stefan Andriopoulous's fascinating book *Possessed: Hypnotic Crimes, Corporate Fiction, and the Invention of Cinema* (2008) deals with the hypnotic criminal in the decades to come, and in those films, as in Smith, we often find double exposure used to represent hypnotic powers. In Fritz Lang's *The Testament of Dr. Mabuse* (1933), for instance, we see the deceased Dr Mabuse's projected will envisioned through double exposures as the half-present spectre that steps forward to possess Professor Baum (Otto Beregi, Sr). As the phantom Mabuse straddles the line between hypnotic projection and supernatural ghost, we witness the survival of conventions that Smith played a significant role in establishing.

Another lost film, *Photographing a Ghost* (1898), has been the subject of considerable interest. One description reads, "Photographer tries to take a picture of a ghost but it won't keep still and finally vanishes" (Barnouw 1981, 89), while another says:

> Scene: A Photographer's Studio. Two men enter with a large box labeled "ghost." The photographer scarcely relishes the order, but eventually opens the box, when a striking ghost of a swell steps out. The ghost is perfectly transparent, so that the furniture, etc., can be seen through his "body." After a great deal of amusing business with the ghost, which keeps disappearing and reappearing, the photographer attacks it with a chair. The attack is amusingly fruitless, but the ghost finally collapses through the floor. (Barnes 1983, 33)

The scene is obviously rooted in the worlds of spiritualism and psychical research with which Smith was intimately familiar. In particular it pokes fun at spirit photography, a practice that will be given more attention in the following chapter.[20] The description's special mention of the ghost's transparency was probably designed to emphasize Smith's signature use of double exposure. A 30 June 1900 article in *Chambers' Journal* by Victor W. Cook described Smith as having "introduced several cunning little devices in spirit-raising," and as a kind of new medium, a specialist in "raising" ghosts (1996, 95), who had even exhibited films for the Queen and Royal Family. At the same time, it alludes to exactly the way ghosts appear in spirit photographs: semi-transparent, half-present wisps only nominally belonging to the image that contain them, resembling (and created via) double exposures. Smith's later *Mary Jane's Mishap* (1903)—itself a subject of attention for scholars from Sadoul to Barnes, and which Jean Mitry praised as "possessing some very precise action cuts outstanding for its time" (2000, 5)—also uses the powers of the double exposure to visualize the spectral in a comic vein. Four minutes long and featuring an impressive 12 shots, including a number of cut-ins, *Mary Jane's Mishap* stars Smith's wife Laura as the low-class housewife who makes the fatal error of pouring paraffin into her stove and is blown up (up the chimney, in fact).

Her headstone reads, "Here Lies Mary Jane Who Lighted the Fire with Paraffin. Rest in Pieces," and mourners are terrified by her ghost stepping from the grave (paraffin bottle in hand), courtesy, again, of Smith's mastery of double exposures.

In *H.G. Wells, Modernity and the Movies* (2007), Keith Williams observes that the insubstantial ghost in Smith's *Photographing a Ghost* is echoed in H.G. Wells's short story "The Inexperienced Ghost" (1902), the titular spectre of which resembles a double exposure in the sense that you can see directly through it (2007, 40), and that it also has certain resonances with Wells's Invisible Man (2007, 52). This is not to suggest that Smith's double exposure ghosts influenced Wells directly, so much as that a broader "photographic" understanding of a ghost found expression in the work of both Smith and Wells. Karen Beckman describes Smith's *Photographing a Ghost* as a meta-commentary on cinema's relationship to photography as means of depicting the supernatural. She says that the film:

> stages a quiet exposure of the inadequacies of the medium of photography in order to assert the supremacy of film in relation to insubstantial matters. As the photographer fails to capture the ghost because of its refusal to stay still, the moving picture delights in the spirit's mobility ... declaring itself the new master of the insubstantial, ectoplasmic body. (2003, 73)

Armed with this interpretation, we can understand the film itself as anticipating the claims that Ricciotto Canudo would make decades later, that cinema does indeed have a special capacity for depicting the spectral that goes beyond those of other media.[21]

Other lost trick films by Smith have titles that speak for themselves: *The Haunted Castle* (1897), *Faust and Mephistopheles* (1898), *Cinderella and the Fairy Godmother* (1898), *Aladdin and the Wonderful Lamp* (1899). Victor W. Cook's aforementioned article in *Chambers' Journal* describes a film called *A Guardian Angel*, where a suicidal gambler is rescued by the spirit of his deceased wife (1996, 95); this film, commonly listed as *The Gambler's Wife* (1899), seems to anticipate the moralistic haunting narratives common in the 1920s. In 1899, Smith produced *The Haunted Picture Gallery*, a version of the pervasive nineteenth-century trope of paintings coming to life, blurring the lines between animate and inanimate. Lynda Nead locates this Pygmalionesque fantasy in locations as diverse as the *tableaux vivant*, Gilbert and Sullivan's *Ruddigore*, magic acts staged at the Egyptian Hall and an 1894 ad campaign for Dewar's Scotch whisky where a deceased Scotsman emerges from a painting to claim his descendant's beverage. Nead refers to Smith's film as "the ultimate nineteenth-century version of *The Haunted Picture Gallery*" (2007, 80) because cinema itself is the full realization of the urge to see pictures come to life. How appropriate that Smith, who had such acquaintance with the world of the supernatural, should be the one to deliver the haunted picture gallery to its "ultimate" medium.

In 1900, Smith also directed the first cinematic version of *The Corsican Brothers*. The 1844 novella by Alexandre Dumas, *père*, tells the story of two Siamese twins separated at birth who retain a psychic link that lasts beyond death. Dion Boucicault's 1852 stage adaptation included a sensational appearance by the ghost of the murdered brother; the trapdoor devised to facilitate the ghost's appearance used "counterweighted platforms and slatted shutters to allow an actor to rise gradually through the floor while simultaneously traveling across it" (Jackson 2004, 6), became known as "the Corsican Trap."[22] A catalogue description of Smith's *The Corsican Brothers* reads as follows:

> One of the twin brothers returns home from shooting in the Corsican mountains, and is visited by the ghost of the other twin. By extremely careful photography the ghost appears *quite transparent*. After indicating that he has been killed by a sword thrust, and appealing for vengeance, he disappears. A "vision" then appears showing a fatal duel in the snow. To the Corsican's amazement, the duel and death of his brother are vividly depicted in the vision, and finally, overcome by his feelings, he falls to the floor just as his mother enters the room. (Heard 2006, 258, original emphasis)

There would be numerous cinematic adaptations of *The Corsican Brothers* with movie stars ranging from Douglas Fairbanks, Jr, to Cheech and Chong, but Smith was first, transposing perhaps the premier ghost melodrama of the nineteenth-century stage to cinema with the help of his well-honed ghost effects that could make a man *quite transparent* and effortless stage visions and other altered states of reality. It is reasonable to suggest, as Gray does (2000, 175), that Smith was attracted to this material because of the role psychic rapport plays in *The Corsican Brothers*, which obviously resonated with a man who played a direct part in the history of telepathy experimentation. A similar case can be made that most of his trick canon, both in terms of subject matter and filmic technique, contains echoes of his earlier life as a stage mesmerist, mentalist and as a psychical researcher.

Smith's Ghosts

This chapter has not exhausted Smith's numerous lives; I have paid little attention, for instance, to his roles as a lanternist or astronomer.[23] I wish to conclude by paying attention to the uses to which he has been put in film studies. The scholar to have written the most on him is certainly Frank Gray, who has brought admirable historical rigour and insight. Gray's 2000 essay "George Albert Smith's Visions and Transformations: The Films of 1898" pays particular attention to the culture of the supernatural as it manifests in Smith's filmmaking. He speaks of a need to locate Smith:

> within a broader cultural history of the supernatural in which it was actively investigated and sought ... As a full participant in this history across the 1880s and 1890s, Smith was actively involved in various means to alter the perception of an audience, either through a mesmerist's live performance, or by creating the fantastic through film production. (2000, 178)

My debt to Gray's article is clear, and I hope to have extended his insights by locating Smith's fascinating career and filmmaking within the late Victorian culture of the supernatural.

One contentious question around Smith's filmmaking is motivation: when Smith reached back into his history as a mesmerist and a psychical researcher in his filmmaking, what were his intentions? Here we find an interesting difference of opinion. During imagines him still in the persona of the charlatan who, partnered with Blackburn, defrauded Gurney and the entire SPR. For During, Smith's trick films continue to mock his gullible previously employers. Describing *Photographing a Ghost*, he says

> Smith's deceptions—his confidence tricks, if you like—have become mere illusions, which mock his old employers ... In Smith's case, a quasi-political resentment was probably at work ... Relatively uneducated assistants like himself were dependent on, and even seduced into fraud by, idealistic and naive 'swells' like Gurney (2002, 276).

This is a substantial change from the usual narrative, where if Smith is understood as having been "seduced" by anyone, it is Blackburn, but no matter—During seems to have taken his impression of Smith's character from Trevor Hall. The evidence is against the claim that Smith is mocking the SPR in his films, because Smith repeatedly and consistently refused to admit fraud even when given opportunities to do so.[24] True, his supernaturally themed films are light-hearted, as are those of Méliès, and do not carry the weightiness with which the prime movers of the SPR approached supernatural matters, but this light touch does not make for mockery. Unlike Méliès, who staged anti-spiritualist scenarios on both the stage and the screen (Solomon 2010, 25–6), Smith apparently refrained from any formal "exposures."

For the opposite viewpoint, we can look to Stacey Abbott. In her article "Spectral Vampires: *Nosferatu* in the Light of New Technology" (2004), Abbott suggests that exposure to the SPR's way of thinking did much to prepare Smith for filmmaking. She writes that:

> Smith embodied a more ambiguous relationship between stage performance, film technology and genuine spiritualism [than Méliès] … the way in which he seamlessly moved between the scientific world of study and analysis of the supernatural to the technological world of stage performance and film magic … suggests an affinity between these worlds. Many of Smith's films … explore his own fascination with the occult and use dissolves, superimpositions and other trick effects in order to convey these supernatural phenomena. (2004, 228)

I welcome Abbott's claim that Smith's choice of supernatural subject matter is rooted in his experiences with the SPR and, less directly, that a familiarity with the claims of psychical researchers helped lead him to filmmaking itself (though the latter claim is obviously more speculative). But I take exception to the implication that Smith is best understood as a spiritualist "true believer" making films to express a belief in genuine supernatural phenomena. Even though Smith certainly did perform stage séances early in his career (as did a great many performers of the time, Houdini included), performing sceptical investigations of mediums like Leonora Piper and Samri Baldwin may have been the closest Smith ever got to the spiritualist community.

Gray has remarked that "History has been unkind to Smith" (2000, 178), and this is true insofar as most of his films are lost to the ravages of history. Ghost texts unto themselves, they can be speculated about and extrapolated upon but never studied directly. If the 93-year-old Smith was there at the opening of the National Film Theatre in 1957 as the standard-bearer for the history of English cinema, "the Father of the British Film Industry" as Michael Balcon called him (Gray 1996, 31), he signified an absence too: not only the loss of so many of his own films, but also the loss of a set of histories that entangled mesmerism, psychical research, spiritualism and magic with filmmaking. Conceiving of him as a deceitful figure making a mockery of his previous employers through films (as During does) or as a true believer using cinema to actualize his view of the afterlife both fall a bit short. It seems certain, however, that a relationship exists between Smith's innovative filmmaking and the extreme possibilities he encountered with the SPR. As will be explored in the next chapter, one of his films, *The X-ray Fiend*, makes this case perhaps the most clearly of all.

NOTES

1. With a few exceptions, his place in each set of histories is rarely acknowledged by the other. For example, in his history of parapsychology, John Beloff merely states, "During the 1890s ... Smith became interested in cinematography" (1993, 87). References to Smith's career in psychical research are even scantier in the literature on cinema, with the exception of Frank Gray's excellent work (esp. 1996, 1998, 2000).
2. His *A Kiss in the Tunnel* (1899) has been called the first edited film in England (Gray 2004). See also Fairservice (2001, 18–22, 32–3).
3. Georges Sadoul and Yvonne Templin (1946) praised Smith as inventor of the close-up as early as 1946, a claim generally made with respect to his films *Grandma's Reading Glass* (1900), *As Seen Through a Telescope* (1900) and *The Sick Kitten* (1903). For more on Smith and the close-up, see Bordwell and Thompson (1979, 147), Brewster (1982, 6), Burch (1990, 89), Hansen (1991, 33), Fairservice (2001, 21), Chapman (2003, 55), Popple and Kember (2004, 103).
4. Working for Charles Urban, Smith invented Kinemacolor, the first economically viable colour process. However, a lawsuit would nullify his patent in 1914. See Thomas (1983), Urban (2003), O'Brien (2012).
5. Reproduced in Gray (1996, 31). Trevor Hall briefly mentions this event in Smith's life, including the detail that Smith was given a picture of the theatre by Lord Hailsham (1964, 173).
6. The popularity of *The Strange Case of Edmund Gurney* was such that BBC adapted it under the name *The Magicians: Edmund Gurney and the Brighton Mesmerist*, which aired in October 1967. Smith was portrayed by Ray Brooks, Gurney by Richard Todd.
7. Whether or not Gurney had facial neuralgia and used chloroform to calm it, thus opening the possibility of an accidental overdose, is

a particular issue of contention. See Coleman (1993) for one attempt to debunk Hall's claims about Gurney's death.
8. The proliferation of documentary paranormal investigation series like *Most Haunted* (2002–10), *Ghost Hunters* (2002–present) and *Celebrity Ghost Hunt* (2012–present) reminds us that this dream is far from dead. See Koven (2007), Williams (2010), Burger (2010), O'Hara (2010), Hill (2011, esp. 66–88), Lauro and Paul (2013), Renner (2013).
9. Peters characterizes Mesmer as a Columbus who "discovered a new world (the continent of the unconscious and the peninsulas of neurosis and hypnosis) yet remained mistaken about its identity to his dying day" (1999, 91).
10. Additional sources on mesmerism/hypnotism and nineteenth-century literature include Kaplan (1975), Tatar (1978), Pick (2000), Thurschwell (2001, 37–64), Melechi (2008, 75–97) and the collection *Victorian Literary Mesmerism* (Wills and Wynne 2006).
11. We know that Smith continued acting as a stage mesmerist as well through at least 1889, well into his tenure with the SPR (Gray 2000, 172).
12. The SPR initially attracted many spiritualists as members but most left in 1886 after a set of exposés of mediums, including the prominent slate medium William Eglinton (Thurschwell 2001, 17–18).
13. For an assessment of Peirce's writings on the supernatural, see Braude (1998).
14. In 1885, James became a founding member of the American Society for Psychical Research. His enthusiastic commitment to psychical research is the major subject of Blum (2006).
15. See Wiley (2012, 110–21) for an account of the Blackburn-Smith experiments.
16. Blackburn published a book called *Thought-Reading, or, Modern Mysteries Explained* in 1884, disclosing some of the secrets of their act. He is often painted as a duplicitous figure who seduced Smith into their joint fraud: "He was bad, dishonest, treacherous and vicious" (Nicol 1966, 25). In the 1890s, Blackburn would relocate to South Africa and have a distinguished literary career there. Stephen Gray, the author of a 1999 book about writing in South Africa, describes Blackburn as "one of South Africa's great writers, and certainly the best of the many colonial Englishmen who recorded life in South Africa at the turn of the century" (Gray 1999, 13).

Gray expresses amazement at discovering that Blackburn "has often been cast a villain and a blackguard, notably by the ... Society for Psychical Research" (1999, 20). Like Smith's, Blackburn's multiple careers seem radically removed from each other.

17. Baldwin, known as "the White Mahatma," was also a pioneer of handcuff escape tricks. He was one of the interesting group of performers who both performed spiritualist exposés and professed a belief in psychic powers himself (Hansen 1990, 53).
18. Sergei Eisenstein would later refer to double exposures as a technique that materializes cinema's basic ability to create the impression of simultaneity, which Eisenstein largely pursued through the linkage of different shots in montage (1947, 79–80).
19. There are other mesmeric scenes in early cinema as well, such as the 1899 Edison film *The Mesmerist and the Country Couple*, which is also a version of the rube film.
20. Other early trick films that seem to overtly mock spiritualism include J. Stuart Blackton and Albert E. Smith's *A Visit to the Spiritualist* (1899), R.W. Paul's *Is Spiritualism a Fraud?* (1906) and certain Méliès films, notably *L'Armoire des frères Davenport* (1902), parodying the American stage museums of Ira and William Davenport, and *Le Portrait spirituel* (1903).
21. Rigby also briefly mentions *Photographing a Ghost* as an early use of trick cinematography in England, implicitly positioning it as the first English horror film (2006, 14); the film receives similar references in Gifford (1973, 14) and Dixon (2010, 5).
22. One might suspect that *The Corsican Brothers* was an excellent candidate for Pepper's Ghost, but this was not the case, since it called for a ghost who delivers dialogue.
23. The latter is surely relevant to the shifts of perspective provided by his close-ups in films like *Seen Through the Telescope*.
24. Tellingly, During (2002, 275) briefly mentions the Blackburn confessions but does not mention Smith's rejection of Blackburn's claims.

Works Cited

Abbott, Stacey. "Spectral Vampires: *Nosferatu* in the Light of New Technology." *Horror Film: Creating and Marketing Fear*. Ed. Stefan Hantke. Jackson: University of Mississippi Press, 2004. 3–20.

Andriopolous, Stefan. *Possessed: Hypnotic Crimes, Corporate Fiction, and the Invention of Cinema.* Chicago: University of Chicago Press, 2008.
[Anon.] "The Brighton Aquarium." *Brighton Herald* 8 July (1882a): 2.
[Anon.] "Cases Received by the Literary Committee." *Journal of the Society for Psychical Research* 7.66 (1891): 7–14.
[Anon.] "The Great Feat. 'A Most Amazing Piece of Invention.'" *London Daily News* 11 September (1911): 1.
[Anon.] "Mesmerism." *Brighton Herald* 23 September (1882b): 3.
Barnes, John. *Pioneers of the British Film.* London: Bishopsgate Press, 1983.
Barnouw, Erik. *The Magician and the Cinema.* New York: Oxford University Press, 1981.
Beckman, Karen. *Vanishing Women: Magic, Film and Feminism.* Durham: Duke University Press, 2003.
Beloff, John. *Parapsychology: A Concise History.* New York: St. Martin's Press, 1993.
Blackburn, Douglas. "Thought-reading Extraordinary." *Light* 86.2 (1882): 392.
Blackburn, Douglas. *Thought-Reading, or, Modern Mysteries Explained.* Field & Tuer: London, 1884.
Blum, Deborah. *Ghost Hunters: William James and the Search for Scientific Proof of Life after Death.* New York: Penguin, 2006.
Bordwell, David and Kristin Thompson. *Film Art: An Introduction.* Reading, MA: Addison-Wesley, 1979.
Braude, Stephen E. "Peirce on the Paranormal." *Transactions of the Charles S. Peirce Society* 34.1 (Winter 1998): 203–14.
Brewster, Ben. "A Scene at the 'Movies.'" *Screen* 23.2 (1982): 4–15.
Burch, Noël. *Life to Those Shadows.* Berkeley: University of California Press, 1990.
Burger, Alissa. "Ghost Hunters: Simulated Participation in Televisual Hauntings." *Popular Ghosts: The Haunted Spaces of Everyday Culture.* Eds. María del Pilar Blanco and Esther Peeren. New York: Continuum, 2010. 162–74.
Chanan, Michael. *The Dream that Kicks: The Prehistory and Early Years of Cinema in Britain.* London: Routledge, 1996.
Chapman, James. *Cinemas of the World: Film and Society from 1895 to Present.* London: Reaktion, 2003.
Coleman, M.H. "The Death of Edmund Gurney." *The Journal of the Society for Psychical Research* 58 (1993): 194–200.
Cook, Victor W. "The Humours of 'Living Picture' Making." *In the Kingdom of Shadows: A Companion to Early Cinema.* Eds. Colin Harding and Simon Popple. London: Cygnus Press, 1996. 94–6.
Coover, John Edgar. *Experiments in Psychical Research at Leland Stanford Junior University.* Sanford, CA: Stanford University, 1997.
Dixon, Wheeler Winston. *A History of Horror.* New Brunswick, NJ: Rutgers University Press, 2010.

During, Simon. *Modern Enchantments: The Cultural Power of Secular Magic.* Cambridge: Harvard University Press, 2002.
Eisenstein, Sergei. *The Film Sense.* London: Harcourt, 1947.
Epperson, Gordon. *The Mind of Edmund Gurney.* Madison, NJ: Fairleigh Dickinson University Press, 1994.
Fairservice, Don. *Film Editing: History, Theory and Practice.* New York: Manchester University Press, 2001.
Gauld, Alan. *The Founders of Psychical Research.* New York: Schocken, 1968.
Gifford, Denis. *A Pictorial History of Horror Movies.* London: Hamlyn, 1973.
Gray, Frank. "From Mesmerism to Moving Pictures in Natural Colours – The Life of G. Albert Smith." *The Hove Pioneers and the Arrival of Cinema.* Ed. Frank Gray. Brighton: University of Brighton, Faculty of Art, Design and Humanities, 1996. 27–31.
Gray, Frank. "George Albert Smith's Visions and Transformations: The Films of 1898." *Visual Delights: Essays on the Popular Projected Image in the 19th Century.* Eds. Simon Popple and Vanessa Toulmin. Trowbridge, Wiltshire: Flicks Books, 2000. 170–80.
Gray, Frank. "*The Kiss in the Tunnel* (1899), G.A. Smith and the Emergence of the Edited Film in England." *The Silent Cinema Reader.* London: Routledge, 2004. 51–62.
Gray, Frank. "Smith the Showman: The Early Years of George Albert Smith." *Film History* 10.1 (1998): 8–20.
Gray, Stephen. *Free-Lancers and Literary Biography in South America.* Amsterdam: Rodopi, 1999.
Hall, Trevor H. *The Strange Case of Edmund Gurney.* London: Duckworth, 1964.
Hamilton, Trevor. *Immortal Longings: F.W.H. Myers and the Victorian Search for Life after Death.* Exeter: Imprint Academic, 2009.
Hansel, Charles Edward Mark. *ESP: A Scientific Investigation.* New York: Scribner, 1966.
Hansen, George. "Magicians Who Endorsed Psychic Phenomena." *The Linking Ring* 70.8 (August 1990): 52–4.
Hansen, Miriam. *Babel and Babylon: Spectatorship in American Silent Film.* Cambridge, MA: Harvard University Press, 1991.
Heard, Mervyn. *Phantasmagoria: The Secret Life of the Magic Lantern.* Hastings: The Projection Box, 2006.
Hill, Annette. *Paranormal Media: Audiences, Spirits and Magic in Popular Culture.* London: Routledge, 2011.
Jackson, Russell. "Victorian and Edwardian Stagecraft: Technologies and Issues." *The Cambridge Companion to Victorian and Edwardian Theatre.* Ed. Kerry Powell. Cambridge: Cambridge University Press, 2004. 52–69.
Kaplan, Fred. *Dickens and Mesmerism: The Hidden Spring of Fiction.* Princeton: Princeton University Press, 1975.

Koven, Mikel J. "*Most Haunted* and the Convergence of Traditional Belief and Popular Television." *Folklore* 118 (August 2007): 183–202.
Lauro, Sarah Juliet and Catherine Paul. "'Make Me Believe!' Ghost-hunting Technology and the Postmodern Fantastic." *Horror Studies* 4.2 (2013): 205–23.
Luckhurst, Roger. *The Invention of Telepathy*. Oxford: Oxford University Press, 2002.
McCorristine, Shane. *Specters of the Self: Thinking about Ghosts and Ghost-seeing in England, 1750–1920*. Cambridge: Cambridge University Press, 2010.
Melechi, Antonio. *Servants of the Supernatural: The Night Side of the Victorian Mind*. London: William Heinemann, 2008.
Mitry, Jean. *Semiotics and the Analysis of Film*. Bloomington: Indiana University Press, 2000.
Nead, Lynda. *The Haunted Gallery: Painting, Photography, Film c. 1900*. New Haven: Yale University Press, 2007.
Nicol, Fraser. "The Silences of Mr. Trevor Hall." *International Journal of Parapsychology* 8 (1966): 3–59.
O'Brien, Charles. "Motion Picture Colour and the Institutionalization of the Cinema." *The Blackwell Companion to Early Cinema*. Ed. André Gaudreault. London: Blackwell, 2012. 298–314.
O'Hara, Jessica. "Making their Presence Known: TV's Ghost-hunter Phenomenon in a 'Post-'world." *The Philosophy of Horror*. Ed. Thomas Fahy. Lexington: University of Kentucky Press, 2010. 72–85.
Oppenheim, Janet. *The Other World: Spiritualism and Psychical Research in English, 1850–1914*. Cambridge: Cambridge University Press, 1985.
Parssinen, Terry M. "Mesmeric Performers." *Victorian Studies* 21.1 (1977): 87–104.
Peters, John Durham. *Speaking into the Air: A History of the Idea of Communication*. Chicago: University of Chicago Press, 1999.
Pick, Daniel. *Svengali's Web: The Alien Enchanter in Modern Culture*. New Haven, CT: Yale University Press, 2000.
Popple, Simon and Joe Kember. *Early Cinema: From Factory Gates to Dream Factory*. New York: Wallflower, 2004.
Renner, Karen J. "Negotiations of Masculinity in American Ghost-hunting Reality Television." *Horror Studies* 4.2 (2013): 225–43.
Rigby, Jonathan. *English Gothic: A Century of Horror Cinema*. Richmond, Surrey: Reynolds & Hearn, 2006.
Sadoul, Georges and Yvonne Templin. "Early Film Production in England: The Origin of Montage, Close-Ups and Chase Sequence." *Hollywood Quarterly* 1.3 (Apr. 1946): 249–59.
Salt, Barry. "The Evolution of Film Form up to 1906." *Cinema 1900–1906: An Analytical Study*. Ed. Roger Holman. Brussels: FIAF, 1982. 281–96.

Smith, George Albert. "Report on a Haunted House in Norwich." *Journal of the Society for Psychical Research* 1 (1885): 313–17.

Smith, George Albert. [Untitled.] *Journal of the Society for Psychical Research* 11 (1895): 225–8.

Solomon, Matthew. *Disappearing Tricks: Silent Film, Houdini, and the New Magic of the Twentieth Century.* Iowa City: University of Iowa Press, 2010.

Spitz, Herman. *Nonconscious Movements: From Mystic Messages to Facilitated Communication.* Mahwah, NJ: Erlbaum, 1997.

Tatar, Maria M. *Spellbound: Studies on Mesmerism and Literature.* Princeton: Princeton University Press, 1978.

Thomas, D.B. *The First Colour Motion Pictures.* London: Her Majesty's Stationery Office, 1983.

Thouless, Robert Henry. *From Anecdote to Experiment in Psychical Research.* London: Routledge, 1972.

Thurschwell, Pamela. *Literature, Technology and Magical Thinking, 1880–1920.* Cambridge: Cambridge University Press, 2001.

Urban, Charles. "Terse History of Natural Colour Kinematography." *Living Pictures* 2.2 (2003): 59–68.

Virilio, Paul. *War and Cinema: The Logistics of Perception.* London: Verso, 1989.

Wiley, Barry H. *The Thought Reader Craze: Victorian Science at the Enchanted Boundary.* Jefferson, NC: McFarland, 2012.

Williams, Karen. "The Liveness of Ghosts: Haunting and Reality TV." *Popular Ghosts: The Haunted Spaces of Everyday Culture.* Eds. María del Pilar Blanco and Esther Peeren. New York: Continuum, 2010. 149–61.

Williams, Keith. *H.G. Wells, Modernity and the Movies.* Liverpool: Liverpool University Press, 2007.

Willis, Martin and Catherine Wynne, eds. *Victorian Literary Mesmerism.* Amsterdam: Rodopi, 2006.

Wilson, Leigh. *Modernism and Magic: Experiments with Spiritualism, Theosophy and the Occult.* Edinburgh: Edinburgh University Press, 2013.

Winter, Alison. *Mesmerized: Powers of the Mind in Victorian Britain.* Chicago: University of Chicago Press, 1998.

CHAPTER 5

Aesthetics of Co-registration: Spirit Photography, X-rays and Cinema

Early cinema's roots in photography are often examined through the chronophotography of Eadweard Muybridge and Étienne-Jules Marey (Braun 1992, 2010; Doane 2002), but instead my approach here will relate cinema to spirit photography and X-ray photography. The former used double exposures to represent contact with the spirit world, and the latter, which made its debut almost at the exact same time as cinema, carried profound supernatural implications in its seeming ability to transform living flesh into a *memento mori*. This chapter explores deep aesthetic and cultural links that spirit photography, X-rays and cinema share through what I refer to as "co-registration," the depiction of different spatialities and temporalities simultaneously, seemingly collapsed onto a single plane. This discussion follows in part from the previous chapter's work on the double-exposure techniques pioneered by G.A. Smith and others, which would become a privileged form for cinematic representations of ghosts, dreams, angels and so on. I have already alluded to the links between cinematic double exposures and the spirit photograph, where the "extras" appear as half-present and insubstantial figures alongside (but not interacting with) the sitters. The major aesthetic feature of most spirit photographs is multiple levels of information displayed together on a photographic surface,

---

The original chapter was corrected: Fig. 5.10, an image from *Bram Stoker's Dracula*, corresponds with the textual reference on p. 118; Fig. 5.11, an image from *The X-Ray Fiend*, corresponds with the reference on p. 121.

the spirit world and the human world of matter both present in a single image but remaining visibly disconnected.[1] It bears a marked similarity to with the X-ray, in which, "The surface of the body, its demarcation from the world, is dissolved and lost in the image, leaving only the faintest trace, while the relation between depth and surface is reversed. Skeletal structures, conventionally thought of as located at the most recessive depth of the body, appear in co-registration with the body's surface" (Waldby 2000, 91). This aesthetic of co-registration provides a concrete visualization of the worldview embraced by many spiritualists and occultists: the spirit world ("Summerland" or "the Seventh Heaven" in spiritualist parlance) as another world largely coterminous with our own but invisible and inaccessible except to those specially equipped, either through mediumship or, as in spirit photography, with technology.

In an article called "The Life and Death of the Superimposition" (1946), André Bazin argued that the cinematic use of double exposures to signify dreams or hallucinations is pure convention:

> Superimposition on the screen signals: "Attention: unreal world, imaginary characters"; it doesn't portray in any way what hallucinations or dreams are really like, or, for that matter, how a ghost would look ... Superimposition can, in all logic, only suggest the fantastic in a conventional way; it lacks the ability to actually evoke the supernatural. The Swedish cinema probably couldn't get the same results from it today as twenty years ago. Its superimpositions wouldn't convince anyone anymore. (1946, 74, 76)[2]

A similar sentiment was expressed by critic and director Curtis Harrington in 1952: "a man double-exposed so that he can be seen through looks not so much as we imagine a ghost might, but rather as a man double-exposed" (1952, 9). These men were correct to the extent that double exposures, so common in the silent era, would on the whole come to represent the supernatural only in comic scenarios, from *Here Comes Mr. Jordan* (1941) and *The Canterville Ghost* (1944) to *Alice* (1990) and *Ghost Dad* (1990)—though there are counter-examples within both horror (including *The House Where Evil Dwells* [1982]) and the art film (Aphichatphong Weerasethakul's *Uncle Boonmee Who Can Recall His Past Lives* [2010]). All the same, there is plenty of evidence to suggest that, in the nineteenth and early twentieth century, the use of double exposure to signify the ghost was more than conventional: people actually believed that ghosts looked that way. A 1903 issue of the magician's journal *Sphinx* ran an article by E.H. Thornton entitled "Ghosts Have No Thickness." It tells us that,

A real ghost has only two dimensions. He may be long or short, or wide or narrow, but he will not be either thick or thin. In fact, he will be so thin that it will not be thinness at all. It won't be anything. This is one of the results of investigations undertaken by the Society for Physical [sic] Research. The society does not affirm that much is known about ghosts and does not explain how the dimensions of ghosts have been established ... The real ghost, the one of two dimensions, is a harmless individual. He looks more like a magic lantern picture than anything else and is about as vicious. (1903, 111)

So entrenched, it seems, was the relationship between the photograph (and other media) and the supernatural that even ghosts were understood as possessing the qualities of photographs. Also striking is the number of ghost stories in the nineteenth century that either narratively involve photography or photographers (like Nathaniel Hawthorne's *The House of the Seven Gables* [1851]) or use photographic imagery to describe ghosts.[3] Allen W. Grove uses the example of the governess in Henry James's *The Turn of the Screw* (1898) seeing the evil ghost Quint "as definite as a picture in a frame," and later seeing him reveal his face against a glass like a portrait subject (1997, 155). Conversely, an early X-ray experimenter named Silvanus Thompson prophesied that "we shall now be able to realize Dickens's fancy when he made Scrooge perceive through Marley's body the two brass buttons on the back of his coat" (Pamboukian 2001, 58), using a metaphor of spectral insubstantiality drawn from a prominent ghost story to characterize the X-ray's powers.[4]

The X-ray, discovered by Wilhelm Conrad Röntgen on 8 November 1895, would quickly become entangled with cinema in ways that went far beyond the historical accident of having debuted in the same year.[5] Röntgen's discovery triggered what one scholar has termed "the most immediate and widespread reaction to any scientific discovery before the explosion of the first atomic bomb in 1945" (Henderson 1988, 324). Even as the X-ray was heralded as a new tool for science that seemed to realize the fantasy of objective, mechanical representations apart from human agency (Daston and Galison 1992, Knight 1986), its gloomy aesthetic fuelled supernatural speculations. The most shocking quality of X-ray images of humans seems not to have been that they showed bones but that they appeared to turn bodies inside out, co-registering depths and surfaces together. Bones appear most prominently in X-ray images of human forms because they are the densest part of our bodies, but they appear surrounded by shadowy impressions of skin and tissue. Writes Akira Lippit:

> The erasure of the surface (which paradoxically renders the world and its depths and interiorities superficial), the disappearance of a discernible interiority, plunges the subject into a "universal depth." A total and irresistible depth, everywhere. The world is no longer only outside, but also within, inside and out ...
>
> In the X-ray image, the body and the world that surrounds it are lost. No longer inside nor out, within nor without, body and world form a heterogeneous one ... You are in the world, the world is in you. The X-ray can be seen as an image of you and the world, an image forged in the collapse of the surface that separates the two. (2005, 43)

In addition to the bodily and spatial collapse that Lippit indicates, we might understand the X-ray as a powerful form of temporal collapse as well. It presents in co-registration the lively present and the "fate that awaits us all" (as Robertson described the image of a skeleton in his Phantasmagoria shows [Barnouw 1981, 19]), showing us life and death, now and the deathly "later," in a single image. Like the spirit photograph and the double-exposure aesthetic in cinema, it brings to the fore the deathly and supernatural subtexts that haunted photography from its inception.

Photographs of the Invisible

A pair of historical anecdotes will help illuminate the hold supernatural photographs had on the cultural imagination around the time of cinema's debut. On 18 June 1896, the *New Zealand Journal* printed an article with the suggestive title "Edison and Rontgen Outdone" (Anon. 1896b). The article shows a photograph of a field that seems to show a pair of shadowy ghost horses and riders jumping over a fence (Image 5.1). It was taken in Waipawa, New Zealand by Mr W.S. Russell, an employee of the Bank of New Zealand. The article explains that a pair of jockey boys died in a jumping accident on the same site, and that the pictures were taken on 13 July, the anniversary of the tragedy. A provocative subheadline reads, "The ghost question settled"; the photograph is understood as presenting positive and indisputable proof of the supernatural. Five months later, however, the article would be reprinted in W.T. Stead's spiritualist journal *Borderland* (Anon. 1896b, 445–6) alongside a letter from another New Zealand photographer dismissing the photo as an accidental double exposure that any photographer might explain. The image is captioned, "A 'faked' spirit photograph" (Anon. 1896b, 446). By Stead's time, the spirit photographs pioneered in the 1860s seemed antiquated and unconvincing, and discussions of photography's super-

A "FAKED" SPIRIT PHOTOGRAPH.

Image 5.1 The alleged New Zealand ghost horses, reprinted in *Borderland* in 1896

natural powers now centred on more exotic images, including "dorchagraphs," images produced by ghosts directly onto photographic plates without a camera, "luminous light photographs" produced from photographic plates left in a darkened séance room, and images purporting to document human thought itself.

Recent scholarship has done much to excavate the significance of spiritualism in the development of modern culture.[6] Spiritualism staked its appeal, as Ann Braude writes, on its ability to "provide empirical proof of the existence of the soul," and "'scientific' evidence of religious truth," asking people to "become 'investigators,' to observe 'demonstrations' of the truth of Spiritualism produced under 'test conditions' in the séance room" (2001, 6). Be they phantom knocks, the voices in séances, phantom writing on slates, mysterious trumpet sounds, full materializations, ectoplasm or any other strange phenomena mediums produced in their long history, spiritualism always invited spectators to judge the evidence personally. Spirit photography provided more tangible and lasting evidence for the supernatural than most practices:

Nothing appeared more objective, after all, than an image captured through the camera's lens. Telekinesis, automatic writing, trance speech, and levitation could be ascribed to the medium's own powers of mind, but the ghostly images in these photographs, which sitters often identified as deceased loved ones, seemed incontrovertible evidence of disembodied souls. (Monroe 2002, 162)

Spirit photographs and other forms of paranormal photography[7] have received considerable attention of late, including numerous gallery exhibitions, a 2003 special issue of *Art Journal,* and books by Martyn Jolly (2006), John Harvey (2007) and Louis Kaplan (2008).[8] Nancy M. West describes the spirit photograph as "a kind of self-reflexive commentary—a means of bringing to the surface photography's uncanny subtexts. Bizarre and often grotesque, these images flaunted the implicit questions the medium has raised about representation and death" (1996, 173). West's observations help locate spirit photography within the history of photography, and in particular the relationship of photography to mortality and loss, famously examined by Roland Barthes (1981) and many others. "In fixing or immobilizing the object," writes Mary Ann Doane, "transforming the subject of its portraiture into dead matter, photography is always haunted by death and historicity" (Doane 1990, 223). The idea that photography "is a mode of bereavement [that] speaks to us of mortification …" (Cadava 1997, 11) has considerable heritage: consider Balzac's assertion in *Cousin Pons* (1847) that the photograph has proved that "a man or a building is incessantly and continuously represented by a picture in the atmosphere, that all existing objects project into it a kind of *spectre* which can be captured and perceived" (1978, 131), and Jules Michelet's reaction to seeing his portrait for the first time in 1850: "The daguerreotype. It saddens me, not to see myself thus with respect to form, but to see myself a corpse, without my inner fire or my spirit" (quoted in West 1996, 174). The photograph, like the X-ray many decades later, was interpreted as supporting long-held occult speculations and seen as a powerful new tool for those who endorsed the supernatural.

In addition, photographs had a long history of creating blurred and half-present images through the exposure and development processes. While most photographers sought to mitigate these technical shortcomings, others embraced them; Julia Margaret Cameron made slightly blurry, ethereal portraits her signature style (Grove 1997, 148–50; Hill 2002). From at least the 1840s, images of transparent ghosts sharing space with living subjects were considered a major challenge for amateur photographers and were often used in magic lantern images. As noted in Chap. 3, the novelty ghost photograph was endorsed by David Brewster himself in his 1856 book *The Stereoscope: Its History, Theory, and Construction*. The photographer's art, Brewster wrote, "enables him to give a spiritual appearance to one or more of his figures, and to exhibit them as 'thin air' amid the solid realities of the stereoscopic picture" (1856, 205).[9] If Brewster stressed these double exposures as effects for the purpose of amusement only (within his broader understanding of optical trickery in service of enlightenment values), the techniques he outlined were nonetheless those used for spirit photography. Popularized (if not precisely invented) in the early 1860s by New York photographer William Mumler,[10] spirit photography would be a spiritualist practice for many decades, not fully dying out until after the First World War.

By the 1897 publication of Albert Hopkins's guide *Magic: Stage Illusions, Special Effects and Trick Photography*, the term "spirit photography" was generic enough to refer to a class of trick photography; anyone could produce a "spirit" photograph without claiming actual supernatural origins. Hopkins's guide denounces spiritualists as frauds and baits them at every occasion, but this was only necessary because there were indeed still spiritualists producing spirit photographs and claiming them as evidence of a world beyond. The practice would still have devotees in the first decades of the twentieth century, notably Ada Deane, William Hope and the "Crewe Circle" in England, though it may be fair to say that the photographs themselves now served more as ritual objects among the faithful than evidentiary documents meant to convert outsiders to spiritualist values.[11] Owen Davies has suggested that the X-ray and cinema helped put an end to spirit photography as a serious practice (2007, 204), and to some extent this may be true. I do not think, however, that it is most productive to conceive of cinema and the X-ray as having usurped the spirit photograph's status as supernatural photography, but rather to regard of the three of them as united through the aesthetic of co-registration.

Seeing Your Own Grave: The X-ray, Death and the Supernatural

On 8 November 1895, a month and a half before the Lumière cinematograph would make its public debut at the Grand Café in Paris, German physicist Wilhelm Conrad Röntgen made a fortuitous discovery. Working in his home laboratory in Würzburg, Röntgen was experimenting with running electrical charges through a variety of vacuum equipment. Running a charge from a Ruhmkorff coil through a Crookes tube in a room that was kept dark to test the opacity of its cardboard cover, Röntgen discovered, quite by accident, a fluorescence left on a nearby bench that "look[ed] like faint green clouds ... Highly excited, Röntgen lit a match and to his great surprise discovered that the source of the mysterious light was the little barium platinocyanide screen lying on the bench. He repeated the experiment again and again" (Glasser 1934, 9). Röntgen named his discovery "*x Strahlen*," "X-rays," a designation that he never expected to outlive their status as "unknown."[12] The persistence of the label in at least some languages speaks to the extent to which a popular understanding of Röntgen's discovery was and remains supernaturally tinged. Biographer Otto Glasser argues that Röntgen initially conducted his experiments in secret because of his awareness of the supernatural implications of the rays made him fear for his professional reputation (Glasser 1934, 38). The first widely distributed X-ray image was a picture of Röntgen's wife's hand, produced on 22 December 1895. Its most prominent feature is a wedding ring, denser than bone; this image would be widely imitated as fashionable women had their own hands X-rayed.[13] As Lippit puts it, "Berthe Röntgen's X-rayed hand in 1895, marked by the exteriority of her wedding band, signaled the entry of light into the human body and the illicit marriage, as it were, of radiation and photographic culture" (2005, 83).

Where most scientific discoveries spread via trade journals and evade major public interest at first, news of the X-ray spread through the popular press and public exhibition, creating great demand in the late Victorian audience hungry for spectacle and novelty (Schedel 1995, 342–3; Mussell 2007, 78). In his non-fiction book *Profiles of the Future* (1974), Arthur C. Clarke separates scientific discoveries into "the expected" and "the unexpected," with the X-ray as a quintessential example of the latter: "No one had ever imagined or predicted such a thing; that one would be able to peer into the interior of the human body ... was something even the most daring prophet had never suggested" (1974, 35–6). Anything could be X-rayed, and, in the first years of the X-ray craze, a great many things were. But the X-rays images that attracted the most widespread interest were those of human bodies: "The sensation of 'seeing one's own death' was probably the most immediate reaction to X-ray images, and, morbid as it is, it was also responsible for the general fascination with X-ray as spectacle" (Tsivian 1996, 84).

Scholars like Grove (1997) and Harvey (2007) have drawn direct connections between X-ray photography and spirit photography. To quote the latter:

> Early radiographic images bore an uncanny resemblance to the soft, milky and translucent apparitions in spirit photographs. Like spirit photographs, radiographs revealed reality beyond the surface of the physical: things that were previously and normally out of sight could now be perceived ... Each represented a vision of our mortality: the radiograph shows a skeletal image (the intimation of our final physical state), which we carry around inside ourselves, even as we live; the "extra" portrays a depth of being that not even X-rays could fathom—the psychical state, the soul or spirit that, it was supposed, survived physical death. (2007, 74)

Aware of these parallels and accustomed to appealing to new technologies and scientific discoveries, spiritualists and occultists found a special value to the X-ray. James Coates's 1911 book *Photographing the Invisible* states:

> To say that the invisible cannot be photographed, even on the material plane, would be to confess ignorance of facts which are commonplace—as, for instance, to mention the application of X-ray photography to the exploration of the muscles, of fractures of bones, and the internal organs. Astronomical photography affords innumerable illustrations of photographing the invisible. (1911, 2)[14]

Photographs of inner and outer words are equally available to the rhetoric of spiritualists and occultists, who claimed that the X-ray confirmed some of their basic premises, including the inadequacy of unaugmented human vision to assess the invisible world that lies around us.

The occult implications of the X-ray may be understood within a new climate of "modern alchemy," to borrow the title of Mark S. Morrisson's 2007 study of the role occultism played in the emergence of atomic science. Occultist thought converged with several exciting scientific discourses in the late nineteenth century. Within months of Röntgen's discovery, Henri Becquerel would discover radiation. The Curies would discover radium the following year, and within the next decade, modern physics and atomic science would begin to take shape. These new discoveries gave fuel to the already thriving modern occult revival, a fact of which scientists were not unaware. Morrisson states that: "the broad revival of interest in alchemy in the late nineteenth and early twentieth centuries ... gave chemists a trope that influenced its public reception and its sense of its own identity and contributed to its early understanding and portrayal of radioactivity's significance" (2007, 9). The scientists ultimately owed the occultists quite a lot, with their *outré* rhetoric doing part of the work of preparing the public for the modern world of scientific wonders. Camille Flammarion wrote in his 1900 work *L'Inconnu*:

> The late discovery of the Röntgen rays, so inconceivable and so strange in its origins, ought to convince us how very small is the field of our usual observations. To see through opaque substances! to look inside a closed box! to see the bones of an arm, a leg, a body, through flesh and clothing! Such a discovery is, to say the least, quite contrary to everything we have been used to consider certainty. (quoted in Henderson 1988, 326)

Likewise, W.T. Stead held that the X-rays represented "the latest inventions and scientific discoveries [that] make psychical phenomena thinkable" (1896, 400), and French spiritist and scientist Hippolyte Baraduc was inspired by the X-rays to investigate what he called "soul photography" (West 1996, 194; Monroe 2002, 249).[15] Others extended the concept of X-rays by postulating "V-rays" (Krauss 1995, 61–4) and "X^x-rays" (1995, 80–6), or tethered X-rays to existing mystical hypotheses like the Odic force, the vital force of life proposed by Baron Dr Karl von Reichenbach in the mid 1840s.

The supernatural heritage of the X-ray can also be traced through the early vacuum tube called the "Crookes tube" in its invention (Grove 1997, 164). Its inventor, William Crookes, was a famed chemist, the discoverer of the element thallium and the inventor of the radiometer. He was also a spiritualist and an early proponent of psychical research (I will discuss his notorious reports on mediums in the next chapter). The Crookes tube and radiometer were invented as part of his profoundly spiritualist scientific investigation into "the fourth state of matter," "Radiant Matter." In a 22 August 1879 speech before the British Association for the Advancement of Science, Crookes's language was draped in exalted mysticism:

> We have actually touched a border land where Matter and Force seem to merge into one another, the shadowy realm between Known and Unknown which for me has always had peculiar temptations. I venture to think that the greatest scientific problems of the future will find their solution in this

Border Land, and even beyond, where it seems to me, lie ultimate Realities, subtle, far-reaching, wonderful. (quoted in Raia-Grean 2008, 71)

As his biographer William H. Brock has noted, Crookes's real and lasting contributions to science were in large part results of his occult explorations (2008, 209). In 1896, Crookes became president of the Society for Psychical Research (SPR) and in his presidential address he framed the discovery of the X-ray as a crux moment in the history of science that will allow it to proceed in supernatural directions (Gunning 2008, 63). Crookes was the living embodiment of the supernaturalized Victorian science, and so his indirect contribution to the discovery of X-rays was amply appropriate.

Advocates for the scientification of the supernatural like Coates, Crookes, Stead, Baraduc and Flammarion all received the X-ray warmly as a tool in their rhetorical arsenal. For others, the register of the X-ray's supernatural qualities was much less positive: it was seen as a disturbing and potentially terrifying portent of death. The most famous invocation of the X-ray image as a spectre of death comes from Thomas Mann's *The Magic Mountain* (1924), with the famous lines "Spooky, isn't it? Yes, there's no mistaking the whiff of spookiness" (1997, 216). So says sanatorium director Behrens just after the protagonist, Hans Castorp, has looked at an X-ray image of his own hand, the paradigmatic X-ray image, bedecked by an heirloom ring:

> Hans Castorp saw exactly what he should have expected to see, but which no man was ever intended to see and which he himself had never presumed he would be able to see: he saw his own grave. Under that light, he saw the process of corruption anticipated, saw the flesh in which he moved decomposed, expunged, dissolved into airy nothingness—and inside was the delicately turned skeleton of his right hand and around the last joint of the ring finger, dangling black and loose, the signet ring his grandfather had bequeathed him: a hard thing, this ore with which man adorns a body predestined to melt away beneath it, so that it can be free again and move on yet other flesh that may bear it for a while. (1997, 215–16)[16]

Though Mann's eloquence is unmatched, the sentiment is not *sui generis*. Legend has it that when Berthe Röntgen first saw the X-ray of her left hand, she shuddered at the image presaging her own death (Glasser 1934, 399); the skeletal hand that Castorp encounters harkens back, of course, to the first widely distributed X-ray image. A newspaper editor in Graz allowed

Professor P. Czermak to make an X-ray image of his head and reported that, "and later, after he had seen the picture, he 'absolutely refused to show the picture to anybody but scientists.' 'He has not closed an eye,' the report continued, 'since he saw his own death'" (Glasser 1934, 40). Another 1896 account of the X-ray appearing in *Transactions of the Colorado Medical Society* said: "As the skeletal fingers came gradually forth from the blank plate, he felt a sort of creepy sensation, as though it was some ghostly hand beckoning him from another world—and it was another world; a new scientific world" (quoted in Howell 1995, 138), and a *Life* magazine cartoon from February 1896 shows a photographer taking the picture of the image of a farmer holding his scythe before a rising sun. The image is friendly and bucolic, but in the inset marked "Röntgen," it becomes a figure of death instead, a skeleton holding a scythe (Glasser 1934, 42).[17] Mann's novel (and perhaps even more strongly, Roger Corman's minor classic *X: The Man with X-ray Eyes* [1963])[18] is also anticipated by a hack story called "Röntgen's Curse" by C.H.T. Crosthwaite that appeared in *Longman's Magazine* in 1896. In this tale, a scientist gives himself X-ray vision that he cannot switch off, and is faced by such horrible visages as his wife:

> Instead of the comely face with its loving smile, a grinning skull, all the more dreadful because it was alive. Instead of the shapely figure, a ghastly skeleton, whose bony hands were outstretched to touch me. In the most tragic events there is sometimes an element of the ludicrous, so there was something of the ridiculous in this horrible travesty of life. There were hairpins hovering, as it were, over the skull, and a necklace of gold floating round the bones of the neck, moved by breathing, yet appearing to touch nothing ... The rings she wore encircled without touching the bones of her fingers. It was a skeleton masquerading in the skeleton of a dress. (Crosthwaite 1896, 478)

Even when these takes on the X-ray are facetious, pulpish or comical, they narrativize the very real anxiety that many people seemed to feel with respect to the X-ray's amazing power to co-register depths and surfaces, life and death, on a single surface, the property it shares with the spirit photograph before it and the cinematic double exposures that followed.

X-RAY AESTHETICS IN MAGIC AND THEATRE

Given the sensational public reactions they provoked and their occult affinities, it seems only natural that X-rays would find a place in the magician's arsenal as well as that of the spiritualist. The aforementioned

Hopkins guide contains a section called "The Neoöccultism" that states: "The X rays, after becoming the indispensable coadjutors of surgeons, and even of physicians, are now competing with the most noted mediums in the domain of the marvellous" (1897, 96). The author suggests that a new form of theatricalized imitation of a séance could be rigged utilizing the X-ray. It calls for a Ruhmkorff coil and Crookes tube hidden from the audience's immediate view behind a wall or curtain, as well as a skeleton covered with zinc sulphide hidden beneath a black curtain (as well as a set of props similarly treated). The trick is described thus:

> a diner (who is doubtless near-sighted, since he wears eyeglasses) is about to do justice to his breakfast. Armed with a knife and fork, he attacks his beefsteak; but he is assuredly a greater eater than drinker, since he contents himself with water, while his light consists of a single candle ... Let us now put out the light and set the Ruhmkorff coil in action. What a surprise! A plate, a glass, a water bottle, and a candle shine in space with the light of glow-worms. A sinister guest in the form of a skeleton sits opposite the place occupied by the near-sighted gentleman, who has disappeared, and whose eyeglasses alone have held their own before this ghastly apparition. (1897, 99)

Whether or not the Neoöccultism was ever put into practice on the stage, or even could be, is uncertain; it would be very elaborate, expensive, and deleterious to the health of the unfortunate actor bombarded with radiation. Nonetheless, Neoöccultism indicates how the figure of the skeleton that had existed in the hands of magicians and lanternists for so long becomes newly relevant and justifiable through the context of the X-ray (a point to which I will return in the next chapter). Hopkins's guide states that "such scenes may naturally be varied to infinity, and the spirit of invention is so fertile, there is no doubt that before long ladies will be giving a place in the programme of their soirées to this up-to-date spiritualism" (1897, 99), displaying the complex links between X-rays, stage magic and spiritualism that existed at the time (Images 5.2 and 5.3).

More often, magic acts did not use actual X-rays but borrowed X-ray aesthetics in service of amazement. In 1897, an X-ray themed act called "Les Rayons Röntgen" was staged at the Théâtre Robert-Houdin under Georges Méliès's management. A striking poster survives, reproduced by Tsivian (1996, 90), which consolidates many key tropes associated with the X-ray (perhaps most pointedly, its gendering) (Image 5.4). It shows a giant X radiating rays towards a well-dressed woman, who also has an X hovering above her head and string of X's along her middle. A man in

ARRANGEMENT FOR A STRIKING EXPERIMENT WITH THE X RAYS.

Image 5.2 Illustrations of the magic trick called "The Neoöccultism," 1897

evening wear stands nearby and points at her with both hands in a highly theatrical fashion. Some glowing scientific apparatus behind him further links the male figure with the magical technology, marking him as an amalgam of scientist and magician. The woman serenely points upwards to the

THE APPARITION.

Image 5.3 Illustrations of the magic trick called "The Neoöccultism," 1897

giant X in the upper left corner; she is simultaneously the subject of the X-rays and their personification. Meanwhile, the omnipresent image of a skeletal hand is displayed on an easel at the front of the image.

Possibly the most elaborate use of X-ray aesthetics for entertainment in the 1890s occurred elsewhere in Paris, at the *Cabaret du Néant*, a sort of up-to-date Phantasmagoria (Image 5.5).[19] Its success in Montmartre was such that a branch opened in New York City, and this venue was the subject of an article in *Scientific American* on 7 March 1896.[20] As the article explains, spectators followed an attendant dressed like a monk to a black-walled

Affiche de spectacle au Théâtre Robert-Houdin
(source : revue *Contrastes* de Guerbet, 1995)

Image 5.4 An advertisement for "Les Rayons Röntgen" stage act, 1897

Image 5.5 Promotional postcard from the Paris *Cabaret du Néant*, c. 1895

Image 5.6 Promotional postcard from the Paris *Cabaret du Néant*, c. 1895

restaurant with coffins as tables, the waiters in funeral garb and a chandelier that appeared to be made of bones and skulls (Images 5.6 and 5.7). The room was decorated with:

IN THE CABARET OF DEATH

Image 5.7 Depiction of the Paris *Cabaret du Néant* from W.C. Morrow's *Bohemian Paris of To-day* (1896)

pictures to which the spectator's attention is called by the lecturer. Seen by the light of the room these pictures are ordinary scenes, but a new aspect is given to each when lights directly behind it are turned on; the figures in it appear as skeletons, each picture being in fact a transparency giving a different effect as it is lighted from the rear or as seen simply by reflected light. (Anon. 1896a, 152)

AN X RAY ILLUSION UPON THE STAGE—CONVERSION OF A LIVING MAN INTO A SKELETON.

Image 5.8 Depiction of transformation trick from New York *Cabaret du Néant* from *Scientific American*, 1896

This is a common register of the X-ray's redefinition of the human body: the dirty secret of bones hiding beneath the facade of flesh cannot be maintained long. In the second chamber, which the spectators would enter to the sounds of a funeral march and tolling bells, an even more dramatic exposure along these lines would occur.

The second chamber, the account tells us, was very dark, the walls painted black, and smoking was not allowed because the trick that transpired within depended on an extremely clear atmosphere. A coffin stood at the back of a small stage. One of the audience members was requested to stand in it. Then, in view of the audience, he would appear to fade away, his image replaced by that of a skeleton. *Scientific American* captions its illustration of this feat with "An X Ray Illusion upon the Stage—Conversion of a Living Man into a Skeleton (Image 5.8)." The skeleton was in fact a painting of a skeleton kept just offstage, illuminated by a set of Argand burners and reflected onto a pane of glass that separates the coffin and the audience. By carefully lowering one burner and increasing the other, one image appeared to replace the other:

The illusion is perfect to the outer audience; the one in the coffin sees absolutely nothing out of the common. His interest, if he knows what is going on, is centered in watching the changing expression of the spectators, being increased by the fact that at their period of greatest astonishment, he is absolutely invisible, although directly before them and seeing them more plainly than ever. After the restoration to life one or more auditors are put through the same performance, so that the recent occupant of the coffin can see what he has gone through. (Anon. 1896a, 152)

The *Cabaret du Néant* coffin trick used a technique derived from Pepper's Ghost and therefore might be said to have as close affinities with (pre-) cinema as with the X-ray (Image 5.9). The third chamber also had an audience member pulled onto the stage, where he would sit in a chamber

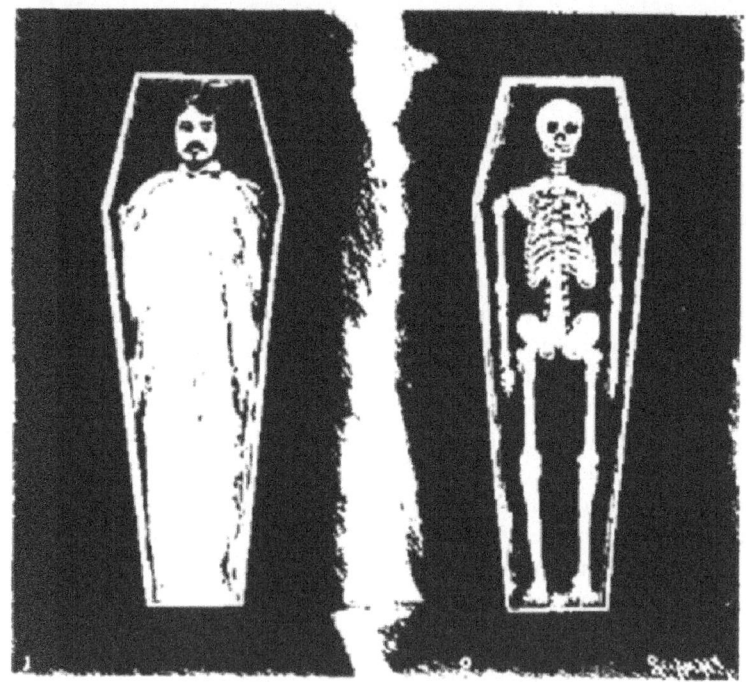

Image 5.9 Depiction of transformation trick from New York *Cabaret du Néant* from *Scientific American*, 1896

and, unbeknownst to him, would appear alongside a sheeted ghost. The *Scientific American* article closes by observing that, "The Röntgen rays are utilized in the advertising matter also, although John Henry Pepper, of the old London Polytechnic, may lay some claim to discovering the full utilization of the rays actually used in the *Cabaret du Néant*" (Anon. 1896a, 153). Through clever new applications of Pepper's Ghost, simple light rays now masquerade as X-rays in the service of entertainment within the *Cabaret*'s morbid attractions.[21]

If the *Cabaret du Néant* is little remembered today, it has received at least one interesting cinematic reference. In Francis Ford Coppola's *Bram Stoker's Dracula* (1992), there is sequence where Mina Murray (Winona Ryder) and the romantic aspect of Count Dracula (Gary Oldman) visit the London Cinematograph.[22] In the Cinematograph, the den of invention that so fascinates the Count, we see a variety of transformation trick films, a backlit puppet show and other modern marvels; posters with the names of inventors, filmmakers and magicians adorn the walls, and one stage is even labelled "Pepper's Ghost." But the place erupts with panic, echoing the myth of the Grand Café, at the appearance of Dracula's wolf Berserker. The Count's predatory approach towards Mina is framed against the 1901 Biograph film *The Ghost Train*, a negative image of a train approaching[23]; Coppola thus represents the Count, a creature of negation, as another such ghost train pulling into the heart of modernity. In this dense, fast-cut sequence there is a brief symbolic intercut to the figure of Mina standing within the white outline of a vertical coffin, shaped *exactly* like those in the *Scientific American* illustrations of the *Cabaret du Néant* (Image 5.10). A skeleton is superimposed on her, never fully replacing her but lingering over her as a sort of ghostly palimpsest. This image foreshadows Mina's own encounter with death as she is infected with Dracula's inhuman blood; it also echoes an earlier sequence where the Count first encounters Mina and we see, from his perspective, blood pumping all through her body as if she were an anatomical model.

Coppola's choice to stage these encounters with mortality within the idiom of the X-ray is in keeping with the film's *fin-de-siècle* setting and also testifies to the continuing power of these images to disquiet. Whether or not Coppola and his collaborators knew it, skeleton imagery has a strange link with Stoker's *Dracula*. In Stoker's initial notes for the writing project that would become *Dracula*, dating from around 1890, the vampire (called "Count Wampyr" before Stoker came across an evocative name linked to a fifteenth-century tyrant in some literature on the history of Transylvania)

Image 5.10 An apparent reference to the *Cabaret du Néant* in *Bram Stoker's Dracula* (1992)

could not be photographed: "could not Codak [sic] him—comes out black or like skeleton corpse" (Stoker 2008, 21). Stacey Abbott writes that "Stoker, drawing upon the language of modern technology, [rewrites] the characteristics of the vampire to embody the increasingly ambiguous relationship between science and the occult" (2007, 17), and the Count's inability to be photographed, even if it does not reach the final draft of the novel, is certainly in keeping with this. Perhaps it is not so much that Dracula's supernatural nature precludes him being photographed as that that the camera, potentially a supernatural device in its own right, reveals his nature more clearly than the naked eye, whether exposing him as a skeleton or as pure absence ("comes out black"). The idea that only bones would be shown in a photograph remarkably forecasts the X-ray, and helps confirm that figure of the skeleton had an occult power in the years immediately before Röntgen's discovery; this perhaps helps us understand why the X-ray mania took the shape it did. Stoker's phrase "skeleton corpse" is curious, reminding one of the X-ray's ability to expose the (even living) body as a skeleton and "corpse" at once, visible on the same photographic surface through an aesthetic of co-registration.

Camera Fiends, X-ray Fiends

In the 1890s, X-rays and cinema were linked as rival novel forms of photography that jointly participated in a certain reconfiguring of the public understanding of materiality and insubstantiality, presence and absence, and life and death. They shared a common exhibition context: Richard Crangle notes that early in 1896, London variety venues exhibited R.W. Paul's Theatrograph and the X-ray side by side, along with new bicycles, military hardware and horseless carriages (1998, 139). Numerous itinerant exhibitors also showed both X-rays and cinema. A notable example is William Paley, who would become known as the "Kinetoscope Man" for the films he made in Cuba during the Spanish-American War, under contract to the Edison Company (Musser 1990, 167).[24] Prior to this, he was an X-ray exhibitor who abandoned this field after a bout of radiation sickness, a problem that numerous experimenters with X-rays would face (Brecher and Brecher 1969, 81–90). Other exhibitors of both X-rays and cinema included William Friese-Greene and Jasper Redfern in Britain, Mark Blow in Australia and Yokota Einosuke in Japan (Condon 2008, 50).[25]

Throughout 1896, commentators often spoke of cinema and the X-ray in the same breath. In his aforementioned "The Kinematograph from a Scientific Point of View," V.E. Johnson indicated that "medicine in all of its branches has, or will very shortly have, three very powerful assistants in the X-rays, the Kinematograph, and the photo-chromoscope" (1996, 6), the latter being an early colour photography process. In a remarkable article that appeared in *New Review* in February 1896, the pseudonymous "O. Winter" draws cinema into his caustic critique of literary naturalism. "Is not Zola the M. Lumière of his art?" asks Winter. "It is the favourite creed of the realists that truth is valuable for its own sake, that the description of a tiresome hat or an infamous pair of trousers has a merit of its own closely allied to accuracy. But life in itself is seldom interesting ..." (1996, 15). The Lumières' cinematograph, for Winter, sharply demonstrates how banal life is when represented realistically, and thus reminds us that art needs unreality to sustain interest (Winter similarly indicts the chronophotography of Eadweard Muybridge). Winter suddenly turns to the X-ray at the close of his essay:

> And now, that Science may ever keep abreast of literature, comes M. Röntgen's invention to play the part of the psychologist. As M. [Paul] Bourget (shall we say?) uncovers secret motivations and inclinations of his

characters, when all you ask of him is a single action, so M. Röntgen bids photography pierce the husk of flesh and blood and reveal to the world the skeletons of living men. In Science the penetration may be invaluable; in literature it destroys the impression, and substitutes pedantry for intelligence. M. Röntgen, however, would commit no worse an outrage than the cure of the sick and advancement of knowledge. Wherefore he is absolved from the mere suspicion of an onslaught upon art. But it is not without its comedy, that photography's last inventions are twin echoes of modern literature. The Cinématograph is but realism reduced to other terms, less fallible and more amusing; while M. Röntgen's rays suggest that, though a too intimate discourse may be fatal to romance, the doctor and the curiosity-monger may find it profitable to pierce through our "too, too solid flesh" and count the rattling bones within. (1996, 17)

Where Winter links cinema to the banality he sees in the realist novels of authors like Zola, he links X-rays to psychological literature, which hones in too closely and exposes too much. Both cinema and X-rays, Winter argues, are ultimately artless, but promise to have scientific utility. Lurking behind Winter's words is panic about the ability of new photographic techniques to penetrate the world too deeply, creating a closeness that seems obscene.

It should be no surprise that several practitioners of the nascent cinematic genre of the trick film staged scenes that were, like the theatrical tricks at the *Cabaret du Néant*, framed around X-rays. Sometimes, the invocation was so general that no skeletal effect need be depicted; Biograph's *The X-ray Mirror* (1899) involves a young *flâneuse* looking into a mirror to see how she looks with a new hat and fainting on seeing herself as a ballerina. Evidently the term "X-ray" could even be used generically for surprising alterations of the human body. Georges Méliès made at least one film clearly about X-rays, known in French as *Les Rayons Röntgen* (1898) (the same name as the theatrical spectacle he staged the year previous) and in English as *A Novice at X-rays*. This lost film features a scientist using an X-ray machine on a patient, causing his skeleton to appear to separate from his body and walk away, before collapsing in a heap. The scientist reverses the experiment and restores the skeleton to the man's body (Ruffles 2004, 14). Near the end of the trick film's popularity, Émile Cohl made *The X-ray Glasses* or *Les lunettes féerique* (1909), where a family dons X-ray glasses that reveal the contents of their soul, and the Italian film *Un ragno nel cervello* (1912) showed X-rays revealing the presence of a spider in a person's brain.

But the definitive example is surely George Albert Smith's 1897 *The X-ray Fiend* (also released as *The X-rays*). It plays out against a stark black background. A long shot shows a well-dressed man and a woman on a park bench. She carries a parasol. He flirts with her and she mildly resists his advances. Unseen by the couple, a black-clad man appears at the back right of the frame. This villain has black beard and a top hat and carries a contraption labelled "X RAYS" at shoulder level (Image 5.11). Rectangular, with a lens-like protruding front, it is shaped distinctly like a movie camera. The fiend takes off the "lens" and immediately (through a substitution cut, the only type of editing in the film) the man and woman become skeletons, and the parasol turns into a wire-frame parody of itself as well. The man and woman are in fact wearing black costumes with bones painted on them, and their skulls, which are clearly the size of human heads, are particularly unconvincing. The man on the bench gesticulates in a much more exaggerated fashion in skeletal form, his legs bouncing up and down, reminding one of the merry dancing skeletons common in lantern displays. The strange intruder disappears, restoring the couple to their previous forms. She rises up from the bench and walks away, though he pathetically falls to his knees in a beggar's posture. He has well and truly been "seen through".

Image 5.11 George Albert Smith's *The X-ray Fiend* (1896)

This comic scene of voyeurism and "undressing" is playfully perverse. *The X-ray Fiend* is one of the earliest examples of what Paul Young (2006) calls "media fantasy films," a term adapted from the "media fantasy" of Carolyn Marvin (1988), who looks to the "fantasies" of a given age to help determine "what 'consciousness' was in a particular age, what thoughts were possible and what thoughts could not be entertained yet or anymore" (Young 2006, 7–8). Young's focus is on electrical media like the wireless, television and internet and he makes only a one-line reference to the X-ray, but the label "media fantasy film" perfectly suits *The X-ray Fiend*, which evokes various themes associated with the X-ray in its first years: an alteration in human perspective, the potential for an excessive, obscene (and inevitably eroticized) closeness, the gloomy and supernatural implications of transforming human bodies into *memento mori*, as well as the fear of the loss of privacy and the rise of voyeuristic new forms of crime. On the latter subject, *The X-ray Fiend* has affinities with H.G. Wells's *The Invisible Man*, published in 1897. Grove writes that Dr Griffin:

> acts out the nightmare that X-rays created in the Victorian imagination. He represents the destructive potential of Röntgen's discovery. He is a robber, a spy, and a murderer, not to mention a ghost, who can use his technology of invisibility to commit his crimes undetected. The Invisible Man represents the ultimate threat to the privacy and security of those he encounters. (1997, 169)

Wells makes it clear that Dr Griffin's transparency is not on account of "those Röntgen vibrations" (2002, 106), but even this disavowal locates Griffin's science within the same modern alchemy as the X-ray. The fiend X-rays other people where his contemporary villain Griffin has pseudo-X-rayed himself, but both are perverse villains using the rays for villainous purposes.[26]

The title *The X-ray Fiend* alludes to the "camera fiend" or "Kodak fiend," an amateur obsessed with documenting the world with the newly portable camera. Between the 1850s and the 1880s, photography was generally seen as a tasteful practice, despite the occasional photographer who would put his craft to less than gentlemanly ends (including the pornographer). Things changed in the 1890s, in part because photography expanded beyond the professional and the well-bred and well-funded amateur, and in part because faster shutter speeds allowed a new kind of intrusive photography. As Bill Jay notes, *"for the first time people could be photographed surreptitiously* ... With the snapshot camera, anyone at any time could be the victim of an embarrassing or even incriminating picture ... the snapshooters ignored the restraints of common decency and good manners" (1991, 222–3, original emphasis). Writes Robert Mensel: "The amateurs were positively Mephistophelean: they belong to a class of minor demons known as 'camera fiend,' or 'Kodak fiends,' and they were said 'to be in league with some evil spirit.' Their activities were mysterious, seductive and intoxicating" (1991, 29). Armed with their weapons, they were thought to go around photographing unsuspecting people and profoundly offending privacy. In 1906, *The American Amateur Photographer* asked "What is to be Done about the Camera Fiend?" and reported that the president's daughter Alice Roosevelt could not shop for her upcoming wedding without being subject to the flashbulbs of overzealous passers-by (the paparazzo is older than we think). A law against photography in public places, the article warns, will be forthcoming if the amateurs do not police their own and rebuke the camera fiend.

Camera fiends were understood as being obsessive almost to the point of derangement. The film *The Camera Fiend* (1903) shows a photographer who is more inclined to take pictures of a drowning boy than to assist in his rescue, only reluctantly helping with his one free hand. Young discusses it as a moralizing allegory for the film industry's fascination with shock: "Its titular devil cares less about human life than about getting a good snapshot of human mortality" (2006, 29). In 1911, Arthur Conan Doyle's brother-in-law Ernest Hornung used *The Camera Fiend* as the title for a sensationalistic novel about a mad scientist obsessed with documenting the human soul.[27] He murders tramps in Hyde Park to try to photograph the soul as it flees the body, even designing a combined camera-firearm to kill and photograph in the same instant, much like Mark Lewis (Karl Boehm) in *Peeping Tom* (1960). Unsuccessful, he turns the device on himself, hoping that his suicide will yield the evidence he was unable to obtain in life.

The camera fiend is easily associated with the supernatural both in terms of his nature (a demon) and his twisted objectives. This is doubly true of Smith's X-ray fiend, who covertly transforms the couple into skeletons for his own perverse, voyeuristic reasons. The fiend in Smith's film is, appropriately, Smith himself; the director plays the high-tech criminal. The other man is Tom Green, the Brighton comedian who appeared in numerous films of the Hove pioneers before directing dozens of films himself, and the woman is Smith's wife Laura, several years before she would play a ghost in *Mary Jane's Mishap* … another version of the wife as the subject of X-ray photography. *The X-ray Fiend* narrativizes anxieties about photography and X-rays, but also has something to say about cinema, in keeping with Young's argument that early cinema was most prone to being reflexive about itself, with its depictions of trains, Kodaks and so on, often serving at least in part to comment on cinema (2006, xxxiii). The fiend's X-ray device strongly resembles a film camera and marks him as a kind of a renegade filmmaker, wandering the streets making illicit photographs of courting couples; indeed the "X-ray effect" is achieved cinematically, through the substitution splice that makes the trick film possible, and only mimics the X-ray. It draws cinema and the X-ray together as surely as O. Winter did, and again within the context of excessive and unwanted intimacy with the image.

There is one aesthetic feature of *The X-ray Fiend* that fascinates me further. When the fiend activates his machine, Laura Smith and Tom Green are wearing black clothes with bones painted on them, and the edges of their clothing are clearly visible against the black backdrop. This is most visible with respect to her dress, which billows noticeably, shades lighter than the backdrop. Perhaps this overlay is a result of technical limitations; Smith's attempt to match the black of their clothes and the black of the set to create the illusion that they are skeletons does not quite work. The film contains none of the double exposures and other camera tricks that Smith would begin to hone the year after in films like *The Mesmerist*, *Photographing a Ghost*, *The Corsican Brothers* and *Santa Claus*. But it may contain seeds of Smith's double-exposure work, and also might be described as more accurately recreating the X-ray aesthetic than theatricalized imitations generally do. Early spectators were not astonished by X-rays simply because that they showed skeletons but because they also reduced flesh and muscle to a wraithlike parody fluttering half-visible alongside it, making depths into surfaces and surfaces into depths. The aesthetic principle shared by the spirit photograph, the X-ray and the cinematic double exposure is co-registration. Coming immediately before Smith's successful pioneering of double-exposure techniques, *The X-ray Fiend* gives us reason to speculate that the aesthetic of the X-ray, with all of its cultural baggage of the supernatural, death and invasion of privacy, played a role in guiding the path of Smith and experimenters like him to the double exposures pioneered by the spiritualists, and which would shortly become the favoured cinematic means of depicting ghosts.

NOTES

1. Discussing Méliès's uses of the double exposure, Gunning refers to the way he treats film space as "a surface bearing the imprint of several images that create an ambiguous area of often contradictory orientations" (1983, 358). Solomon (2010, 104) also draws attention to the use of double exposures to represent disembodied spirits in Houdini's *The Man from Beyond* (1922), as a point of continuity with the spirit photograph and as evidence of Houdini's ambiguous position relative to spiritualism.
2. For a discussion of superimpositions, Bazin and Godard, see Morgan (2011).
3. See Curtis (2008, esp. 123–37) for a discussion of photographic imagery in ghost films, as well as more general thoughts about the relationship of photography and haunting. The eccentric British film *The Ashpyx* (1973) and the Thai film *Shutter* (2004) are particularly good examples.
4. We might reflect here too that Pepper's Ghost, which appeared on a pane of glass to the amazed audience, must have had a two-dimensional appearance as well as a wispy, half-present figure seeming to interact and yet be apart from the theatrical space. It too had aesthetic connections to the spirit photograph, which debuted at almost the same time across the Atlantic.
5. For treatments of early cinema's relationship with the X-ray, see Cartwright (1995), Crangle (1998), Jülich (2000, 2008), Tsivian (1996), Lippit (2005), Tosi (2005), Natale (2006), and Elder (2008). The X-ray and cinema shared presentation venues and personnel, and were so linked in the public mind that it is common to find them mentioned the same breath by commentators of the time. If anything, the X-ray's initial profile was superior: it, not cinema, was dubbed "the New Photography" by the press.
6. Useful sources on spiritualism not otherwise cited in this volume include Owen (1989), Cottom (1991), Pimple (1995), Morita (1999), Weinstein (2004), Weisberg (2004), Tromp (2006), Blum (2006), Herman (2006), Bennett (2006, 2007), Gomel (2007), McGarry (2008), Kontou (2009) and Vinitsky (2009).
7. This expanded label would include ectoplasm photography (see Schoonover 2003), aura photography, Kirlian photography, thoughtography, *nensha* and so on. Krauss (1995) is likely the

most broad and inclusive treatment of paranormal photography available.
8. Sources on spirit photography include Jay (1991, 7–29), Gunning (1995, 2003, 2008), Monroe (2002, esp. 162–8, 171–3, 180–5), Cox (2003, 112–35), Tucker (2005, 159–93), Leja (2006, 21–58), Cadwallader (2008), Wojcik (2009), Arias (2009) and Natale (2016, esp. 109–134).
9. See Kaplan (2008, 27–31), Tucker (2005, 71–3) and Gunning (2007, 112) for the relationship of spirit photograph to other novelty photographic techniques.
10. For Mumler's predecessors, see Krauss (1995, 99–101). The heyday of the spirit photograph was in the 1860s and 1870s, when they were at the centre of extensive debates about authenticity and even legality. William Mumler was acquitted after a sensational trial in 1869 due to lack of evidence, but his French equivalent, Édouard Buguet, would not be so lucky, and received a year in prison and a stiff fine after confessing to fraud (Monroe 2002, 180–5).
11. For a thorough treatment of the "later life" of spirit photography, see Jolly (2006, 90–139).
12. Seventeen years would pass before the nature of X-rays was firmly determined to be waves like light waves but with a shorter wavelength than visible light. Prior to that there were several competing theories. Other terms used for X-rays images included "shadowgraphs," "skiagraphs" and the slightly more general "radiographs."
13. An 1896 article in *Pearson's Magazine* features the X-rayed hand of the wife (unnamed) of Professor Spies of the Urania Institute of Berlin, reflecting the pervasiveness of the image of *female* hands (Dam 1896, 413), and, as I shall explore in the subsequent chapter, female skeletons.
14. Similarly, the article entitled "Psychic Photography" written by Andrew Glendinning for the July 1896 issue of *Borderland* contains subheadings like "From the Roentgen Rays to the Existence of the Soul" and "The Faith of Science in the Invisible."
15. See also Gibbons (1981, 139–40) and Krauss (1995, 51–7).
16. See Danius (2000, 196–202) for a thorough discussion of Mann's use of X-ray imagery.
17. Of course, the "deathly" qualities of the X-ray would take on a different inflection once it became clear that the rays were in fact dangerous, capable of inscribing themselves on the bodies of their

subject in unexpected ways, causing nausea, hair loss, skin peeling and burning and equally unpleasant symptoms. Most early experimenters would display these symptoms to some degree or another. The victims of the X-ray were numerous, and became recorded in the annals of medical history as martyrs who suffered or even died to further the cause science (Herzig 2005, 85–100).

18. Fantasies about X-ray vision circulated long before Superman's 1938 debut: an 1899 article in the *Aberdeen Weekly Journal* claimed that a Massachusetts boy named Afley Leonel Brett has gained the power to see "with all the wonderful faculties of the Röntgen Rays" (Anon. 1899, 6), but only for 15-minute intervals when hypnotized by his father.

19. The *Cabaret* fits perfectly with the gloomy character of *fin-de-siècle* Paris described by Schwartz (1998, esp. 44–88).

20. See Pierson for a treatment of *Scientific American*'s significance in the late nineteenth century (2002, 33–46), including a brief treatment of the *Cabaret du Néant* article (2002, 43). For a description of the Paris venue, see Morrow (1899, 264–76).

21. For other discussions of the *Cabaret du Néant*, see Nadis (2005, 15–16) and Simon (2004, 277–8).

22. For more on this much-discussed sequence, see Gelder (1994, 88–9), Stewart (1999, 241–4), Thomas (2000, 303–7), Moore (2000, 48–9), and Joyce (2007, 105–7).

23. F.W. Murnau famously used negative film to convey the vampire's unnatural and inverted status in *Nosferatu*. Hans Richter put it to more playful supernatural uses in *Ghosts Before Breakfast* (1927).

24. This William Paley is not to be confused with the same-named CBS president, who was born in 1901.

25. Excluded from the present discussion is the X-ray film proper, the actual use of X-ray images in cinematography, pioneered by Scottish scientist James MacIntyre in 1897. See Cartwright (1995, esp. 131–41), Tosi (2005, 169–71).

26. If Wells's Dr Griffin seems remarkably chaste in his use of his powers, at least in comparison with the invisible rapist Sebastian Caine (Kevin Bacon) in *Hollow Man* (2000) or even the perverse version of Griffin from Allan Moore's *The League of Extraordinary Gentlemen*, Grove reminds us of the paedophilic implications of the passage: "I looked about the hillside, with children playing and girls watching them, and tried to think of all the fantastic advan-

tages an invisible man would have in the world" (1997, 169). In "Now You See Him: The Invisible Man Revealed" (2002), a special feature for Universal's Legacy Collection of *The Invisible Man* series, David J. Skal opines that invisible man films are popular because they are covertly about nudity. This claim is particularly borne out with respect to *The Invisible Woman* (1940), where the transparent titular character (Virginia Bruce) takes a shower on screen. This censor-friendly gag appeared previously with a female ghost in *Topper* (1937).

27. Arthur Conan Doyle would defend twentieth-century spirit photographers like William Hope and wrote a book defending the infamous Cottingley Fairy Hoax; see Wynne (1998).

Works Cited

Abbott, Stacey. *Celluloid Vampires: Life After Death in the Modern World.* Austin: University of Texas Press, 2007.
[Anon.] "The Cabaret du Néant." *Scientific American* 7 March (1896a): 152–3.
[Anon.] "Edison and Rontgen Outdone: A Waipawa Photographer Takes the Picture of Two Phantom Horses and Riders." *Borderland* 4:3 (October 1896b): 446.
[Anon.] "A Human X Ray." *Aberdeen Weekly Journal* 17 July (1899): 6.
[Anon.] "What is to be Done about the Camera Fiend?" *The American Amateur Photographer* XVIII (March 1906): 4–5.
Arias, Rosario. "(Spirit) Photography and the Past in the Neo-Victorian Novel." *Literary Interpretation Theory* 20 (2009): 92–107.
Balzac, Honoré de. *Cousin Pons.* London: Penguin, 1978.
Barnouw, Erik. *The Magician and the Cinema.* New York: Oxford University Press, 1981.
Barthes, Roland. *Camera Lucida: Reflections on Photograph.* New York: Hill and Wang, 1981.
Bennett, Bridget. "Spirited Away: The Death of Little Eva and the Farewell Performances of 'Katie King.'" *Journal of American Studies* 40 (2006): 1–16.
Bennett, Bridget. *Transatlantic Spiritualism and the Nineteenth-century American Literature.* Houndmills, Basingstoke, Hants: Palgrave Macmillan, 2007.
Blum, Deborah. *Ghost Hunters: William James and the Search for Scientific Proof of Life After Death.* New York: Penguin, 2006.
Braude, Ann. *Radical Spirits: Spiritualism and Women's Writers in Nineteenth-century America.* Bloomington: Indiana University Press, 2001.
Braun, Marta. *Eadweard Muybridge.* London: Reaktion, 2010.

Braun, Marta. *Picturing Time: The Work of Étienne-Jules Marey (1830–1904)*. Chicago: University of Chicago Press, 1992.

Brecher, Ruth and Edward Brecher. *The Rays: A History of Radiology in the United States and Canada*. Baltimore: Wilkins & Wilkins, 1969.

Brewster, David. *The Stereoscope: Its History, Theory and Construction, With Its Application to the Fine and Useful Arts and to Education, Etc*. London: John Murray, 1856.

Brock, William H. *William Crookes (1832–1919) and the Commercialization of Science*. Aldershot, Hants: Ashgate, 2008.

Cadava, Eduardo. *Words of Light: Theses on the Photography of History*. Princeton: Princeton University Press, 1997.

Cadwallader, Jen. "Spirit Photography and the Victorian Culture of Mourning." *Modern Language Studies* 37.2 (2008): 8–31.

Cartwright, Lisa. *Screening the Body: Tracing Medicine's Visual Culture*. Minneapolis: University of Minnesota Press, 1995.

Clarke, Arthur C. *Profiles of the Future: An Inquiry into the Limits of Possibility*. London: Victor Gollancz, 1974.

Coates, James. *Photographing the Invisible: Practical Studies in Spirit Photography, Spirit Portraiture, and Other Rare but Allied Phenomena ... with 90 Photographs*. London: L.N. Fowler, 1911.

Condon, Denis. *Early Irish Cinema 1895–1921*. Dublin: Irish Academic Press, 2008.

Cottom, Daniel. *Abyss of Reason: Cultural Movements, Revelations, and Betrayals*. New York: Oxford University Press, 1991.

Cox, Robert S. *Body and Soul: A Sympathetic History of American Spiritualism*. Charlottesville: University of Virginia Press, 2003.

Crangle, Richard. "Saturday Night at the X-rays—The Moving Picture and 'The New Photography' in Britain, 1896." *Celebrating 1895: The Centenary of Cinema*. Ed. John Fullerton. Sydney: John Libbey & Company Pty Ltd, 1998. 138–44.

Crosthwaite, C.H.T. "Rontgen's Curse." *Longman's Magazine* 28.167 (September 1896): 469–84.

Curtis, Barry. *Dark Places: The Haunted House in Film*. London: Reaktion, 2008.

Dam, H.J.W. "A Wizard of To-Day." *Pearson's Magazine* 1.4 (April 1896): 413–9.

Danius, Sara. "Novel Visions and the Crisis of Culture: Visual Technology, Modernism, and Death in *The Magic Mountain*." *Boundary 2* 27.2 (Summer 2000): 177–211.

Daston, Lorraine and Peter Galison. "The Image of Objectivity." *Representations* 40 (Autumn 1992): 81–128.

Davies, Owen. *The Haunted: A Social History of Ghosts*. New York: Palgrave Macmillan, 2007.

Doane, Mary Ann. *The Emergence of Cinematic Time: Modernity, Contingency, the Archive.* Cambridge, MA: Harvard University Press, 2002.
Doane, Mary Ann. "Information, Crisis, Catastrophe." *Logic of Television: Essays in Cultural Criticism.* Ed. Patricia Mellencamp. Bloomington: Indiana University Press, 1990. 222–239.
Elder, R. Bruce. *Harmony + Dissent: Film and Avant-garde Movements in the Early Twentieth Century.* Waterloo: Wilfred Laurier University Press, 2008.
Gelder, Ken. *Reading the Vampire.* London: Routledge, 1994
Gibbons, Tom H. "Cubism and 'The Fourth Dimensions' in the Context of the Late Nineteenth-Century and Early Twentieth-Century Revival of Occult Idealism." *Journal of the Warburg and Courtauld Institutes* 44 (1981): 130–47.
Glasser, Otto. *Wilhelm Conrad Rontgen and the Early History of the Roentgen Rays.* San Francisco: Norman, 1934.
Glendinning, Andrew. "Psychic Photography." *Borderland.* 3.3 (July 1896): 313–321.
Gomel, Elana. "'Spirits in the Material World': Spiritualism and Identity in the Fin De Siècle." *Victorian Literature and Culture.* 35.1 (2007): 189–213.
Goodman, Philip C. "The New Light: Discovery and Introduction of the X-ray." *American Journal of Roentgenology* 165 (1995): 1041–45.
Grove, Allen W. "Röntgen's Ghosts: Photography, X-rays and the Victorian Imagination." *Literature and Medicine* 16.2 (Fall 1997): 141–73.
Gunning, Tom. "Haunting Images: Ghosts, Photography and the Modern Body." *The Disembodied Spirit.* Brunswick, Maine: Bowdoin College Museum or Art, 2003. 8–19.
Gunning, Tom. "Invisible Worlds, Visible Media." *Brought to Light: Photography and the Invisible, 1840–1900.* San Francisco: San Francisco Museum of Modern Art, 2008. 51–63.
Gunning, Tom. "Phantom Images and Modern Manifestations: Spirit Photography, Magic Theatre, Trick Films and Photography's Uncanny." *Fugitive Images: From Photography to Video.* Ed. Patrice Petro. Bloomington: Indiana University Press, 1995. 42–71.
Gunning, Tom. "To Scan a Ghost: The Ontology of Mediated Vision." *Grey Room* 26 (Winter 2007): 94–127.
Gunning, Tom. "An Unseen Energy Swallows Space: The Space in Early Film and Its Relation to American Avant-garde Film." *Film Before Griffith.* Ed. John Fell. Berkeley: University of California Press, 1983. 355–66.
Harrington, Curtis. "Ghoulies and Ghosties." *Horror Film Reader.* Eds. Alain Silver and James Ursini. New York: Limelight Editions, 2000. 9–20.
Harvey, John. *Photography and Spirit.* London: Reaktion Books, 2007.
Henderson, Linda Dalrymple. "X Rays and the Quest for Invisible Life in the Art of Kupka, Duchamp, and the Cubists." *Art Journal* 47 (Winter 1988). 323–340.

Herman, Daniel. "Whose Knocking? Spiritualism as Entertainment and Therapy in Nineteenth-Century San Francisco." *American Nineteenth Century History* 7.3 (September 2006): 417–42.
Herzig, Rebecca M. *Suffering for Science: Reason and Sacrifice in Modern America.* New Brunswick, NJ: Rutgers University Press, 2005.
Hill, Marylu. "'Shadowing Sense at War with Soul': Julia Margaret Cameron's Photographic Illustrations of Tennyson's 'Idylls of the King." *Victorian Poetry* 40.4 (Winter 2002): 445–62.
Hopkins, Albert. A. *Magic: Stage Illusions and Scientific Diversions Including Trick Photography.* New York: Munn & Co., 1897.
Howell, Joel. *Technology in the Hospital: Transforming Patient Care in the Early Twentieth Century.* Baltimore: The Johns Hopkins University Press, 1995.
Jay, Bill. *Cyanide & Spirits: An Inside-out View of Early Photography.* Munich: Nazraeli Press, 1991.
Johnson, V.E. "The Kinematograph from a Scientific Point of View." *In the Kingdom of Shadows: A Companion to Early Cinema.* Eds. Colin Harding and Simon Popple. London: Cygnus Press, 1996. 25.
Jolly, Martyn. *Faces of the Dead: The Belief in Spirit Photography.* London: British Library, 2006.
Joyce, Simon. *Victorians in the Rearview Mirror.* Athens: Ohio University Press, 2007.
Jülich, Solveig. "Media as Modern Magic: Early X-ray Imaging and Cinematography in Sweden." *Early Popular Visual Culture* 6.1 (April 2008): 18–33.
Jülich, Solveig. "Seeing in the Dark: Early X-ray Imaging and Cinema." *Moving Images: From Edison to the Webcam.* Eds. John Fullerton and Astrid Söderbergh Widding. London: John Libbey, 2000. 47–58.
Kaplan, Louis. *The Strange Case of William Mumler, Spirit Photographer.* Minneapolis: Minnesota University Press, 2008.
Knight, Nancy. "'The New Light': X-rays and Medical Futurism." *Imagining Tomorrow: History, Technology, and the American Future.* Ed. Joseph J. Corn. Cambridge, MA: The MIT Press, 1986. 10–30.
Kontou, Tatiana. *Spiritualism and Women's Writing: From the Fin de Siècle to the Neo-Victorian.* Houndmills, Basingstoke, Hants: Palgrave Macmillan, 2009.
Krauss, Rolf H. *Beyond Light and Shadow: The Role of Photography in Certain Paranormal Phenomena: A Historical Survey.* Portland, OR: Nazraeli Press, 1995.
Leja, Michael. *Looking Askance: Skepticism and American Art from Eakins to Duchamp.* Berkeley: University of California Press, 2006.
Lippit, Akira Mizuta. *Atomic Light (Shadow Optics).* Minneapolis: University of Minnesota Press, 2005.
Mann, Thomas. *The Magic Mountain.* New York: Alfred A. Knopf, 1997.
Marvin, Carolyn. *When Old Technologies Were New: Thinking About Electric Communication in the Late Nineteenth Century.* New York: University of Oxford Press, 1988.

Mensel, Robert E. "'Kodakers Lying in Wait: Amateur Photography and the Right of Privacy in New York, 1885–1915." *American Quarterly* 43.1 (Mar 1991): 24–45.

McGarry, Molly. *Ghosts of Futures Past: Spiritualism and the Cultural Politics of Nineteenth-Century America*. Berkeley: University of California Press, 2008.

Monroe, John Warne. *Laboratories of Faith: Mesmerism, Spiritism and Occultism in Modern France*. Ithaca: Cornell University Press, 2002.

Moore, Alan and Kevin O'Neil. *League of Extraordinary Gentlemen*. V1. La Jolla, CA: American's Best Comics, 2000.

Moore, Rachel O. *Savage Theory: Cinema as Modern Magic*. Durham: Duke University Press, 2000.

Morgan, Daniel. "The Afterlife of the Superimposition." *Opening Bazin: Postwar Film Theory and Its Afterlife*. Eds. Dudley Andrew and Hervé Joubert-Laurencin. Oxford: Oxford University Press, 2011. 127–141.

Morita, Sally. "Unseen (and Unappreciated) Matters: Understanding the Reformative Nature of 19th-century Spiritualism." *American Studies* 3.2 (Fall 1999): 99–135.

Morrisson, Mark S. *Modern Alchemy: Occultism and the Emergence of Atomic Theory*. Oxford: Oxford University Press, 2007.

Morrow, W.C. *Bohemian Paris of To-day*. London: Chatto and Windus, 1899.

Mussell, James. *Science, Time and Space in the Late Nineteenth-century Periodical Press: Movable Types*. Aldershot, Hants: Ashgate: 2007.

Musser, Charles. *The Emergence of Cinema: The American Screen to 1907*. New York: Maxwell Macmillan International, 1990.

Nadis, Fred. *Wonder Shows: Performing Science, Magic and Religion in America*. New Brunswick, NJ: Rutgers University Press, 2005.

Natale, Simone. "Le specttacolari origini di cinema e radiografia." *Mondo Niovo*. 2 (2006). 55–62.

Natale, Simone. *Supernatural Entertainments: Victorian Spiritualism and the Rise of Modern Media Culture*. University Park, PN: Pennsylvania State University Press, 2016.

Owen, Alex. *The Darkened Room: Women, Power, and Spiritualism in Late Nineteenth Century England*. London: Virago Press, 1989.

Pamboukian, Sylvia. "'Looking Radiant': Science, Photography and the X-ray Craze of 1897." *Victorian Review* 27.2 (2001): 56–74.

Pierson, Michele. *Special Effects: Still in Search of Wonder*. New York: Columbia University Press, 2002.

Pimple, Kenneth D. "Ghosts, Spirits and Scholars: The Origins of Modern Spiritualism." *Out of the Ordinary: Folklore and the Supernatural*. Barbara Walker, ed. Logan: Utah State University Press, 1995. 75–89.

Raia-Green, Courtenay. "Picturing the Supernatural: Spirit Photography, Radiant Matter, and the Spectacular Science of Sir William Crookes." *Visions of the Industrial Age, 1830–1914: Modernity and the Anxiety of Representation in*

Europe. Eds. Minsoo Kang and Amy Woodson-Boutlon. Aldershot, Hants: Ashgate, 2008. 55–80.

Ruffles, Tom. *Ghost Images: Cinema of the Afterlife.* Jefferson, NC: McFarland, 2004.

Schedel, Angelika. "An Unprecedented Sensation—Public Reaction to the Discovery of X-Rays." *Physics Education* 30.6 (1995): 342–47.

Schoonover, Karl. "Ectoplasms, Evanescence, and Photography." *Art Journal* 63.3 (Autumn 2003): 30–43.

Schwartz, Vanessa. *Spectacular Realities: Early Mass Culture in Fin-de-siècle Paris.* Berkeley: University of California Press, 1998.

Simon, Linda. *Dark Light: Electricity and Anxiety from the Telegraph to the X-ray.* Orlando: Harcourt, 2004.

Solomon, Matthew. *Disappearing Tricks: Silent Film, Houdini, and the New Magic of the Twentieth Century.* Iowa City: University of Iowa Press, 2010.

Stead, W.T. "Suggestions from Science for Psychic Students: Useful Analogies from Recent Discoveries and Inventions." *Borderland* 3.4 (October 1896): 400–11.

Stewart, Garrett. *Between Film and Screen: Modernism's Photo Synthesis.* Chicago: University of Chicago Press, 1999.

Stoker, Bram. *Bram Stoker's Notes for Dracula.* Eds. Robert Eighteen-Bisang and Elizabeth Miller. Jefferson NC: McFarland, 2008.

Thomas, Ronald R. "Specters of the Novel: *Dracula* and the Cinematic Afterlife of the Victorian Novel." *Victorian Afterlife: Postmodern Culture Rewrites the Nineteenth Century.* Eds. John Kucich and Dianne F. Sadoff. Minneapolis: University of Minnesota Press, 2000. 288–310.

Thornton, E.H. "Ghosts Have No Thickness." *The Sphinx* 2.10 (December 1903): 111.

Tosi, Virgilio. *Cinema Before Cinema: The Origins of Scientific Cinematography.* London: British Universities Film & Video Council, 2005.

Tromp, Marlene. *Altered States: Sex, Nation, Drugs and Self-Transformation in Victorian Spiritualism.* Albany: SUNY Press, 2006.

Tsivian, Yuri. "Media Fantasies and Penetrating Vision: Some Links between X-rays, the Microscope, and Film." *Laboratory of Dreams: The Russian Avant-Garde and Cultural Experiment.* Eds. John E. Bowlt and Olga Matich. Stanford: Stanford University Press, 1996. 81–99.

Tucker, Jennifer. *Nature Exposed: Photography as Eyewitness in Victorian Science.* Baltimore: The Johns Hopkins University Press, 2005.

Vinitsky, Ilya. *Ghostly Paradoxes: Modern Spiritualism and Russian Culture in the Age of Realism.* Toronto: University of Toronto Press, 2009.

Waldby, Catherine. *Visible Human Project: Informatic Bodies and Posthuman Medicine.* London: Routledge, 2000.

Weart, Spencer R. *Nuclear Fear: A History of Images.* Cambridge, Harvard University Press, 1988.

Weinstein, Sheri. "Technologies of Vision: Spiritualism and Science in Nineteenth-Century America." *Spectral America: Phantoms and the National Imagination.* Ed. Jeffrey Andrew Weinstock. Madison, WI: University of Wisconsin Press, 2004. 124–40.

Weisberg, Barbara. *Talking to the Dead: Kate and Margaret Fox and the Rise of Spiritualism.* San Francisco: Harper, 2004.

Wells, H.G. *The Invisible Man.* New York: Signet, 2002.

West, Nancy M. "Camera Fiends: Early Photography, Death, and the Supernatural." *The Centennial Review.* 40.1 (1996): 170–206.

Winter, O. "The Cinematograph." *In the Kingdom of Shadows: A Companion to Early Cinema.* Eds. Colin Harding and Simon Popple. London: Cygnus Press, 1996. 13–17.

Wojcik, Daniel. "Spirits, Apparitions, and Traditions of Supernatural Photography." *Visual Resources* 25.1–2 (2009): 109–136.

Wynne, Catherine. "Arthur Conan Doyle and Psychic Photographs." *History of Photography* 22.4 (1998): 385–92.

Young, Paul. *The Cinema Dreams Its Rivals: Media Fantasy Films from Radio to the Internet.* Minneapolis: University of Minnesota Press, 2006.

CHAPTER 6

Méliès's Skeleton: Gender, Cinema's *Danse Macabre* and the Erotics of Bone

It is a familiar sight to students of early cinema. The magician steps onto the stage, a set ornately decorated in Louis XV style, from a door at the right of the screen, his female assistant in tow. Both are elegantly dressed with the trappings of wealth and class: the magician in black evening wear, the assistant in a white dress and carrying a white fan. He lays a sheet of newspaper on the floor, picks up a chair and puts it on top of the paper, first twirling the chair around in a dexterous gesture of the sort that magicians use to deflect audience suspicions of trickery. The assistant sits on the chair and idly fans herself as the magician places a blanket over her. She disappears; the magician beams at his successful trick. He makes an elaborate gesture to rematerialize her, but she instead reappears a skeleton, blackened and inert, sitting upright in the chair. Momentarily horrified, he makes two quick "shooing" gestures in its direction. Picking up the blanket, he covers the skeleton, pulls back the blanket and finds the lovely assistant in place again. They stand and leave the stage, but then step back to take a bow to the audience, and walk out of the door, leaving the stage and the audience's view. The first audiences would have recognized this act as typical, except in two crucial respects: it occurs not on stage but on the screen, and it adds the skeleton to what had previously been a simpler vanishing act. The magician is Georges Méliès, the director of the film, and the assistant is Jehanne D'Alcy, his usual assistant on both stage and screen. She was also, in a long magic tradition, his mistress, and would later become his wife following the death of the first Madame Méliès (Images 6.1, 6.2, 6.3 and 6.4).

Image 6.1 Georges Méliès's *The Vanishing Lady* (1896)

Few one-minute films have attracted as much discussion as this one, Méliès's *Escamotage d'une dame chez Robert-Houdin* or *Escamotage d'une dame au théâtre Robert-Houdin*, known in English as *The Vanishing Lady* (1896). Its disappearances and appearances may not represent the first examples of substitution cutting in cinema history (that distinction appears to go to Edison's *The Execution of Mary, Queen of Scots* the previous year) but rather represent the first place where such a cut was used to approximate an effect from the magical stage. This is the significance of *The Vanishing Lady*; not the first film containing a trick effect, but nevertheless the first *trick film*, not only using the magic show as subject matter but allowing its logic of vanishing and appearance to decide on cinematic technique. In many ways, it set the tone for the rest of Méliès's career in filmmaking. And if imitation is the sincerest form of flattery, *The Vanishing Lady* was successful indeed: both R.W. Paul and Thomas Edison would produce films of the same title and theme within the next two years. With one foot in the heritage of the magical stage and one in cinema's future, *The Vanishing Lady* reflects "the defamiliarization and violent reconstruction of the human subject" (Hurley 1996, 4) common

MÉLIÈS'S SKELETON: GENDER, CINEMA'S *DANSE MACABRE*... 137

Image 6.2 Georges Méliès's *The Vanishing Lady* (1896)

to texts of its cultural moment, something we may recognize in the transformation scenes common in the trick film.[1]

This chapter tracks a visual motif, the skeleton (particularly the female skeleton), over a range of time and through a variety of media. Though it discusses a longer history of skeletons in the iconographies in European culture prior to era of cinema's debut (and finally subsequent to it), it focuses on the peculiarities of what I term the "skeleton vogue" of the 1890, when, "formerly [skeletons] were out of the sight in the living world, [but] they were now ever present" (McGrath 2002, 191). Even a cursory survey of early cinema finds that filmmakers were positively fascinated by skeletons: they appear frequently in trick films by Walter R. Booth, Edwin S. Porter,[2] Émile Cohl, Segundo de Chomón and others, as well as Méliès and Smith. To explain this phenomenon, we can look in two directions at once: to the traditions of the *danse macabre* stretching back to the Middle Ages, and to the new context of the X-ray. We need not choose one of these explanations over the other; in fact, a balanced assessment must take them both into account. But what is certain is that, in the 1890s, something changes with respect to the figure of the skeleton. If it sometimes

Image 6.3 Georges Méliès's *The Vanishing Lady* (1896)

retains the merry aspect familiar from the dancing skeletons of the magic lantern tradition, something dark and sinister frequently intrudes too. Where the skeleton was once substanceless and ghostly, it could now be corporeal, with a visceral and potentially erotic charge. And, perhaps most strikingly of all, where skeletons were once predominantly genderless, the new skeleton vogue finds them to be female more often than not.

A canonical early film, Méliès's *The Vanishing Lady* has naturally been the subject of much analysis, especially in terms of gender. The skeleton itself has gone largely ignored, beyond Elizabeth Ezra's astute but passing comment that its "hide and seek anatomy lesson perfectly emblematized the popular combination of masculine scrutiny (masquerading as 'X-ray vision') and sensationalized eroticism" (2006, 127). Criticism about gender in trick film goes back at least to Lucy Fischer's "The Lady Vanishes: Women, Magic and the Movies" (1979; a revised version appeared in Fischer's book *Cinematernity: Film, Motherhood, Genre* [1996]). Fischer argues that trick films, particularly those of Méliès, are premised on the relationship of a powerful, authoritative male figure in the magician, and the woman or women upon whom the magic is performed. Women are

Image 6.4 Georges Méliès's *The Vanishing Lady* (1896)

transformed into decorative objects, are dematerialized and decorporealized and thus transformed into "spirit," and are often envisioned as a figment of the male imagination (1979, 31–2). This gender dynamic, argues Fischer, is a holdover from the magical stage. She goes on to interpret the trick films as an expression of a cultural need to contain women that discloses a masculine weakness and fear of female power, and a desire to appropriate female powers of procreation (evident in magic's fondness for fertility symbols like eggs and doves). Perceptive in its observations about the fluid corporeal status of the female assistant on both the stage and the screen, "The Lady Vanishes" was one of the first articles to consider the role of women in early cinema and spotlight the inadequacy of the theories of gender and spectatorship that emerged in the 1970s to deal with cinema's earliest years.[3] In 1981, Linda Williams argued against the reproductive paradigm in Fischer's argument, suggesting an alternate reading on the status of women in Méliès:

> While Lucy Fischer emphasizes the envious male's appropriation of female procreative powers in the construction of this machine that gives "birth"

to women, I would stress instead that this spewing forth of identical female bodies only calls attention even more to the status of these bodies as totally mastered, infinitely reproducible *images* whose potential threat of castration has been disavowed by the fetish object of the machine with which they are associated. (1981, 33)

Fischer responded to this criticism, asserting that she and Williams share a common point—the replacement of woman by her male-fabricated image (1996, 39). In both Fischer's and Williams's approaches, however, the historical specificity of the vanishing woman trick is secondary to broader theoretical concerns about the nature of cinema itself and the status of the female image. My approach comes closer to that of Karen Beckman (2003), who tracks *The Vanishing Lady*'s relationship to a broader fascination with disappearing woman throughout the latter half of the nineteenth century, which she relates to a panic about the surplus female population at a time when census data began to reveal that women outnumbered men. Writes Beckman, "[The vanishing woman trick] exploded onto the cultural scene with a forcefulness and panache unrivalled by other stage tricks at any point in the century. Never had a magic trick been so prominent, so revered" (2003, 47–9).

The skeleton transformations so common in early cinema have a curious relationship to the scenes of animation and the overall obsession with vitalism that Lynda Nead finds everywhere at the time of cinema's debut. Nead states:

At the end of the nineteenth century the search for the spirit or life within the inert art object was evident across all forms of visual media. The exquisite passage from stasis to movement, the hesitation and moment of delay prior to motion, became the fool's gold of representational practices in the period. In an age when lovelorn sculptors could no longer pray to benign goddesses to animate their creations, the power to endow the image with life was handed over to magicians, lanternists and film-makers. (2007, 53)

However, these fantasies of animation that cinema seemed to satisfy are haunted by their inverse: the transition from motion to inertia and death. Nead offers one example to which the female body is central:

In the many transformation films of this period, the sexualized female body provides the matter through which the power of film magic is displayed. Women's bodies are fragmented and annihilated and their flesh turned to bone. In the American Mutoscope and Biograph Company's *The Artist's Dream* (1899), a beautiful, fleshy life model in a leotard is transformed into a skeleton, while an artist dozes at his easel. (2007, 90)[4]

Early filmmakers were well aware of the paradox that cinema, in its potential for giving life and animating its subjects, even bestowing a sort of immortality, was at the same time a brand of living death. The figure of the skeleton, especially when it is gendered female, can serve to emblematized that paradox.

Locating the Cinematic in the Skeleton

As the first of the trick films that would make him famous, Méliès's *The Vanishing Lady* is often mentioned as part of long-standing debates about Méliès and intermediality. Academic treatments of Méliès often stress continuities between the theatrical illusions he staged at the Théâtre Robert-Houdin and his filmmaking, arguing that Méliès imported the conventions of the magical theatre into cinematic form, and consequently his work remains essentially rooted in the theatrical (see Vardac 1949; Kovács 1984; Gaudreault 2007; Solomon 2008, 2010). His films tend to replicate proscenium staging and his sets often include windows, bookcases, fireplaces and so on painted onto the walls. Characters frequently address the audience, like a magician bowing to acknowledge applause. But acknowledging the theatrical qualities of Méliès's filmmaking does not mean disparaging him as *merely* theatrical and therefore uncinematic, as certain early critics did. Elizabeth Ezra's (2000) book on Méliès makes a particularly detailed analysis of the varied cinematic techniques throughout Méliès's body of work, concluding that:

> Méliès did not merely produce "filmed theatre" but used a number of cinematic techniques such as close-ups, multiple exposures and continuity editing. The special effects that he developed were often innovative and always sophisticated … In addition, Méliès sometimes used deep staging, with characters moving back and forth along the camera access, and he created the illusion of camera movement through the use of moving backdrops and matte shots of objects approaching the camera. (2000, 150)

Few of these innovations are manifest in *The Vanishing Lady*, which only uses three simple substitution tricks, but through these it accomplishes feats that could not have been done on stage. The film depends on being *both* theatrical and cinematic for its effect, on both acknowledging a familiar theatrical tradition and departing from it.⁵ As John Frazer writes:

> The first part of the trick substituted a film device for a stage device. However, when the skeleton appears out of nowhere, a different order of thinking is involved. There is no longer a stage drape to cover the action. The magical appearance is entirely dependent on the ability of the camera to interrupt and reconstruct time. (1979, 60; see also Solomon 2010, 34–5)

The film's French title locates it within the heritage of stage magic.⁶ *The Vanishing Lady* was not filmed in the Théâtre Robert-Houdin, but at Méliès's outdoor studio at Montreuil-de-Bois,⁷ so the name declares a certain relationship to magical traditions, perhaps securing a retroactive imprimatur from Jean-Eugène Robert-Houdin, the great legitimizer of modern magic (Robert-Houdin 1859; Fechner 2002; Jones 2008, 2010; Leeder 2010). The film declares itself as an exact transliteration of a stage act, but, as we shall see, that is not so. The cinematic Méliès lays down the newspaper, which never moves throughout the film, to defray speculation about a trap door, but the film's trick requires no trap door. The convention of the newspaper comes from the vanishing woman act pioneered by Hungarian-French conjurer Buatier de Kolta in 1886; the "newspaper" would actually be a rubber sheet carefully split in two to allow the magician to slide through the trapdoor beneath it. But instead Méliès utilizes, in Dan North's apt phrase, "a *temporal* trap door" (2008, 55), depending on an interruption of time rather than the theatrical trick's disjuncture of space.

The presence of the newspaper in *The Vanishing Lady* is an intriguing vestige of the trick's theatrical roots, remaining as pure adornment, or even misdirection. If audiences by and large understood the basics of the venerable and pervasive vanishing woman act, they would have been surprised by the skeleton's sudden appearance. The cinematic, then, takes as its emblem a (female) skeleton, perhaps in recognition of the current overlap between cinema and the X-ray. So surprising is the appearance of the skeleton that even Méliès's internal conjurer is taken aback. Gaby Wood writes,

> If you play the film again and slow it down at the moment when the skeleton appears, you notice that Méliès, the magician himself, is shocked by

its arrival. He looks surprised shakes his head, and tries to shoo the skeleton away, as if that wasn't supposed to happen. Clearly, even he thinks he has unintentionally killed the woman, instead of simply making her vanish. (2002, 194)

I concur with Wood's impression—the effect of the film is indeed predicated on the notion of a "trick gone wrong," which complicates Fischer's claim that the magician in the trick film represents masculine authorial power.[8]

Cinematic substitution tricks like the one we see in *The Vanishing Lady* have their own apocryphal origin story, just as cinema has the myth of the Grand Café. As Méliès wrote in 1907:

> One day, when I was photographing as usual in the *Place de l'Opéra*, the camera ... jammed and produced an unexpected result. It took a minute to disengage the film and to start the camera up again. In the meantime, the passers-by, a horse trolley and other vehicles had, of course, changed positions. When I projected the film strip, which I had glued back together at the point of the break, I suddenly saw a Madeleine-Bastille horse trolley change into a hearse and men become women. The substitution or stop-camera trick had been discovered. Two days later, I produced the first metamorphoses of men into women and the first sudden disappearances which, in the beginning, had such great success. (1988, 44)

This story is suspect for a number of reasons, not the least being that Méliès did *not* invent the substitution cut. Edison's *The Execution of Mary, Queen of Scots* was filmed in August 1895, at least 15 months before *The Vanishing Lady* was filmed, and there is every reason to believe Méliès was familiar with it. The story is fanciful and improbable (Gaudreault 2007, 170–1), and more than a little morbid, and has occasionally even been used as evidence of film's ghostliness (Michaels 1998, 76–7). The image of the trolley changing into a hearse invokes the danger of modern life, perhaps one of those traffic accidents that sent curious spectators flooding into the Paris Morgue (Schwartz 1998, 44–88). Scholars like Kristen Whissel (2008) and Ben Singer (2001) have linked the emergence of cinema to traffic as sensationalistic phenomena of urban modernity, with skeletons frequently representing such dangers in newspaper cartoons. Méliès's mythical, self-aggrandizing, apocryphal yet still foundational "first cut" implicates death; it is perhaps appropriate that the first time he used it in a film, in *The Vanishing Lady*, it is to slip in death's emblem. As

Michael Mangan writes, "The essence of the live trick is maintained but elaborated upon by the camera in the figure of Death" (2007, 130). We can further note that the use of the substitution cut (pun intended) in *The Execution of Mary, Queen of Scots* also signifies death, occurring when the executioner's axe strikes the queen's neck.

Skeletons appear with great frequency in Méliès's later trick films.[9] Sometimes, as in *The Haunted Castle* (1897), a skeleton appears as one of a number of menacing elements in a gothic setting. Sometimes, as in *The Wizard, the Prince and the Fairy* (1900) and *The Doctor and the Monkey* (1900), a non-ambulatory skeleton marks the setting as a sorcerer's workplace. In *The Magician's Cavern* (1901), a display skeleton is given flesh and turned into a young woman by the magician. Like the magician's assistant she is, the newly embodied woman is then subjected to a levitation trick, and turned back into a skeleton in the process. The skeleton then does a lively dance, and though it may be an imperfection in the special effects, the visible outline of the actor surrounding the skeleton suggests an X-ray image akin to Smith's *The X-ray Fiend*. In *The Monster* (1903), an Egyptian prince, before an elaborate backdrop of the Sphinx and the pyramids, takes the skeleton of his dead princess and recruits a dervish to restore her to life. The skeleton is garbed in linens and a mask by the dervish and then comes to life, doing a dance, and then growing distended and grotesque. The dervish pulls back the robes and reveals the princess as she was in life, but only for an instant before she turns into skeleton again and collapses in his arms.[10] As Ezra notes, what we see in *The Monster* is an inversion of *The Vanishing Lady*, moving from bone to flesh to bone, instead of flesh to bone to flesh (2000, 41). Without exception, these skeletons are immaculate and white, unlike the charred brown appearance of their forebear in *The Vanishing Lady*, which looks more like an old skeleton from an anatomical collection, blackened over time. It is also striking in these films that, the vast majority of the time a skeleton is clearly gendered: it is female.[11]

One can find many instances in the trick film beyond Méliès as well. One of the best examples is in Walter R. Booth's *Undressing Extraordinary* (1901). It is one of the innumerable "haunted hotel" films, in which a traveller is comically beset by supernatural forces.[12] In *Undressing Extraordinary*, a man attempts to undress but continually finds himself fully dressed again, in a wide variety of costumes, through the magic of substitution cutting. At one point he is happy to find himself in sleepwear but when he moves towards the bed, a skeleton appears waiting for him, sitting upright on the edge of the bed. Lest we miss the sexual implications, its legs are widely splayed apart. After rearing back in horror, he grabs and tries to strangle it; thereupon it transforms into a chair, the sexualized skeleton evoked and disavowed once again.

THE DANSE MACABRE

Paying attention to the role that the figure of skeleton has traditionally played in western culture can help us better understand Méliès's skeletons. The skeleton became the pre-eminent allegorical figure of death in the late medieval period, with the emergence of the *danse macabre*. Death was often figured as a skeleton carrying a scythe or an hourglass, mocking earthly ambitions in the face of the inexorability of death. These images fit into the broader European tradition of the *memento mori*, where bones and skulls are a reminder of death's inexorability (Binion 2004). Leonard P. Kurtz writes that skeletons were a familiar sight to many at the time, since many cities maintained ossuaries where the bones of the dead were exhibited:

> The ossuaries were necessary because of the preference of the people for a particular cemetery, regarded as the holiest burial ground ... The people insisted on being buried there, and hence the skeletons had to be removed to the charnier to make way for new dead. Skeletons were then on general display at all times and the people came to regard them as an integral part of the landscape. (1975, 189)

The *danse macabre* dates back at least to 1376 (1975, 178), initially existing in both theatrical forms and visual artistic forms like frescoes in churches. It is thought to initially derive from the deuterocanonical book 2 Maccabees and the martyrdom of a mother and her seven sons, a common artistic subject in the grim Black Plague-ravaged late medieval world. One of the most famous manifestations of the Dance of Death was Hans Holbein's *La Danse macabre*, first appearing in 1538. It featured 41 woodcuts of Death, figured as a skeleton, visiting a varied series of figures, from the Pope to a Peddler, the King to an Old Woman. Friedrich Kittler reproduces the oldest known depiction of a print shop, dating from 1499 (1999, 5), featuring a startling *danse macabre*. A triad of skeletons cavorts around the shop, disturbing a compositor, a bookseller and two men working a printing press; even Gutenberg's invention, promising new permanence for the words of man, is mocked by Death. These images stay with us in such figures as the Grim Reaper and the Death card of the Tarot deck.

The magic lantern became a major venue for images of Death embodied. In 1659, Christiaan Huygens drew the earliest known representation of a moving slide of a magic lantern: ten images of a dancing skeleton. As Laurent Mannoni writes, "paradoxically, the first illuminated artificial recreation of life was a representation of death" (2000, 40). One of the images in Kircher's *Ars Magna Lucis et Umbra* has a skeleton carrying a scythe and an hourglass (Heard 2006, 37). These images lasted into the Phantasmagoria era, with Robertson conventionally ending performances with a projection of the skeleton and the words "The fate that awaits us all" (Barnouw 1981, 19) and referring to the skeleton as being "the only real horror … See what is in store for all of you, what each of you will become one day" (Castle 1995, 37). Mervyn Heard's *Phantasmagoria: The Secret Life of the Magic Lantern* (2006) reproduces numerous nineteenth-century lantern sides featuring skeletons … one sitting on a baby, another holding a mirror up to the face of another skeleton, and so on. One skeleton rides a skeletal horse highly reminiscent of the one from Méliès's *The Merry Frolics of Satan* (1906) (2006, 282). In the nineteenth century, the skeleton was a popular figure in new optical technologies of all sorts. The choreutoscope, an improved phenakistiscope invented by L.S. Beale in 1866, often featured a dancing skeleton jugging its own detachable head (Heard 2006, 236). Indeed, the image of the skeleton seems to have particular utility for such comic effects; the 1833 lantern manual *Fun for Winter Evenings* says:

> A curious effect is produced by drawing out the tube, and slipping it in suddenly to the focus: this is easily done, by holding the tube tight at the proper place, a shivering motion may be given to the figures, by giving the lantern a sudden shake, a skeleton is made to tumble to pieces by means of a slide made for the purpose. By standing at the bottom of the stairs, a figure may be made to appear going up. The figure of a skeleton is a very good one for this purpose. (Herbert 2004, 173-4)

Skeletons would also appear in theatrical illusions not dependent on lanterns, such as the elaborate "Black Art," made famous by Harry Kellar and Alexander Herrmann, in which "a life-size skeleton … appears and dances around the stage, becomes dismembered, the separated parts floating about, but they finally rearticulate themselves, and the skeleton vanishes" (Hopkins 66). In this case, the skeleton is constructed of *papier maché* and was worked by assistants dressed in dark clothes so as to be unseen against the black drapery. It is on the pervasive image of the dancing and dislocating skeleton that the Lumière brothers would draw for their early stop motion experiment, *Le Squelette joyeux* (1897), where the dancing skeleton loses limbs and collapses into a pile of bones but always re-forms.[13] As we have seen, dancing skeletons appear in Méliès's work with considerable frequency, contrasting strongly with the immobile bones we see in *The Vanishing Lady*.

In the nineteenth century, the line between the ghost and the ambulatory skeleton was a fine one. Anatomists once drew skeletons standing on terra firma, but by the nineteenth century the convention had shifted to drawing them standing in mid air, appearing to float in space, like ghosts. The seemingly paradoxical ghostliness of skeletons stems from the fact that "up until the end of the nineteenth century, the notion of 'living bones' was a contradiction in terms. Bones were dead and the skeleton was a relic" (McGrath 2002, 111).[14] The "ghosts" of Pepper's Ghost were often skeletons as well. The first public presentation, staged by John Henry Pepper at the Polytechnic in 1863, featured "a ghostly skeleton robed in a shroud" that disappears (rather than tumbling into a pile of bones) when attacked with a sword. "The ghost's dramatic appearances and actions were conducted by an assistant clothed from head to foot in black, and holding a white-painted skeleton in his arms" (Lamb 1976, 44). The first ghost to "haunt" the New York stage was the skeleton of an old miser come back to take revenge on his wicked nephew as the spectacular finale of a play called *True to the Last* (Posner 2007, 192–3).

Phantom skeletons, meanwhile, periodically appear in the literature on spiritualism and psychical research; they represent something that people experienced (or at least claimed to). A letter from a Miss Emma Foy of Manor Park, Essex, to the Literary Committee of the Society for Psychical Research (SPR) appeared in the January 1891 issue of the SPR's *Journal*:

> Towards the end of the year 1872, I saw a tall human skeleton enter the bedroom, dragging a coffin which it brought close to me. Over its right arm was a pall. Then it pointed to the coffin, it threw the pall over me, causing a feeling of suffocation which left me very weak. Continued its visits almost every night about 10:30 for the space of about two years, then gradually

disappeared. Tried in many ways to dispel the illusion; did not believe in supernatural occurrences; have always been of lively disposition; excellent spirits which seemed to affect; never saw a real skeleton; nor up to that time any representation of one; nor had any dread of death.

... The phantom appeared again suddenly in August 1879, either the last week in August or the first in September. This time there were eight persons present. *Two persons saw the vision besides* myself—a poor woman and an educated gentleman, the gentleman being thrown into a very nervous state for some time after and experiencing similar sensations to myself. Was out of health this time. Time 9:30 pm. (Anon. 1891, 10, original emphasis)

Here again a skeleton is essentially a ghostly, insubstantial figure, in this case maintaining an ability to disquiet that belies the comic depictions of skeletons we find elsewhere at the time. The fact that it appears in Miss Foy's bedroom and violates her in a strange, phantasmal way, rather as Dracula and other nineteenth-century vampires do, would appear to be a reflection of the pervasive sexualization of the skeleton I will discuss in detail shortly. As hard as it may be to disagree with Noël Carroll's statement that "Skeletons, on the face of it, are not sexy" (2010, 230), it appears to be the case that skeletons have nonetheless held sexual significance in the late Victorian mind.

Skeletal imagery booms in popularity in the 1890s and 1900s. This is not only a reaction to the discovery of the X-ray but strangely seems to anticipate it as well, allowing the speculation that the sensation provoked by Röntgen's discovery was nourished by (and in turn fed back into) a pre-existing skeleton mania. As seen in the previous chapter, magic acts involving skeletons were now often explicitly framed around X-rays, with the *Cabaret du Néant* as a key example. If the X-ray did not create the skeleton vogue, it undeniably cemented it and, critically, reshaped it. One obvious change is that, far from the wispy phantom skeletons of previous time, the skeleton could now be a figure of embodied horror. One famous example is Gaston Leroux's *The Phantom of the Opera*, initially published in serial form in 1909 and 1910. Erik, the titular phantom, is actually a flesh and blood, if highly disfigured, mad genius living in the opera house's bowels, who poses as the "Opera ghost." His appearance is consistently described as skeletal; as Joseph Buquet, the opera's chief scene setter and major source of conjecture about the Phantom, explains: "He is extraordinarily thin and his dress-coat hangs on a skeleton frame. His eyes are so deep you can hardly see the fixed pupils. You just see two big black holes, as in a dead man's skull ... the *absence* of that nose is a horrible thing *to look at*" (Leroux 1994, 11, original emphasis). At one point Erik conceals himself amid the skulls in the ossuary of a Breton church, his skull-face at home amid icons of death and decay. The framing device in *The Phantom of the Opera* deals with Leroux's own (fictional) discovery of Erik's body, now a more conventional skeleton beneath the Opera House, and the book ends with: "And, now, what do they mean to do with that skeleton? Surely they will not bury it in the common grave! ... I say that the place of the skeleton of the Opera ghost is in the archives of the National Academy of Music. It is no ordinary skeleton" (1994, 348). This is perfect ending for a novel from a time in which skeletons so rarely seem to be ordinary.[15]

A more literal living skeleton appears in Perceval Landon's 1908 short story "Thurnley Abbey." The ghost of the tale is that of a murdered nun walled up in the abbey, who appears as walking a skeleton that, like the Phantom of the Opera, proves highly material. The narrator's confrontation with the revenant is spectacularly visceral:

> I tore at the robed skeleton—how well the whole thing had been carried out, I thought—I broke the skull against the floor, and stamped upon its dry bones. I flung the head away under the bed, and rent the brittle bones of the trunk in pieces. I snapped the thin thigh-bones across my knee, and flung them in different directions. The shin-bones I set up against a stool and broke with my heel. I raged like a Berserker against the loathly thing, and stripped the ribs from the backbone and slung the breastbone against the cupboard ... At last my work was done. There was but a raffle of broken bones and strips of parchment and crumbling wool. (2003, 42)

What a change from the skeletal ghosts of earlier periods, who disappeared like vapour when struck by the hero's sword! The one in "Thurnley Abbey" is thoroughly corporeal, all bone, and must be violently subdued. If the female skeleton in *The Vanishing Lady* is less horrific and less animate than the undead nun who haunts Thurnley Abbey, they are on the same lineage, and that this new visibility of female skeletons reveals something about attitudes about death, spirit and sexuality around the turn of the century.

Sexualized Skeletons and Female Assistants

The significance of the female skeleton has been explored most thoroughly by Roberta McGrath (2002). For the majority of medical history, female skeletons were ignored and never described. Drawings and descriptions of female skeletons began to emerge in the eighteenth century, but female skeletons were rarely collected: only female pelvic bones, understood as the only key point of distinction between the genders on the skeletal level, were studied (2002, 105). The fact that the skeleton of the 1890s seems to be *predominantly* female is a striking change that must have everything to do with changing attitudes towards the female body. Cinema and the X-ray debuted into a society of shifting gender roles and extensive debates over sexual identity, the period of, in Elaine Showalter's famous phrase, "sexual anarchy." The so-called "Woman Question"—the title of an 1885 paper by Karl Pearson—was present in most every aspects of life, from politics to education to labour to trade and foreign policy (Showalter 1990, 49–55). A particular flashpoint for all of these issues was women's bodies, in an age when women seem to exist in "surplus," as discovered by census around the mid-nineteenth century (Beckman 2003, 19–31). A complex and contradictory set of attitudes towards the female body emerged, turning it into a cultural text caught between antimonies of corporeality and incorporeality, and when Méliès invokes in a single motion the vanishing trick and the X-ray in *The Vanishing Lady*, he exposes an essential connection between both practices: both take their fascination from a new reconfiguration of the nature of corporeality in a world where the line between the visible and the invisible became increasingly uncertain. And while both can be and were used on any subject, it is obviously the case that female subjects, as vanishing women or female skeletons, were understood to be the most effective subjects.

In the previous chapter, I discussed William Crookes as the man who merged spiritualist and scientific sensibilities more clearly than any other figure in Victorian Britain. His most famous misadventure in psychical research, an investigation of the medium Florence Cook and her famed alter ego Katie King in 1873 and 1874, is relevant to the present discussion of women, spirit and (dis)embodiment. Cook was a teenage medium from London, and King was a "control," a friendly denizen of the Other Side.[16] British mediums of the 1870s favoured "full materializations": trumping the previous table-rappings and disembodied voices, a physically embodied ghost would appear to the séance-goers, even as the medium was locked away in a "spirit cabinet," bound and immobilized to prevent any suggestion of fraud. A particularly beautiful and personable spectre, Katie King could manifest physically in the séance room and meet, flirt with and even kiss guests … even as her medium Florence Cook was (apparently) tucked away in the spirit cabinet. Crookes's 1874 report on mediumship, which so scandalized his scientific peers that there was talk of removing him from the Fellowship of the Royal Society, contained a series of 44 photos of King, who, despite Crookes's claims to the contrary, looks much like Cook (Image 6.5). Scholarship has generally concluded that Crookes was a wilful party in Cook's hoax, most likely because they were having an affair (Crookes being married with eight children, and Cook's senior by decades) (Tromp 2006, 37–46; Fischer 2004, 172–4; Raia-Green 2008; Lyons 2009, 97–105; Lehman 2009, 149–159).[17] Crookes certainly described King with love-struck superlatives: "Photography is inadequate to depict the perfect beauty of Katie's face, as words are powerless to describe her charms of manner. Photography may indeed give a

Image 6.5 William Crookes with "Katie King" in 1874

map of her countenance; but how can it reproduce the brilliant purity of her complexion, or the ever varying expressions of her most mobile features?" (quoted in Hall 1963, 86).

In the embarrassment resulting from the release of a report fully embraced by no one,[18] Crookes backed away from psychical research for decades. Cook retired Katie King as well, but not before an extensive set of "farewell appearances" (Bennett 2006); King would subsequently re-manifest through other mediums (Lehman 2009, 160–7). Crookes composed a poem as a sort of eulogy for Katie on her departure, ending with the couplet: "Her overpowering presence made you feel/It would not be idolatry to kneel" (quoted in Hall 1963, 86). Lofty praise indeed, but, such praise was often reserved for dead women. In the assessment of Courtenay Raia-Grean, Crookes started the experiments with scientific integrity, but was co-opted by a practised con-woman and manipulator:

> At some point it seems reasonably clear that Crookes became Cook's collaborator, the passive object of his research coming to fully implement him in an experiment, or rather gamble, of her own … [Crookes became] more of an "impresario" exhibiting the spirit phenomena in question than a scientist investigating them. (2008, 68)

The line between magician and spiritualist has often been a thin one, and in the surviving images of Crookes standing arm in arm with the full materialization of Katie King, we see striking resonances with the duo of the magician and female assistant, and a similar sexual dynamic. It is plainer here than in most cases that, even as the man stands as the embodiment of formal authority, the woman has the real power. Crookes was clearly more in love with King than Cook:

> "Katie" was not a woman at all but an eternal, undemanding, sexually flamboyant being, who had nothing to do with the world of Mrs. Crookes (who seems to have had little interest in his work) or Florence Cook (who was manipulating him for his own ends) … he was "infatuated" with "a substantial spirit" and like many men before him, meshed in this massive experience of love, he became wholly irresponsible. (Osmond 1963, 209)

I would add that Katie King was not just a disembodied, idealized woman but also a *dead* one. In the last year of his life, Crookes would appear alongside the dead woman again, this time through a spirit photograph (as opposed to a photograph of full materialization). In 1919, spirit photographer William Hope produced an image of Crookes with his own deceased wife (Jolly 2006, 102–3). To explain these images of dead women, we must investigate the late Victorian fascination with sexualized female death and particularly the imagery thereof, of which the aforementioned vogue for X-ray images of women's hands was perhaps one of the milder expressions.

Certainly, associations of the X-ray with furtive voyeurism and eroticism emerged almost immediately. A contributor to the *Pall Mall Gazette* wrote in March 1896 wrote: "We are sick of the Röntgen Rays ... you can see other people's bones with the naked eye, and also see through eight inches of solid wood. On the revolting indecency of this there is no need to dwell" (quoted in Goodman 1945, 1043). A London firm even tried to sell X-ray-proof undergarments (Weart 1988, 45). A 1900 German caricature entitled "Declaration of Love, as Photographed with the Röntgen Camera" displayed an image reminiscent of Smith's *The X-ray Fiend*: a male skeleton, phallic sword at his belt, kneeling dramatically before a dainty female skeleton, all while a goat-hoofed satyr photographs it from outside of the frame (Tsivian 1996, 87–8). The eroticization of the skeleton that runs through the reception of X-ray images was in keeping with the death-obsessed character of Victorian pornography and erotica (Lutz 2011), and we see it in a number of other places. A striking souvenir postcard from the Paris *Cabaret du Néant* shows a black skeleton against a white background, posed with its arms behind its head and looking (though fleshless) distinctly feminine and distinctly erotic, rather like a skeletal showgirl (Image 6.6). In the less famous of his two articles reviewing the Lumière programme, Maxim Gorky suggested that, "Possibly tomorrow X rays will also appear on the screen at Aumond's [sic], used in some way or other for 'belly dances'" (1985, 231); facetiously or otherwise, Gorky endorses a kind of skeleton pornography. A poem by Lawrence K. Russel that appeared in *Life* magazine on 12 March 1896 facetiously considered the X-ray's erotic potential:

> She is so tall, so slender, and her bones—
> Those frail phosphates, those carbonates of lime—
> Are well produced by cathode rays sublime,
> By oscillations, amperes and by ohms.
> Her dorsal vertebrae are not concealed
> By epidermis, but are well revealed.

Image 6.6 Promotional postcard from the Paris *Cabaret du Néant*, c. 1895

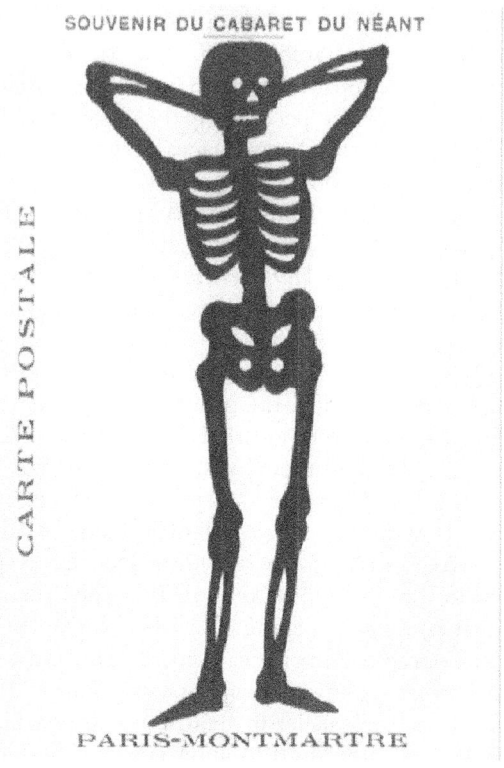

Around her ribs, those beauteous twenty-four,
Her flesh a halo makes, misty in line,
Her noseless, eyeless face looks into mine,
And I but whisper "Sweetheart, Je t'adore."
Her white and gleaming teeth at me do laugh.
Ah! Lovely, cruel, sweet cathodograph! (1896, 191)

The poem describes a skeleton with the erotic care usually reserved for a woman's body, and carries more than a few implications of the *fin-de-siècle* fascination with dead and dying women,[19] the definitive treatment of which is perhaps Bram Dijkstra's *Idols of Perversity: Fantasies of Feminine Evil in Fin-de-siècle Culture* (1988).

Dijkstra describes the late Victorian culture of misogyny as a widespread reaction to emerging feminist movements that took Darwinian theory as a pretext for insisting that women's prescribed roles and positions are natural and preordained. Artists were alternatively fascinated by tragic women like Ophelia and Tennyson's Lady of Shallot, and vicious and predatory female vampires, Medusas and Sphinxes; the ideal woman is substanceless, disembodied or dead. A quintessential example is Lucy Westenra in *Dracula*, who goes from a "horrid flirt" (1975, 91) to a vampire who preys on children, but who regains her purity in death after being staked by her husband-to-be Lord Godalming: "There in the coffin lay no longer the foul Thing ... But Lucy as we had seen her in her life, with her face of unequalled sweetness and purity" (1975, 255). As Dijkstra writes, Lucy is transformed into "that ideal creature of feminine virtue by the mid-nineteenth century: the dead woman" (1975, 346).[20] One is reminded of William Crookes's insistence that the spectral beauty of the Katie King could not be captured by photography, that she was indeed a kind of Platonic ideal beauty precisely because she was disembodied. Though Dijkstra's explorations do not extend to subjects like magic shows, X-rays or cinema, it is not hard to find echoes of his thesis in *The Vanishing Lady* and other skeletal transformation scenes. Dijkstra gives extensive treatment to paintings of dead women, often naked. German artist Albert von Keller visited morgues to perfect his photorealistic portraits of corpses, and reported that:

> in the case of girls and women who had died a natural death ... [if one] studied their faces intensively one could see them take on an expression of pain so noble and almost so sympathetic by their suffering that it allowed an otherworldly happiness to shine through which could often only be compared to the miraculous expression of a woman who is in love to the point of ecstasy. (qtd. in Dijkstra 1988, 56)

Dijkstra notes that von Keller's observation "shows how literal an equation late nineteenth century males made between virtuous passivity, sacrificial ecstasy, and the erotic death as indicative of 'feminine fulfillment'" (1988, 56). When one looks at von Keller's 1885 painting *Study of a Dead Woman*, every rib of its nude subject bulging through her pallid skin, one sees how the skeleton vogue participated in this culture of necrophilia, and how Dijkstra's premise may easily be extended to the romance of bone.

Further, as Ludmilla Jordanova notes, there is a body of paintings representing the dissection of a beautiful, young, nude woman (1989, 98–104)[21] with one or more doctor standing around the supine corpse, and often with a symbolic skeleton of death looking on as well. One is again reminded of the staking of Lucy in *Dracula*, where four male characters crowd around her coffin to drive the stake home. Jordanova argues that western society consistently genders science (and more broadly, culture itself) as male, with nature being gendered female. The statue *Nature Unveiling Herself Before Science*, sculpted by Louis-Ernest Barrias in 1899, is a famously literal example: a young woman covered in a veil, lifting it to expose her breasts and face, "implies that science is a masculine viewer, who is anticipating full knowledge of nature, which is represented as the naked female body" (1989, 87). The relevance of this unveiling metaphor to the transformation of a woman into a skeleton we see in *The Vanishing Lady* and elsewhere is clear: masculine (scientific) magic transforms the woman into a medical specimen through a process of (profound) unveiling or undressing.[22] Asks Jordanova:

> Why ... is it the *female* in particular that is to be (un)veiled? First, covering [her] implies shame and modesty ... Modesty was a concept through which ... the contradictory effects of seeing women's bodies were negotiated. Second, veiling implies secrecy. Women's bodies, and by extension feminine attributes, cannot be treated as fully public, something dangerous might happen, secrets might be let out, if they were open to view. Yet, in presenting something as inaccessible and dangerous, an invitation to know and to possess is extended. (1989, 92–3)

Indeed, this unveiling may be forced on a woman by masculine science, her inner secrets penetrated and exposed, precisely as a punishment for a breach of modesty. A stunningly misogynistic (and anti-Semitic) example is "A Photograph of the Invisible" by George Griffith, where the link between the sexualized female skeleton and the X-ray becomes explicit. This hack story appeared in the same April 1896 issue of *Pearson's Magazine* as a profile of Röntgen entitled "A Wizard of To-day," the text of which even makes reference to "A Photograph of the Invisible" (Dam 1896, 414). The story tells of a young man named Denton who speaks with his friend Professor Grantham about his desire for revenge on a woman named Edith, who jilted him in favour of a millionaire German Jew named Goldsberg, who is described as "phenomenally homely and vulgar" (Griffith 1896, 379). Grantham is the only person in command of a new kind of trick photography that employs a very particular aesthetic of co-registration:

He could photograph people with a ghostly double of themselves looking over their shoulder, and by means of photographs of a man, and his parents, and his grandparents, he had produced a composite picture that was an excellent likeness of a remote ancestor, as proved by an ivory miniature that he had never seen.

Of course he never did this kind of thing for money, but as a matter of favour; and, for the sake of his pet art, he had now and then taken the photographs of some of the most noted beauties of Society by his unknown process, and the results, with their exquisite blending of light and shade and tinting, were the pride and glory of their origins and the envy and despair of every professional in the world. (Griffith 1896, 378)

Grantham is a master of manipulating double exposures in a way that strongly echoes Mumler's art. After educating Denton about X-rays (Denton had been travelling and missed the initial flurry of excitement), Grantham proposes a scheme for revenge against Edith that even Denton finds horrifying and excessive. According to Grantham, the punishment fits the crime:

The woman has committed a crime against herself and all true womanhood, and to punish her you shall wound her in the tenderest spot in such a woman's being, her vanity and the vainglory which she takes in the beauty she has sold. You shall teach her, in a word—yes, and that millionaire purchaser of hers too, that beauty is but skin deep. (Griffith 1896, 379)

Indeed, it is with skin, or lack thereof, that Grantham's plan is concerned. He invites Edith to a session where he photographs her in complete darkness. He then sends the resulting images to her and her husband. What they see causes "the blood [to] rush to his face till it was almost purple, and died out of hers till it was grey and white and ghastly—the face of a corpse, but for the two bright glaring eyes that stared out of it" (Griffith 1896, 379). Just what unspeakable horror stared out at them from Grantham's photograph?

The photograph seemed, as it were, to be in three layers—all transparent save the third. It was a vignette, just showing the head and neck and shoulders. The dress, a most dainty morning costume, in which she had elected to be taken, was perfect in pattern, but diaphanous and transparent. Under this were the skin and flesh, transparent also.

Above were her features, perfect in their likeness, and the wreathed crown of golden brown hair of which she was so proud, but they were the face and hair not of a living woman, but of a ghost, and, beneath all, sharp in outline and perfect in every hideous detail, a fleshless skull—her own skull—poised on the jagged vertebrae of her neck, and supported on the bare bones of her chest and shoulders, grinned at her through the transparent veil of flesh, and seemed to stare at her out of the sockets in which two ghostly eyes seemed to float. (Griffith 1896, 379–80)

Like Smith's X-ray fiend, Grantham's modus operandi is secretly X-raying people for nefarious purposes. Here we see the aesthetic of co-registration taking on its most horrifying aspect. At the sight of this skeletal portrait, both Mr Goldsberg and his wife go insane. But only her delusion is characterized: "She imagines that she is a skeleton, and that her clothing and skin are nothing more than transparent shadows which everybody can see through" (1896, 380). Her physicians confine her to live in total darkness, for she cannot tolerate even the faintest light. Edith's feminine vanity is punished by her reduction to a fleshless wraith of herself, and her "crime against true womanhood" through her sexual betrayal of Denton is repaid with an eternity of nudity, right down to the bone.

Jehanne D'Alcy in *The Vanishing Lady* is denied such a fate of living death and eternal nudity, but her transformation into bone has a distinctly sexual edge nonetheless. One review of *The Vanishing Lady* on the Internet Movie Database, authored by the late science fiction writer F. Gwynplaine MacIntyre, carries the title, "Now, if he'd made her CLOTHES disappear ..." in recognition of the erotic implications of the female skeleton, reminding us of all the nervous reactions to the "indecent" and potentially pornographic X-ray. We may read in the magician's surprised reaction on unveiling the skeleton something of the giddy thrill of unexpected, unauthorized voyeurism that connects it with the emerging genre of the stag film, the paradigmatic example of which, Esme Collings's *A Victorian Lady in Her Boudoir*, was also made in 1896 (see Nead 2007, 186–94). Méliès directed at least one stag film himself, *After the Ball* (1897), very much in the mould of Collings's film. It shows a society woman who sheds her clothes with the help of a maid and, clad only in her flesh-coloured leotard, stands with her back to the camera as the maid pours bathwater down her back. At the end of the scene, the maid looks at the camera, seemingly acknowledging her complicity with the viewer's voyeurism; the film suddenly takes place in the same presentational mode that *The Vanishing Lady* does, in the regime of exhibitionist confrontation. That the undressing woman in *After the Ball* is Jehanne D'Alcy, Méliès's vanishing woman, confirms the link between the two scenes of "undressing."

The fact that D'Alcy was also Méliès's mistress is itself part of a long tradition of the female assistant also being the magician's lover.[23] Adelaide Herrmann, Gay Blackstone, Nani Darnell and Bess Houdini were notable examples from the early history of stage magic of the combined assistant-lover. The memoirs of Carl Hertz, magician and early cinema exhibitor, describes the beginnings of his relationship with his assistant: "The [oath of secrecy] was duly administered, and the contract signed, and thus Emelie D'Alton became the original Vanishing Lady, and, a little later, to make my secrets more secure, she became Mrs. Carl Hertz" (1924, 29). Hertz here articulates several dimensions of the magician's relationship to his assistant. His description, however facetious it may be, of marrying Mademoiselle D'Alton to secure his secrets, attests to the essential danger women pose in their ability expose the magician and the need to contain that danger through strictures like marriage. And, further, no matter how many illusions she might participate in, her identity *is* the "vanishing lady."

The vanishing woman trick has a history going back into the eighteenth century, but there was a boom in its popularity in the 1880s. Buatier de Kolta premiered his version, "L'Escamotage d'une Dame en Personne Vivante," at the Egyptian Hall on 6 August 1886. It quickly became perhaps the only trick that virtually all magicians performed and, more than any other trick, it was responsible for cementing the convention of the female assistant (Robert-Houdin was generally assisted by his sons). The female assistant is a complex and contradictory figure. Francesca Coppa argues that magic is superficially constructed as an epistemological matter, with the magician as a possessor of secret and rarefied knowledge that the audience is denied. The assistant, especially when she acts as a shill pulled "unexpectedly" onto the stage, must appear as unschooled in magic as the audience, but in fact she know its secrets intimately and in many cases is as skilful a performer as the magician himself (Coppa 2008, 89–92). Most tricks depend on the illusion of female passivity. In the vanishing woman illusion, the woman must *appear* still, but actually speedily slips away into a trapdoor, her status as a labouring body concealed. Like a magical sylph, the assistant's corporeality is always fluid and unstable, and she floats between life and death, embodiment and disembodiment. She embodies Kelly Hurley's observation that late Victorian thinkers were perfectly capable of "identifying women as dangerously defined by their bodies on the one hand and ethereal, essentially disembodied creatures on the other"

(1996, 10). The spectacle of thinly veiled misogynistic violence in the Vanishing Woman trick anticipates the trick that would come to represent magic in the following century: Sawing a Woman in Half. Magicians were not subtle about the relish they took in seeming to dismember women: in a 1921 publicity stunt, British magician P.T. Selbit even challenged feminists Christabel and Sylvia Pankhurst to subject themselves to being sawed in half on his stage (Steinmeyer 2003, 292–3).[24]

The paradoxes of the female assistant (and more broadly of women in the Victorian imagination) are manifest in *The Vanishing Lady*, where Jehanne D'Alcy ranges from being extremely disembodied, vanishing into thin air, to being grotesquely embodied as an inert, blackened skeleton. It is worth reiterating that, in this respect, the skeleton in *The Vanishing Lady* is not like the bulk of the cinematic skeletons that would follow it. It does not get up and dance or bow, tipping its head in the process—rather it sits there, testifying to its deadness. Perhaps this is simply a reflection of the technical limitations placed on Méliès at the time; he certainly wasted no time in creating lively skeletons in his later films. But seen another way, *The Vanishing Lady* is a meaningful relic of a moment when the skeleton had a particular power to shock and titillate. It accords with Garrett Stewart's points about cinema's tendency to refer to the photographic image, cinema's inert base, to convey the death of a character, either with freeze framing or a photograph within the film: "filmic textuality has one foot in its own graven image as a photogram ... Photography is a death in replica, cinema a dying away process" (1999, 152). In this case, the image of death borrows the image of the doubly haunted X-ray image. At any rate, by the end of the film Jehanne D'Alcy is back in the flesh, restored, the skeleton disavowed ... or is it? Even with her flesh restored, we spectators have seen her in the ultimate state of undress. She carries those bones with her, and to those bones she will return ... the skeleton is, as Robertson told his audiences a century before, "the fate that awaits us all."

The Survival of Skeletons

This book principally limited its focus to early cinema, but I am compelled to continue tracking representations of the skeleton throughout the twentieth century and to our contemporary moment, in part because the conventions of the skeleton on display in early cinema so resolutely inform the rest of its history. This narrative culminates with a new version of the sexualized female skeleton that makes Méliès's look modest by comparison, but which is still very much on its lineage. If skeletons would never again appear as commonly as in early cinema, the image does persist, often (as in Bergman's *Persona* [1966]) making reference to early cinema in the process. In D.W. Griffith's fascinating *The Avenging Conscience* (1914), a bridge between the trick film and the emerging conventions of the silent horror film, a laurelled skeleton appears as the ultimate horrific image conjured by the guilt-ridden unconscious of the murderer (Henry B. Walthall); Walthall again hallucinated a skeletal figure of death while playing Edgar Allan Poe in *The Raven* (1915). A comparable image appears in Carl Theodor Dreyer's *Vampyr* (1932). Disney's *The Skeleton Dance* (1929) and other cartoons would update lanternic traditions of choreographed, self-dislocating skeletons, often with the skeletons playing their ribcages like xylophones. Indeed, animation, including stop-motion in such films as *Jason and the Argonauts* (1963), *Army of Darkness* (1992) and *The Nightmare Before Christmas* (1993), would keep *danse macabre* imagery alive all through the twentieth century and beyond. The Oscar-nominated animated short *This Way Out* (2008) provides its own variation on the centuries-old dancing skeletons motif. If Michael Jackson's famous 1983 music video *Thriller* is another point of continuation for *danse macabre* traditions, the imagery is even stronger in its less-known follow-up *Ghosts* (1997), where special effects make Jackson into a literal dancing skeleton (Hogle 2002, 221-4).

In my essay "Collective Screams: William Castle and the Gimmick Film" (2011), I contend that Castle's desire to provoke audiences with his sometimes extra-filmic gimmicks led him to cast himself as a new incarnation of early cinema's trick filmmakers, a fact Castle signals through his repeated use of skeletons. The walking skeleton that menaces Annabel Loren (Carol Ohmart) at the climax of *House on Haunted Hill* (1959), actually a trick rigged by her husband Frederick (Vincent Price), was accompanied by the pop-out skeleton Emergo that flew from the front of the theatre to hover over (hopefully) terrified audiences. Castle consciously drew on the iconographies of the trick film in order to position himself (and Price, his internal avatar) as a master horror showman, albeit with his tongue firmly in his cheek. We find Castle playing Méliès most egregiously during his customary first-person appearance in the opening sequence of *13 Ghosts* (1960); in this sequence the gendering of the "magician" and the skeleton is particularly interesting. We see an office door marked "William Castle," and silhouetted on the other side is the shadow of skeleton's head and upper chest (looking quite like an X-ray image). The skeleton, having made appearances in *House on Haunted Hill* and *The Tingler* (1959), was Castle's symbol by this point and, inside the office, we find Castle at a desk alongside hokey horror props like a skull and a test tube on a Bunsen burner; the effect is an amusing clash of the gothic and the mundane. The skeleton turns out to be his secretary. He says "No more dictation today" and she raises her pen. Castle explains the gimmick of *13 Ghosts*, "Illusion-O" and its special ghost viewer, and in so doing affects magical changes to the film itself at will (drawing attention to the "magical" qualities of film form generally suppressed by the classical model). At the end of the sequence, he says "Goodbye for now" to the audience, and then turns to the skeleton secretary. "Shall we go?" he asks the female skeleton, and they both vanish. In this sequence, Castle returns to the trope of the vanishing female skeleton in order to make a statement about his own "magical" powers of authorship, providing strong evidence for the lasting cultural visibility of this trope.

Lest we think of the sexualized skeletons and intrusive X-rays as quaint footnotes from a time long gone, the issues associated with them continue to resonate with debates about corporeality, technology, privacy and exposure. One point of continuity lies with current debates around the use of full-body scanning technology (millimetre wave scanners and backscatter X-ray scanners) in airports in the post-11 September world. The American Civil Liberties Union condemns these devices as virtual strip searches and *The Guardian* has claimed that the scanners violate child pornography laws through their ability to create indecent images of children (Travis 2010, 1). Issues as old as the X-ray's discovery return in full force. Backscatter technology can:

> [pinpoint] not only weapons, drugs and contraband, but also the traveler's breasts, buttocks and genitalia. In fact, the resolution is so clear that the operator can literally count the hairs on a man's chest or measure the depth of a woman's navel. At the same time the machines are checking for contraband, they can produce an X-rated image comparable in quality to those found in Playboy magazine. (Murphy and Wilds 2001, 334)

The preceding quote comes from an article entitled "X-Rated X-Ray Invades Privacy Rights"[25] which argues that these intrusive security scans are unreasonably intrusively and objectifying an airline passenger's body by giving it the same status as a piece of luggage. These debates are important ones, but I find it interesting to find them framed in terms so similar to the moral panics inspired by the arrival of the X-ray more than a century ago. Arguments against full-body scans embrace eroticized language: scanners are "X-rated," expose genitals, breasts and buttocks, produce images which are likened to those in *Playboy* magazine and are even described as operating with a kind of "voyeur vision" (2001, 340). This rhetoric is not so removed from the angry letter in the *Pall Mall Gazette* in 1896 decrying the X-ray as revolting, indecent and voyeuristic … but the extent to which such debates are contingent on eroticization helps us see the titillation that underpins moral such outrage. "X-rated X-ray Invades Privacy Rights" might work as a subtitle for Smith's *The X-ray Fiend*, or even Méliès's *The Vanishing Lady*.

In the summer of 2010, a new lady skeleton caused a stir on the internet and in the mass media. (Image 6.7) The monitor manufacturer EIZO put out a calendar to promote the use of their products in medical imaging. It contains twelve pinup images of a female body, all rendered with X-rays, or at least approximating X-ray aesthetics. They all appear to show the same model wearing nothing but a pair of high heels in a variety of

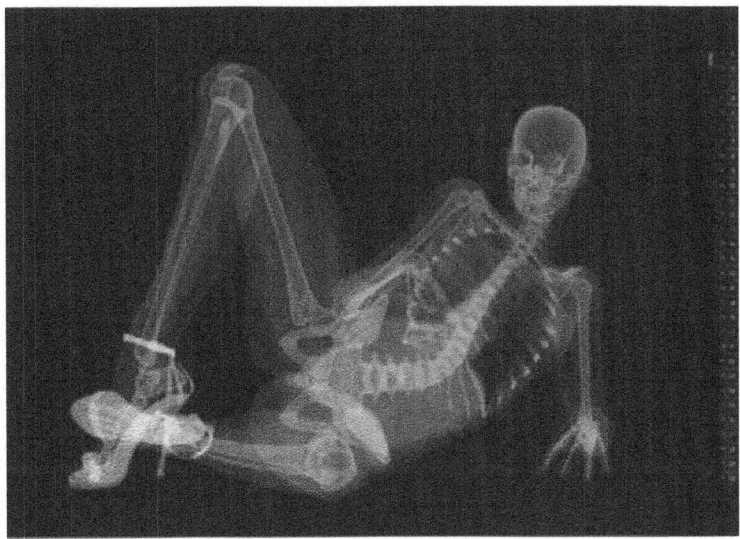

Image 6.7 "Miss November" from the EIZO's pin-up skeletons calendar (2010)

classic pornographic poses: lying with her back arched, or legs splayed with her hands at her crotch. Occasionally she is posed so that the fleshy outline of her breast juts into the frame, or her buttocks appear as a shapely halo framing her pelvic bones.[26] But little titillation is to be found in that death's head skull starring out at the camera. As Phil Plait, blogger for *Discover Magazine*, writes in an article waggishly titled "X-rayted pinups":

> But seriously, would someone consider these to be racy pictures? ... In many of the pictures, you can see a hint of flesh, and in many cases, those particular body parts are considered to be, um, secondary sexual characteristics—and as it is well known by the lingerie industry, hinting at skin can be more interesting than simply exposing it. In a lot of the pictures the model is posed provocatively. In most of them she's wearing some killer stilettos, which is more of a pinup thing than medical imaging thing.
> On the other hand, *these are freaking X-rays.* (2011, 1)

For whatever discussion and titillation EIZO's images produced (including a presence on sites like MSNBC.com that would certainly not normally reproduce images of a nude woman!), it seems obvious that a naked man's skeleton would not have the same impact. In their constellation of nudity, erotic display and "scientific" dismemberment, the images of EIZO's skeleton pin-up carry strong echoes of Méliès's *The Vanishing Lady* and the other sexualized skeletons of the late Victorian skeleton vogue. Whether or not they represent conscious homage, they are evidence of the skeleton vogue's impact lingering on in the twenty-first century, which continues to be felt especially where questions of masculine scientific authority and female corporeality and incorporeality are concerned.

Notes

1. For an excellent treatment of transformations in early cinema, see Solomon (2000).
2. Porter's *The Mystic Swing* (1900) is an intriguing variation on *The Vanishing Lady*, where a magician and Mephisto compete to dematerialize and rematerialize a woman. The magician triumphs when he turns her into a skeleton that Mephisto cannot make disappear.
3. The article has been criticized for not paying enough attention to films with female magicians (Salt 1992, 16). A fuller treatment of female conjurers in the trick film would have to wait until Solomon

(2010, 66–8). For other takes on gender in Méliès, see Ezra (2000, 89–116) and Waldow (2010).
4. A slightly different gender dynamic is in play in *The Startled Lover* (1899), where woman seemingly transforms herself into a skeleton to frighten her quarrelling lover.
5. André Gaudreault's useful neologism "trickality" breaks the distinction between narrativity and theatricality (2011, 37–8).
6. "*Escamotage*" comes close to meaning disappearance, but with some untranslatable connotations of thievery and trickery (Beckman 2003, 49). In a reflection of the pervasiveness of the vanishing woman trick, "*escamoteur*" was a key synonym for magician in French. As Solomon notes, part of Méliès's strategy in replicating known tricks on screen was to be able to sell his films to other illusionists and fairground exhibitors, which may explain the presence of his theatre's name in the film's title (2008, 39).
7. Méliès's first studio was, however, modelled on the Robert-Houdin stage, both in its dimensions and in features like trapdoors, rollers, winches and mattes (Jacobson 2010, 195–6).
8. See Lamont and Wiseman (1999, 119–20) for staged failure as a tradition in stage magic.
9. Tsivian identifies nine human/skeleton transformation tricks before 1904 (1996, 293 n. 41); subsequent discoveries such as *The Prolific Magical Egg* (1902) extend this list.
10. For the importance of the figure of the mummy in late Victorian fiction and culture, see Daly (1999, 84–116), Day (2006, 19–62), Luckhurst (2006), Briefel (2008) and Macfarlane (2010). For an approach specific to cinema, see Lant (1992).
11. Exceptions include the aforementioned *Les Rayons Röntgen/A Novice at X-rays* and *The Prolific Magical Egg* (1902), where Méliès transforms himself into a skeleton.
12. Key haunted hotel films include Edwin S. Porter's *Uncle Josh in a Spooky Hotel* (1900), J. Stuart Blackton's *The Haunted Hotel* (1907), Segundo de Chomón's *The House of Ghosts* (1908), with the ur-example being Georges Méliès's *The Bewitched Inn* (1897).
13. See North (2008, 53, 190), for notes on this and other Lumière trick films.
14. See Ebner and Jenkins (1983) for more on depictions of skeletons in anatomical manuals.

15. For a treatment of *The Phantom of the Opera*'s echoes of the *danse macabre*, most evident in the famous *bal masqué* sequence, see Hogle (2002, 5–6, 126–7).
16. Katie was herself purported to be the daughter of another notable control, a seventeenth-century Welsh pirate named John King.
17. Some dispute this claim; biographer William H. Brock absolves Crookes of sexual immodesty but concludes that he was at least hoodwinked by a variety of enterprising mediums (2008, 203).
18. It gave considerable ammunition to spiritualism's opponents and debunkers. Magician John Nevil Maskelyne wrote, "The 'scientist' who writes like this—and clasps the beautiful and substantial spirit in his arms—is much too far gone for investigation" (quoted in Brock 2008, 179).
19. Slightly later, in Mann's *The Magic Mountain*, we find Hans Castorp making a fetish object of an X-ray image of Clavdia Chauchat, keeping it in his breast pocket near his heart and kissing it frequently. For more on the sexual implications of the X-ray, see Kevles (1997, 28–30).
20. See also Tracy (1990), Pike (1991) and Christ (1993).
21. Elisabeth Bronfen offers an analysis of Gabriel von Max's 1869 painting *Der Anatom*, where a doctor looks down on a beautiful young female corpse. Von Max, himself a spiritualist, had a special interest in women on the threshold of life and death (Bronfen 1992, 3–6).
22. Rae Beth Gordon notes the frequency of Méliès films in which "the feats of magicians and magnetizers are interchangeable with those of doctors and physicians" (2001, 189); see also Frayling (2005, 48–55).
23. Méliès was apparently a philanderer who engaged in numerous affairs with the young women who are featured in many of his films. Frazer writes that, "One gets the impression that Méliès may have been the most happy when making films such as *Ten Ladies in One Umbrella* (1903), in which he is the only man on a stage surrounded by his obedient harem" (1979, 128).
24. The ultimate cinematic expression of this misogynistic convention would have to be Herschell Gordon Lewis's *The Wizard of Gore* (1970). Other films to explore the gender implications of the sawing-a-woman-in-two trick include Susan Seidelman's *Desperately Seeking Susan* (1985) and Claude Chabrol's *La Fille*

coupée en deux (2007). Warren Zevon used a magical metaphor to characterize his love life in "For My Next Trick, I'll Need a Volunteer," a track off his excellent 2000 album *Life'll Kill Ya*. Zevon sings "I can saw a woman in two/But you won't want to look in the box when I'm through/I can make love, disappear/For my next trick, I'll need a volunteer."

25. This irresistible pun has also been used by David A. Mackey for his article "The 'X-rated X-ray': Reconciling Fairness, Privacy, and Security" (2007).
26. Similarly, in 2001 the Belgian neo-conceptualist artist Wim Delvoye produced a series of X-ray images of people having sex. In 1921, Franz Fiedler published a set of images of women in various sexualized poses alongside skeletons.

Works Cited

[Anon.] "Cases Received by the Literary Committee." *Journal of the Society for Psychical Research* 7:66 (1891): 7–14.

Barnouw, Erik. *The Magician and the Cinema*. New York: Oxford University Press, 1981.

Beckman, Karen. *Vanishing Women: Magic, Film and Feminism*. Durham, NC: Duke University Press, 2003.

Bennett, Bridget. "Spirited Away: The Death of Little Eva and the Farewell Performances of 'Katie King.'" *Journal of American Studies* 40 (2006): 1–16.

Binion, Rudolph. "Europe's Culture of Death." *The Psychology of Death in Fantasy and Horror*. Ed. Jerry S. Piven. Westport, CT: Greenwood Press, 2004. 119–36.

Briefel, Aviva. "Hands of Beauty, Hands of Horror: Fear and Egyptian Art at the Fin de Siècle." *Victorian Studies* 50.2 (2008): 263–71.

Brock, William H. *William Crookes (1832–1919) and the Commercialization of Science*. Aldershot, Hants: Ashgate, 2008.

Bronfen, Elisabeth. *Over Her Dead Body: Death, Femininity and the Aesthetic*. Manchester: Manchester University Press, 1992.

Carroll, Noël. "The Fear of Fear Itself: The Philosophy of Halloween." *Zombies, Vampires, and Philosophy: New Life for the Undead*. Eds. Richard Greene and K. Silem Mohammed. Chicago: Open Court, 2010. 223–35.

Castle, Terry. *The Female Thermometer: 18th Century and the Invention of the Uncanny*. New York: Oxford University Press, 1995.

Christ, Carol. "Painting the Dead: Portraiture and Necrophilia in Victorian Art and Poetry." *Death and Representation*. Eds. Sarah Weber Goodwin and

Elisabeth Bronfen. Baltimore: The Johns Hopkins University Press, 1993. 133–151.

Coppa, Francesca. "The Body Immaterial: Magician's Assistants and the Performance of Labour." *Performing Magic on the Western Stage: From the Eighteenth-Century to the Present.* Eds. Francesca Coppa, Lawrence Hass, James Peck. New York: Palgrave Macmillan, 2008. 85–106.

Daly, Nicholas. *Modernism, Romance and the Fin de Siècle: Popular Fiction and British Culture.* Cambridge: Cambridge University Press, 1999.

Dam, H.J.W. "A Wizard of To-day." *Pearson's Magazine.* 1.4 (April 1896): 413–9.

Day, Jasmine. *The Mummy's Curse: Mummymania in the English-speaking World.* London: Routledge, 2006.

Dijkstra, Bram. *Idols of Perversity: Fantasies of Feminine Evil in Fin-de-siècle Culture.* New York: Oxford University Press, 1988.

Ebner, Ingrid D. and Glen P. Jenkins. *Skeletons in Our Closet: Skeletal Illustration as Represented in the Rare Book Collection of the Cleveland Health Sciences Library.* Cleveland: History Division, the Cleveland Health Sciences Library. 1983.

Ezra, Elizabeth. "Becoming Woman: Cinema, Gender and Technology." *A "Belle Epoque"? Women in French Society and Culture, 1890–1914.* Eds. Diana Holmes and Carrie Tarr. New York: Berghahn Books, 2006. 125–36.

Ezra, Elizabeth, *Georges Méliès and the Birth of the Auteur.* Manchester: Manchester University Press, 2000.

Fechner, Christian. *The Magic of Robert-Houdin.* Boulogne, France: Edition F.C.F., 2002.

Fischer, Andreas. "'The Reciprocal Adaptation of Optics and Phenomena': The Photographic Recording of Materializations." *The Perfect Medium: Photography and the Occult.* Eds. Clément Chéroux, Andreas Fischer, Pierre Apraxine, Denis Canguilhem and Sophie Schmit. New Haven: Yale University Press, 2004. 171–89.

Fischer, Lucy. *Cinematernity: Film, Motherhood, Genre.* Princeton: Princeton University Press, 1996.

Fischer, Lucy. "The Lady Vanishes: Women, Magic, and the Movies." *Film Quarterly* 33 (Fall 1979): 30–40.

Frayling, Christopher. *Mad, Bad and Dangerous? The Scientist and the Cinema.* London: Reaktion, 2005.

Frazer, John. *Artificially Arranged Scenes: The Films of Georges Méliès.* Boston: G. K. Hall, 1979.

Gaudreault, André. "Méliès the Magician: The Magical Magic of the Magic Image." *Early Popular Visual Culture* 5.2 (July 2007): 167–74.

Gaudreault, André. "Theatricality, Narrativity, and Trickality: Reevaluating the Cinema of Georges Méliès." *Fantastic Voyages of the Cinematic Imagination:*

Georges Méliès's Trip to the Moon. Ed. Matthew Solomon. Albany: SUNY Press, 2011. 31–48.
Goodman, Philip C. "The New Light: Discovery and Introduction of the X-ray." *American Journal of Roentgenology* 165 (1995): 1041–45.
Gordon, Rae Beth. *Why the French Love Jerry Lewis: From Cabaret to Early Cinema.* Stanford: Stanford University Press, 2001.
Gorky, Maxim. "Gorky on the Films, 1896." *New Theatre and Film 1934 to 1937.* Ed. Herbert Kline. San Diego: Harcourt Brace Jovanovich, 1985. 227–31.
Griffith, George. "A Photograph of the Invisible." *Pearson's Magazine* 1.4 (April 1896): 376–80.
Hall, Trevor H. *The Spiritualists: The Story of Florence Cook and William Crookes.* New York: Helix Press, 1963.
Heard, Mervyn. *Phantasmagoria: The Secret Life of the Magic Lantern.* Hastings: The Projection Box, 2006.
Herbert, Stephen. *A History of Pre-Cinema.* Volume 2. London: Routledge, 2004.
Hertz, Carl. *A Modern Mystery Merchant: The Trials, Tricks and Travels of Carl Hertz, the Famous American Illusionist.* London: Hutchinson, 1924.
Hogle, Jerrold E. *The Undergrounds of* The Phantom of the Opera: *Sublimation in Leroux's Novel and its Progeny.* New York: Palgrave, 2002.
Hopkins, Albert. A. *Magic: Stage Illusions and Scientific Diversions Including Trick Photography.* New York: Munn & Co., 1897.
Hurley, Kelly. *The Gothic Body: Sexuality, Materialism, and Degeneration at the Fin de Siècle.* Cambridge: Cambridge University Press, 1996.
Jacobson, Brian R. "The 'Imponderable Fluidity' of Modernity: Georges Méliès and the Architectural Origins of Cinema." *Early Popular Visual Culture* 8.2 (May 2010): 189–207.
Jolly, Martyn. *Faces of the Dead: The Belief in Spirit Photography.* London: British Library, 2006.
Jones, Graham M. "The Family Romance of Modern Magic: Contesting Robert-Houdin's Cultural Legacy in Contemporary France." *Performing Magic on the Western Stage From the Eighteenth Century to the Present.* Ed: Francesca Coppa, Lawrence Hass and James Peck. New York: Palgrave Macmillan, 2008. 33–60.
Jones, Graham M. "Modern Magic and the War of Miracles in French Colonial Culture." *Comparative Studies in Society and History* 52.1 (2010): 66–99.
Jordanova, Ludmilla. *Sexual Visions: Images of Gender in Science and Medicine between the Eighteenth and Twentieth Centuries.* Madison, WI: University of Wisconsin Press, 1989.
Kevles, Bettyann Holtzmann. *Naked to the Bone: Medical Imaging in the Twentieth Century.* New Brunswick, NJ: Rutgers University Press, 1997.
Kittler, Friedrich A. *Gramophone, Film, Typewriter.* Stanford, CA: Stanford University Press, 1999.

Kovács, Katherine Singer. "Georges Méliès and the Féerie." *Film before Griffith*. Ed. John Fell. Berkeley: University of California Press, 1984. 244–57.
Kurtz, Leonard P. *The Dance of Death and the Macabre Spirit in European Literature*. Geneva, Switzerland: Slatkine Reprints, 1975.
Lant, Antonia. "The Curse of the Pharaoh, or How Cinema Contracted Egyptomania." *October* 59 (Winter 1992). 86–112.
Lamb, Geoffrey Frederick. *Victorian Magic*. London: Routledge & Kegan Paul, 1976.
Lamont, Peter and Richard Wiseman. *Magic in Theory: An Introduction to the Theoretical and Psychological Elements of Conjuring*. Hatfield: University of Hertfordshire Press, 1999.
Landon, Perceval. "Thurnley Abbey." *The Dark Horse Book of Hauntings*. Ed. Scott Allie. Milwaukee: Dark Horse, 2003. 32–46.
Leeder, Murray. "Collective Screams: William Castle and the Gimmick Film." *Journal of Popular Culture* 44.4 (2011): 774–96.
Leeder, Murray "M. Robert-Houdin Goes to Algeria: Spectatorship and Panic in Illusion and Early Cinema." *Early Popular Visual Culture*. 8.2 (2010): 187–203.
Lehman, Amy. *Victorian Women and the Theatre of Trance: Mediums, Spiritualists and Mesmerists in Performance*. Jefferson, NC: McFarland, 2009.
Leroux, Gaston. *The Phantom of the Opera*. Charlottesville, VA: University of Virginia Library, 1994.
Luckhurst, Roger. "The Mummy's Curse: A Genealogy." *Magic, Science, Technology and Literature*. Eds. Jarmila Mildorf, Hans Ulrich Seeber and Martin Windisch. Berlin: LIT Verlag, 2006. 123–38.
Lutz, Deborah. *Pleasure Bound: Victorian Sex Rebels and the New Eroticism*. New York: Norton, 2011.
Lyons, Sherrie Lynne. *Species, Serpents, Spirits, and Skulls: Science at the Margins in the Victorian Age*. Albany: SUNY Press, 2009.
Macfarlane, Karen E. "Mummy Knows Best: Knowledge and the Unknowable in Turn of the Century Mummy Fiction." *Horror Studies* 1.1 (2010): 5–24.
MacIntyre, F. Gwynplaine. "Now, if only he'd made her CLOTHES disappear ..." *Internet Movie Database*. July 5, 2005. http://www.imdb.com/title/tt0000075/usercomments Accessed June 18, 2009.
Mackey, David A. "The 'X-rated X-ray': Reconciling Fairness, Privacy, and Security." *Criminal Justice Studies*. 20.2 (June 2007): 149–59.
Mangan, Michael. *Performing Dark Arts: A Cultural History of Conjuring*. Bristol: Intellect, 2007.
Mannoni, Laurent. *The Great Art of Light and Shadow: The Archaeology of Cinema*. Exeter: University of Exeter Press, 2000.
McGrath, Roberta. *Seeing Her Sex: Medical Archives and the Female Body*. New York: Manchester University Press, 2002.

Méliès, Georges. "Cinematographic Views." *French Film Theory and Criticism, 1907–1939.* Volume 1. Ed: Richard Abel. Princeton: Princeton University Press, 1988. 35–46.

Michaels, Lloyd. *The Phantom of the Cinema: Character in Modern Film.* Albany: SUNY Press, 1998.

Murphy, Michael C. and Michael R. Wilds. "X-rated X-ray Invades Privacy Rights." *Criminal Justice Policy Review* 12.4 (December 2001): 333–343.

Nead, Lynda. *The Haunted Gallery: Painting, Photography, Film c. 1900.* New Haven: Yale University Press, 2007.

North, Dan. *Performing Illusions: Cinema, Special Effects and the Virtual Actor.* London: Wallflower, 2008.

Osmond, Humphry. "Victorian Imbroglio." *International Journal of Parapsychology* 5.2 (Spring 1963): 203–12.

Pike, Judith Eloise. *Exquisite Corpses: The Fetish of the Female Dead Body in Late Eighteenth and Nineteenth Century Literature.* Diss. University of California, Irvine, 1991.

Plait, Phil. "X-rayted pinup." *Discover Magazine.* June 21, 2010. http://blogs.discovermagazine.com/badastronomy/2010/06/21/x-rayted-pinup. Accessed June 23, 2011.

Posner, Dassia N. "Spectres on the New York Stage: The (Pepper's) Ghost Craze of 1863." *Representations of Death in Nineteenth-century U.S. Writing and Culture.* Ed. Lucy Elizabeth Frank. Aldershot, Hants: Ashgate, 2007. 189–204.

Raia-Grean, Courtenay. "Picturing the Supernatural: Spirit Photography, Radiant Matter, and the Spectacular Science of Sir William Crookes." *Visions of the Industrial Age, 1830–1914: Modernity and the Anxiety of Representation in Europe.* Eds. Minsoo Kang and Amy Woodson-Boutlon. Aldershot, Hants: Ashgate, 2008. 55–80.

Robert-Houdin, Jean Eugène. *Memoirs of Robert-Houdin, Author, Conjurer, Ambassador.* Philadelphia: G.G. Evans, 1859.

Russel, Lawrence K. "Lines on an X-ray Portrait of a Lady." *Life* 27.689 (March 12, 1896): 191.

Salt, Barry. *Film Style & Technology: History & Analysis.* Second Edition. London: Starword, 1992.

Schwartz, Vanessa. *Spectacular Realities: Early Mass Culture in Fin-de-Siècle Paris.* Berkeley: University of California Press, 1998.

Showalter, Elaine. *Sexual Anarchy: Gender and Culture at the Fin de Siècle.* New York: Viking, 1990.

Singer, Ben. *Melodrama and Modernity: Early Sensational Cinema and Its Contexts.* New York: Columbia University Press, 2001.

Solomon, Matthew. *Disappearing Tricks: Silent Film, Houdini, and the New Magic of the Twentieth Century.* Iowa City: University of Iowa Press, 2010.

Solomon, Matthew. "Fairground Illusions and the Magic of Méliès." *Travelling Cinema in Europe: Source and Perspectives*. Ed. Martin Loiperdinger. Frankfurt: Stœmfeld/Roter Stern, 2008. 35–46.

Solomon, Matthew. "'Twenty-five Heads under One Hat: Quick-change in the 1890s." *Meta Morphing: Visual Transformation and the Culture of Quick-change*. Ed. Vivian Sobchack. Minneapolis: University of Minnesota Press, 2000. 3–20.

Steinmeyer, Jim. *Hiding the Elephant: How Magicians Invented the Impossible and Learned to Disappear*. New York: Carol & Graf Publishers, 2003.

Stewart, Garrett. *Between Film and Screen: Modernism's Photo Synthesis*. Chicago: University of Chicago Press, 1999.

Stoker, Bram. *The Annotated Dracula*. Ed. Leonard Wolf. New York: Ballantine, 1975.

Tracy, Robert. "Loving Your All Ways: Vamps, Vampires, Necrophiles and Necrofiles in Nineteenth-Century Fiction." *Sex and Death in Victorian Literature*. Ed. Regina Barreca. Bloomington: Indiana University Press, 1990. 9–31.

Travis, Alan. "New scanners break child porn laws." *guardian.co.uk*. January 4, 2010. http://www.guardian.co.uk/politics/2010/jan/04/new-scanners-child-porn-laws Accessed June 29, 2010.

Tromp, Marlene. *Altered States: Sex, Nation, Drugs and Self-transformation in Victorian Spiritualism*. Albany: SUNY Press, 2006.

Tsivian, Yuri. "Media Fantasies and Penetrating Vision: Some Links Between X-rays, the Microscope, and Film." *Laboratory of Dreams: The Russian Avant-garde and Cultural Experiment*. Eds. John E. Bowlt and Olga Matich. Stanford: Stanford University Press, 1996. 81–99.

Vardac, A. Nicholas. *Stage to Screen: Theatrical Method from Garrick to Griffith*. Cambridge: Harvard University Press, 1949.

Waldow, Stephen. "Women Objectified, Manipulated, and Exploited: The Central Attractions in the 'Cinema of Attractions.'" *Film Matters* 1.3 (July 2010): 20–5.

Weart, Spencer R. *Nuclear Fear: A History of Images*. Cambridge, MA: Harvard University Press, 1988.

Whissel, Kristen. *Picturing American Modernity: Traffic, Technology, and the Silent Cinema*. Durham: Duke University Press, 2008.

Williams, Linda. "Film Body: An Implantation of Perversions." *Cinétracts* 12 (Winter 1981): 19–35.

Wood, Gaby. *Edison's Eve: A Magical History of the Quest for Mechanical Life*. New York: Alfred A. Knopf, 2002.

CHAPTER 7

"Living Pictures at Will": Projecting Haunted Minds

This chapter focuses on the idea of thought's externalizability and its relationship to the history of the supernaturalization of projection. Terry Castle has influentially historicized Freud's uncanny, noting that the very term "phantasmagoria," moved from describing this external spectacle to:

> the phantasmic imagery of the mind. This metaphoric shift bespeaks ... a very significant transformation in the human consciousness over the past two centuries ... the spectralization or "ghostifying" of mental space ... Thus in everyday conversation we affirm that our brains are filled with ghostly shapes and images, that we "see" figures and scenes in our minds, that we are "haunted" by our thoughts. (1995, 141–3)

This internalization of thought also suggests its potential externalizability. Those haunting thoughts do not necessarily stay contained with the mind, but can be projected outward into cinema-like displays. This chapter draws attention to several nineteenth-century examples, one fiction, one a prominent hoax and one an earnest declaration of a spiritualist, and ultimately suggests the persistence of the theme of externalized thought into twenty-first century cinema.

"Unsubstantial, Impalpable,—Simulacra, Phantasms": Bulwer-Lytton's Phantoms

As we have seen, cinema emerged into the late-Victorian world obsessed with magic and the supernatural. The previous half century had seen the emergence of stage magic as respected middle-class entertainment, the rise of spiritualism as a modern, purportedly scientific religion, the occult revival and the emergence of psychical research. It is perhaps no surprise, then, to find early commentators using supernatural metaphors to characterize cinema's curious qualities. But the mind is never that far away, either: Gorky qualified his initial description of cinema's grey, silent netherworld with "[h]ere I shall try to explain myself, lest I be suspected of madness or indulgence in symbolism" (1960, 407). Again, the ghostly space of cinema is tied in (albeit by the way of a disclaimer) with mental states. This section will provide a new angle on the backstory of the film/mind/ghost triad through examining a similar dynamic in Edward Bulwer-Lytton's 1859 novella "The Haunted and the Haunters; or, The House and the Brain."

Today probably most famous for having penned the definitive line of purple prose, "It was a dark and stormy night,"[1] Bulwer-Lytton (later the 1st Baron Lytton) was not only a well-known writer in his time but also an early participant in the Victorian "occult revival." This fact manifests clearly in certain of his writings. While fiction, "The Haunted and the Haunters" reflects some contemporaneous theorizations of the supernatural, and its narrator often serves as a mouthpiece for Bulwer-Lytton's ideas. In fact, such was Bulwer-Lytton's credibility in occultist circles that Madame Blavatsky herself reportedly claimed that no author ever wrote about supernatural beings so truthfully (van Schlun 2007, 136). The story's narrator takes it upon himself to investigate an infamous London haunted house where no visitor lasts more than a few hours without fleeing in terror—though no two people relate the same experience. The story is considered an influential example of the Victorian "scientification" of the supernatural, in which hauntings are justified with references to electromagnetism, mesmerism, telegraphy and so on. Alison Milbank refers to it as "the apogee of the naturalized supernatural in the Victorian age" (2002, 163).[2] In contrast to such familiar Victorian haunting narratives as Henry James's *The Turn of the Screw* (1898) or Charlotte Perkins Gillman's *The Yellow Wallpaper* (1892), there is no theme of madness—quite the opposite, in fact, as the narrator is defined as utterly rational and sane. Nor is there much of what Tzvetan Todorov would call "fantastic hesitation," where we might wonder if its phenomena are real or imaginary: in "The Haunted and the Haunters," ghostly phenomena do indeed originate in the human mind, but not in the sense of a hallucination.

The ghosts that the narrator observes in the haunted space have a distinctly proto-cinematic (or "Phantasmagorical" or "lanternic") character. These spectres are shadowy approximations of the human form that seem to re-enact a recorded scene, and the narrator appears to both share and not share space with them simultaneously:

> Suddenly [...] there grew a shape,—a woman's shape. It was distinct as a shape of life,—ghastly as a shape of death [...] As if from the door, though it did not open, there grew out another shape, equally distinct, equally ghastly,—a man's shape, a young man's. It was in the dress of the last century, or rather in a likeness of such dress (for both the male shape and the female, though defined, were evidently unsubstantial, impalpable,—simulacra, phantasms) [...] Just as the male shape approached the female, the dark Shadow started from the wall, all three for a moment wrapped in darkness. When the pale light returned, the two phantoms were as if in the grasp of the Shadow that towered between them; and there was a blood-stain on the breast of the female; and the phantom male was leaning on its phantom sword, and blood seemed trickling fast from the ruffles, from the lace; and the darkness of the intermediate Shadow swallowed them up,—they were gone. (1980, 46–7)

Though his servant flees in panic and his dog dies of fright, our intrepid narrator manages to stay steady by telling himself, "my reason rejects this thing; it is an illusion,—I do not fear" (1980, 44). And indeed, the ghosts prove unable to affect him.

The use of "Shadow" here is of interest. It takes us, of course, back to Gorky's description of "the kingdom of shadows" and "not life but its shadow" in 1896 (1960, 407), but "photographic shadows," "shadow-images" and simply "shadows" were privileged descriptors in late nineteenth- and early twentieth-century periodicals for both photochemical film and X-ray images (Borden 2012, 168). The title of the 2011 documentary about the American Film Registry, *These Amazing Shadows*, attests to the persistence of this rhetoric. In Bulwer-Lytton's tale, the shadow-play seems to be imprinted onto the environment of the haunted house, as if playing and replaying through some quasi-mechanical means. And the explanation is technological, albeit an occult technology: a mysterious device, described as a compass floating in a clear liquid on top of a thin tablet, with astrological symbols in place of cardinal directions. With this object destroyed, the haunting ceases, the house becoming inhabitable. Nonetheless, the narrator theorizes that a living human agency was behind these hauntings, and that ghosts are less the motivated, intelligent, ensouled spirits of the dead than residual thoughts and memories willed into a semblance of being by mysterious forces. The narrator reflects on the fact that no two persons told the same tale of their experiences in the haunted house:

> If this were an ordinary imposture, the machinery would be arranged for results that would but little vary; if it were a supernatural agency permitted by the Almighty, it would surely be for some definite end. These phenomena belong to neither class; my persuasion is, that they originate in some brain now far distant; that that brain had no distinct volition in anything that occurred; that what does occur reflects but its devious, motley, ever-shifting, half-formed thoughts; in short, that it has been the dreams of such a brain put into action and invested with a semi-substance. That this brain is of immense power, that it can set matter into movement, that it is malignant and destructive ... (1980, 58)

Alongside the device, our narrator discovers a miniature portrait dated from 1765, featuring a man described as resembling "some mighty serpent transformed into a man, preserving in the human lineaments the old serpent type" (1980, 68). He is identified as a notorious man who fled London on the suspicion of a double murder. This man is presumably the architect of the haunted space, but no more information is provided in the most familiar version of the story, which ends with the information that the house is inhabitable again.

However, in the longer, original version of the story,[3] the responsible party is revealed to be an evil, immortal mesmerist named Mr Richards. Mr Richards is heavily associated with empire: the owner of the house encountered him under another name in India, where he was a corrupt adviser to a Rajah, and he now presents himself as an Orientalist residing in Damascus. Mr Richards is a man of great will, who has willed himself not to die. The narrator tracks him to a London gentleman's club and boldly questions him: "To what extent human will in certain temperaments can extend?" Mr Richards's answer again invokes empire, "To what extent can thought extend? Think, and before you draw breath you are in China!" The narrator replies, "True. But my thought has no power in China," and Mr. Richards replies, "Give it expression, and it may have: you may write down a thought which, sooner or later, may alter the whole condition of China. What is a law but a thought? Therefore thought is infinite—therefore thought has power ..." (1980, 75).

Though this discussion of the projectability of though may not seem supernatural per se, the conclusions the narrator draws from it are:

> Yes; what you say confirms my own theory. Through invisible currents one human brain may transmit its ideas to other human brains with the same rapidity as a thought promulgated by visible means. And as thought is imperishable—as it leaves its stamp behind it in the natural world even when the thinker has passed out of this world—so the thought of the living may have power to rouse up and revive the thoughts which the dead—such as those thoughts *were in life*—though the thought of the living cannot reach the thoughts which the dead *now* may entertain. (1980, 75–6)

For several pages, the narrator spells out his (and, by implication, Bulwer-Lytton's) theories of the supernatural and the mind, eventually confronting Mr Richards for his evils and declaring "execrable Image of Death and Death in Life, I warn you back from the cities and homes of healthful men; back to the ruins of departed empires; back to the deserts of nature unredeemed!" (1980, 81).

Reflecting the paradoxical impressions of travel and immobility, motion and stillness, emerging from cinema and other modern media, Mr Richards responds to this attempt at banishment by wresting his and the narrator's consciousnesses into another place: "As he spoke I felt as if I rose out of myself upon eagle wings. All the weight seemed gone from the air—roofless the room, roofless the dome of space. I was not in the body—where I knew not—but aloft over time, over earth" (1980, 81-2). The subsequent sequence plays out almost entirely in dialogue, as the narrator witnesses an allegorical (one assumes) depiction of Mr Richards's ultimate grim fate, the lone survivor of a ship in the frozen north, pursued by foes under an iron sky. Mr Richards then impels the narrator to sleep, and commands him not to tell any of this story to anyone, while he presumably flees the country and changes his identity.

"The Haunted and the Haunters" is a fascinating muddle, especially in the longer version, but one central recurring theme is projection: the projection of Mr Richards's will that causes the ghosts to haunt the house, the projection of his and the narrator's consciousness out of their bodies and into an allegorical space, and of course, the shadowy, ineffable phantoms that the narrator confronts in the haunted house. That sequence anticipates many hallmarks of accounts of early cinema spectatorship: uncanny figures that resemble human beings but are shadowy phantasms divested of life force, the traceless appearance from and disappearance into nothingness, the uncertain line between presence and absence, and the demarcation between the naïve, overwhelmed spectator who succumbs to panic and the sophisticated one capable of saying some version of "it is an illusion—I do not fear." These parallels are more than anecdotal, and demonstrate the extent to which these themes were not necessarily unique to cinema, but rather illustrate consistencies between early cinema and the broader history of projected media, especially its entanglement with the supernatural.

THE LESSON OF SYMPSYCHOGRAPHY

From Bulwer-Lytton's occult projections of 1859, we move two examples of the mystical projection of thought from 1896 and the immediate aftermath of the unveiling of cinema and the X-ray. In September 1896, *Popular Science Monthly* carried an article by scientist David Starr Jordan entitled "The Sympsychograph: A Lesson in Impressionist Physics." Jordan was one of the most respected scientists in the United States at the time and the president of Stanford University. The article concerned a curious image, rather resembling a later surrealist photograph: a blurry collage of a series of images of cats. Image 7.1. The picture, the text tells us, was produced by the seven members of the "Astral Camera Club of Alcalde," inspired by Röntgen's experiments. With a specially designed

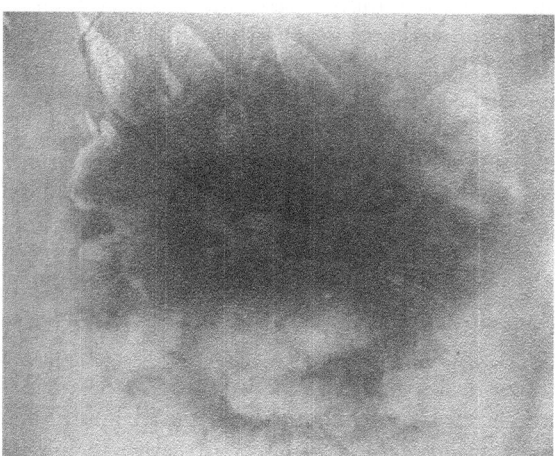

Image 7.1 David Starr Jordan's "Sympsychograph" (1896)

camera, the Club devised a way to capture on a sensitive plate, "as the rays of light are gathered in ordinary photography," those "electric and odic impulses [that] could be transferred from the brain or retina through the eye of each different observer" (1896, 600).

The sympsychograph itself claims to record mental impressions of the concept "cat" from each member of the Club:

> They were not to think of any particular cat, but of a cat as represented by the innate idea of the mind or ego itself ... One man's thought of a cat would be individual, ephemeral, a recollection of some cat which he had some time seen, and which by the mind's eye would be seen again ... The personal equation would be measurably eliminated in sympsychography, while the cat of the human innate idea, the astral cat, the cat which "never was on land or sea," but in accordance with which all cats have been brought into incarnation, would be more or less perfectly disclosed. (1896, 600–1)

Again, mystical discourse (buoyed by the sympsychograph's aesthetic resemblance to a spirit photograph), mental spaces and the image smoothly coexist. The fact that the article tells us that the Astral Camera Club's experiment was conducted on 1 April ought to have been a giveaway (or failing that, the claim that "The next experiment will be by similar means to photograph the cat's idea of man" (1896, 601)), and the following issue confirmed that it was a hoax. By then, however, the idea had taken root with some credulous readers. Jordan would recall in his autobiography that, "One clergyman even went so far as to announce a series of six discourses on 'The Lesson of Sympsychography,' while many others said they welcomed the discovery as verifying what they had long believed" (Jordan 1922, 599). Though a hoax, sympsychography stands near the beginning of a tradition of attempted or purposed thought photography or "thoughtography," famously manifesting in the *nensha* experiments of Tomokichi Fukurai in Tokyo[4] and, later, the work of the controversial American photographer Ted Serios.[5]

In sympsychography, the purported act of mental projection onto undeveloped film is justified with references to the recent discovery of X-rays; the article argues that "the invisible rays of Rontgen are not light in the common sense, but akin rather to brain emanations, or odic forces, which pass from mind to mind without the intervention of forms of gross matter as a medium" (1896, 598). The reference here is to a discredited concept: the odic or odylic force (also sometimes called the von Reichenbach force after its purported discoverer, Baron Karl von Reichenbach), a hypothetic life force used to justify mesmeric *rapport*. What Jordan suggests facetiously, other writers proposed in earnest: an article entitled "Röntgen's Vindication of Reichenbach" appeared in an 1897 issue of the spiritualist/occultist journal *Borderland*, arguing that X-rays were none other than the odic force.

The idea that thought itself can be conceived as a kind of emanation that can stretch beyond the body into the world around us, and even imprint itself as a kind of photography, is born of both science's recent unveiling of new unseen worlds and of the "ghostification" of mental space. And those haunting thoughts so stubbornly failed to remain confined to one's head.

"The Kinetiscope of the Mind"

Tropes of projection and the externalizability of thought also operated in the nascent field of psychical research. Frederic W.H. Myers, offered a redefinition of the ghost less as a motivated, intelligent being than as a lingering psychic phenomenon (estranging many spiritualists in the process). As McCorristine notes, Myers's conception of "the ghost as an automatic phenomenon implied a radically phantasmagorical and haunted world, a site of previous events, memories and dreams that never disappear from the visual world, but can be relayed through hallucinatory vision" (2010, 179).

A similar sensibility, tied explicitly to cinema and other media technologies, is on display in the article appearing *Borderland* in October 1896, entitled "Suggestions from Science for Psychic Students: Useful Analogies from Recent Discoveries and Inventions," authored by the journal's founder, W.T. Stead. Regarded as the founder of the "New Journalism," the forerunner of both tabloid journalism and investigative journalism, Stead would die in 1912 on the *RMS Titanic*. He was also an enthusiastic spiritualist and employed medium Ada Goodrich Freer as *Borderland*'s co-editor. Running from 1893 to 1897, *Borderland* published widely on new developments in psychical research, spiritualism, theosophy and eastern religions, palmistry, precognition, astrology, haunted houses, psychic photography, and even psychic messages received from Mars.

Stead's article began by noting that "The discovery of the Röntgen rays has compelled many a hardened sceptic to admit, when discussing Borderland, that 'there may be something in it after all'" (1896, 400). Stead frames various new discoveries, including electricity, the phonograph, the telephone, the photograph, the X-ray, the (far from new) camera obscura and, critically for our purposes here, the kinetoscope, as "helpful analogies, claiming only that they at least supply stepping stones that may lead to a rational understanding of much that is now incomprehensible" (1896, 400).[6] Stead consistently misspells Edison's invention as "kinetiscope"— he may be thinking of the earlier kinetiscope designed by Austrian inventor Franz von Uchatius, which projected moving drawings. Stead divides his section on the kinetoscope into the "Kinetiscope of Nature" (based around the idea of nature spontaneously recording traumatic events and replaying them when appropriately sensitive spectators are near) and the "Kinetiscope of the Mind," which deals with the projectability or externalizability of inner images and states. He introduces the latter thus: "The possibility of visualizing the phantoms of the imagination is possessed by some persons in such a high degree that they can compel clairvoyants and sensitives to see as if they were real persons the purely imaginary heroes and heroines of an unwritten romance" (1896, 403). Here, Stead assembles a set of shorter anecdotes. The first, entitled "Living Pictures at Will," describes a Frenchman who purchased a sixteenth-century chateau and furnished it in Renaissance style. The decor included a portrait of a nobleman of the House of Valois pictured alongside some "charming girls," and the owner found that by focusing his mental energies on the portrait, it was possible to will its originals to manifest "in a visible and tangible form." A dull vapour would fill the room and become:

> the originals of the portraits sitting there clothed in costumes of the olden times, seated in the armchairs. They were alive, or at least they so appeared, so entire was the illusion (if illusion it was). Their faces were those of persons talking, their eyes moving, their lips opening as if they were conversing together, but the magician could not distinguish an articulate word, the most being a light murmur of voices. The marvellous scene lasted half an hour, then melted into a mist. (1896, 403)

This scenario is, of course, another recapitulation of the haunted gallery motif Lynda Nead has surveyed, identifying paintings and other inanimate works coming to life as a key fantasy of the nineteenth century, culminating in cinema:

> The haunted gallery is a powerful metaphor for the uncanny magic of early film. Every still is haunted by the photographic likenesses of those who are no longer there; each time the project is set in motion the figures step out of their frames and come to life. There is, however, an instant of hesitation

and doubt—does the image move, can it live?—but the moment cannot be held for long. (2007, 204)

In Stead's anecdote, a parallel moment of hesitation is implied in the parenthetic "if illusion it was." Are these actually the ghosts of the portrait models, or merely apparitions that look like them, willed to that shape by the gentleman's mind?

Stead then reproduces a letter from Madame Marie de Manasseine, who claims that she has always possessed "the faculty of representing to myself vividly and objectively all that I desired … on reading the history of a disease, I could at will see the patient and all the pathological phenomena of his disease. On reading the description of a journey, I not only saw mentally, but, as it were, objectively, the scenery described, &c." (1896, 403). She honed the skill to conjure and manipulate hypnagogic hallucinations (phenomena of the indeterminate mental state between sleep and waking life), but also notes that:

> during my entire conscious life I have, from time to time, a visual phantom or apparition which remains completely independent of my will, and which appears sometimes several times a day, and sometimes more rarely, after longer or shorter periods. This visual phantom consists in a very brilliant star, having the apparent size of the planet Venus. It appears to me ordinarily at a certain distance, suspended in the middle of the room: but sometimes it approaches me and begins to shine over my shoulder, sometimes over my breast. (1896, 403)

This phantom often shines above her daughter's head. It interestingly blurs the line between those images born of the human mind (the talent Madame de Manasseine professes to possess in great degree) and the supernatural (she regards the hallucinogenic star as portending "some success or pleasure") (1896, 403).

Lastly, Stead reproduces some comments by theosophist C.W. Leadbeater that concern "the projection to the desired spot of a thought-form—that is to say, an artificial elemental moulded in the shape of the projector and ensouled by his thought. Thus form would receive whatever impressions there were to be received, and would transmit them to his maker, not along an astral telegraph-wire, but by sympathetic vibration" (1896, 403). Leadbeater goes on to address the question of whether an astral body can be solidified into material forms; he says that yes, it can, and it is even possible to produce perfect illusions of the human form, but that "No one connected with any school of white magic" (1896, 403) would deign to do such a thing. The astonishing idea of creating a double of oneself and sending it out into the world, relaying its sensory impressions back to one's body, is an extreme incarnation of modern technology's ability to create lifelike but lifeless doubles of the human form, wedded to the occult speculations triggered by telegraphy and its descendants.

Mind/Film/Ghost: "Just Like an Old-Time Movie"

Stead's article displays how "cinematic" metaphors became available almost immediately to supernatural discourses. Here, the medium is mined for analogic value, both in terms of the recording and the replaying of reality, that is, the projectability of phantasmic images through the mind's eye into observable reality. Stead does not contend that they are themselves supernatural, but rather places them within the stock of media metaphors that had served spiritualists for a half century. It was also in 1895-6 that Sigmund Freud began to formulate his version of "projection" (Laplanche and Pontalis 1973, 354).[7] In his 1901 *The Psychopathology of Everyday Life*, Freud asserted:

> I believe that a large part of the mythological view of the world, which extends a long way into the most modern religions, is nothing but psychology projected into the external world. The obscure recognition ... of psychical factors and relations in the unconscious is mirrored ... in the construction of a supernatural reality, which is destined to be changed back once more by science into the psychology of the unconscious. (1965, 258-9)

Again, "projection," in all of its many senses, hangs stubbornly around both the supernatural and the mind, here again understood as being, on some level, interchangeable.[8] Of course, to return to Castle, this retreat of the supernatural into the unconscious serves to supernaturalize thought.

One also thinks of that key strand of early film theory that connects cinematic conventions to mental processes. The key example is Hugo Münsterberg:

> [Film] can act as our imagination acts. It has the mobility of our ideas which are not controlled by the physical necessity of outer events but by the psychological laws for the association of ideas. In our mind past and future become intertwined with the present. [Film] obeys the laws of the mind rather than those of the outer world. (1916, 41)

Münsterberg was an anti-spiritualist, though his thinking was somewhat informed by spiritualist ideas (Natale 2010; see also Cooper 2013, 28–38). He would perhaps not have welcomed the comparison, but his theories of cinema materializing the workings of the inner mind work in parallel to contemporaneous supernatural theorizations. In his theories, film becomes just that projected externalization of thought, no less so than Mr Richards's shadow-phantoms, the sympsychograph's mind cats, or Stead's anecdote of "Living Pictures at Will," Madame de Manasseine's brilliant star and the ensouled, projected doubles of theosophist fantasies.

It is no surprise, then, that the co-registration aesthetic of the superimposition effects praised by Camille Flammarion and later lambasted by André Bazin would enter cinema not only to represent ghosts but also memories, dreams, hallucinations and other states of alterity, especially in the silent era.[9] D.W. Griffith's *The Avenging Conscience* (1914) provides a succinct example, where the putative ghost of the murdered uncle—either a "real" ghost or a hallucinatory manifestation of the protagonist's guilt (buoyed by the ghost's visitation to him in bed)—is visualized through double exposures; in the end, the bulk of the film turns out to be a dream. Even in the non-supernatural *Sherlock Jr.* (1924), the dreaming projectionist's entering of the film is preceded by a dislocation of spirit from body that resembles an out-of-body experience and borrows the conventional language of the cinematic ghosts, with the superimposition serving to literalize Münsterberg's logic.

Writes Castle, "By the end of the nineteenth century, ghosts had disappeared from everyday life, but as the poets intimated, human experience had become more ghost-ridden than ever. Through a strange process of rhetorical displacement, thought itself had become phantasmagorical" (1995, 144). The entanglement of the projected image with thought and the supernatural illustrated here is intimately linked to that process, and is clearly not limited to the nineteenth century. In one case from 1976, experimental psychologist Alvin G. Goldstein published an account of his own visual hallucinations, which he described as "[i]n every respect resembl[ing] a Hollywood version of the ghost" (1976, 425). While acknowledging that the hallucination originated in his mind, Goldstein also makes it clear that media conventions of depicting ghosts gave them shape.

A song haunts this discussion: 1970's "If You Could Read My Mind," in which Gordon Lightfoot deploys cinematic haunting imagery from "an old-time movie" to characterize his own troubled inner spaces. It is a song replete with invocations of the cinematic to convey this paradoxical interplay of embodiment and bondage, insubstantiality and invisibility, within mental space. In his mind, the singer is a ghost, bound in a gothic fortress from an old-time movie, needing to be set free but cannot be so long as the (presumably female) addressee of the song cannot truly see him ("I'm a ghost you can't see"); this image, drawn from an "old-time movie," characterizes his essential vulnerability and, presumably, his consequential emotional unavailability. The scenario the song describes echoes Plato's Cave, itself famously linked to both cinema and mental space by Jean-Louis Baudry (1974–5, 42),[10] except the singer is not the one doing the looking. Rather, he needs to be seen but cannot be. The lyrics evoke those narratives of ghosts desperate to be put to rest, going back at least to Pliny the Younger's tale of the Greek philosopher Athenodorus's investigation of a ghost that stalked an Athenian house "with fetters on his legs and chains on his wrists" (2006, 182). "If You Could Read My Mind" is a relationship song, certainly, but the metaphors it deploys unobtrusively tap into a triad with considerable lineage: cinema (or the projected image more broadly), the ghost and the inner spaces of the mind.

I will conclude with a much later example I have explored before (Leeder 2012), from *Stir of Echoes* (1999), a film made long after the general obsolescence of the double-exposure aesthetic, to illustrate the persistence of the triadic link between cinema, mental spaces and the supernatural. As a party trick, Tom Witzky (Kevin Bacon) agrees to be hypnotized by his sister-in-law Lisa (Illeana Douglas). She says, "Close your eyes," and we see a wipe effect approximate the closing of his eyes. What follows is a rare dream/hallucination sequence to play out entirely in point-of-view, the way dreams generally do. The audience explicitly shares Tom's perspective, but not his vision per se, since his eyes are closed; it is more the case that we are invited to share the gaze of his mind's eye. For a time, the screen is black. We hear Lisa's sonorous voice: "Now, just listen for a moment. Listen to the sounds of the room around you." Her voice dictates what appears in Tom's imagination *and* the film's imagetrack. She instructs him "Now, I want you to pretend you're in a theatre." The lights come up on a bare proscenium, seen from the audience with eight or nine other spectators present. She clarifies, "A movie theatre," and a huge screen momentously rolls down in front of the stage. "You're the only one there," she says, and the rest of the audience fade away. She says, "It's one of those great old movie palaces," and the bare white screen is replaced by opulent red curtains. "You look around," Lisa says. "It's a huge empty theatre." The camera tracks rapidly backwards in mid air—a movement that is impossible for the human body, but possible for the camera's eye, for a dreamer unpinned from a physical body, or for a ghost. Lisa says that the walls and chairs are covered in black, and blackness crawls down them, wiping out the redness.

"In the whole, pitch black theatre," she says as the camera's gaze again points to the screen, "there's only one thing you can see, and that's the white screen." The light appears, flickering and roiling, and she notes the presence of letters on the screen, black and indistinct. "You begin to drift closer to them in your chair," she says, and the camera does so, until it seems like it must be hovering in the middle of the theatre (an image we later see visualized in one of Tom's flashbacks). The letters remain hazy until (Tom's) screen fills (our) screen, and Lisa commands them into focus: "The letters spell 'SLEEP.'" She repeats, "Sleep ..." and the screen returns to blackness. What follows are two quick, nightmarish flashes, not from his memory, but that of Samantha (Jennifer Morrison), the murdered girl whose spirit occupies his house. Later in the film Tom receives a vision of her death; both images are finally revealed as point-of-view shots from Samantha's perspective.

Throughout the rest of the film, Samantha invisibly haunts not only Tom's house but also his mind, as a consequence of this hypnotic trip into the movie theatre—the Phantasmagoria—of imagination. This is represented later in the film when Lisa re-hypnotizes Tom and he sees Samantha as a faceless figure sitting in this supposed vacant movie palace of the mind, an ideal visualization of the haunted space of the modern mind. She is there, inexorably, despite Lisa's insistence that he is alone in his mindspace. Despite gender-swapping the hypnotizing in-law, the initial hypnotism sequence plays much as it does in Richard Matheson's source novel *A Stir of Echoes* (1958), except that there, the hypnotic space *is* a proscenium theatre. The film effectively restages the sequence reflexively, in a cinema within cinema, and evokes a whole set of powerful associations in the process.

I have suggested that early cinema's supernatural affinities are as attributable to continuities with older media as much as to its newness and novelty. These continuities stretch forward to this day. The discourse around "oldness" (Lightfoot's "old-time movie," *Stir of Echoes*'s picture palace) localizes cinema's ghostliness in older forms and styles; in novels like Theodore Roszak's *Flicker* (1991), Ramsay Campbell's *Ancient Images* (1989) and Gemma Files's *Experimental Film* (2015), as well as films like *John Carpenter's Cigarette Burns* (2005), *Sinister* (2012), *Playback* (2012), *The Canal* (2014) and *The Quiet Ones* (2014), older films and film formats prove to be figurative or literal repositories of supernatural power or gateways to alternate worlds. Perhaps old movies, old movie theatres and even older media forms help to inspire more reflection on the triadic relationship between the mind, the supernatural and projected light. This makes sense if it is truly the case that, as Alice Rayner writes, "[t]echnology has provided the means to make ghosts an ordinary part of consumer culture but in doing so has familiarized and inured the culture against the absences and losses that the medium projects ..." (2006, 157). But just as the supernatural affinities of early cinema cannot be explained only through its novelty value, so too the ghost's purported domestication fails to explain its enduring appeal and uncanny power. So long as our minds remain haunted, one ventures to say, we will continue projecting our ghosts, onto our screens or elsewhere.

Notes

1. So began Bulwer-Lytton's 1830 novel *Paul Clifford*.
2. See also Knight (2006). I explore the connections between Bulwer-Lytton's story and Richard Matheson's novel *Hell House* (1971) and its adaptation *The Legend of Hell House* (1973) in Leeder (2014).
3. All citations here are from the longer version of the story. For information on the two versions, see Wyse (2004, esp. 33–4, 55–7).
4. These experiments inspired Kōji Suzuki's 1991 novel *Ring* and its various adaptations (*Ring/Ringu* [1998], *The Ring Virus* [1999], *The Ring* [2002]). See Enns (2010).
5. See Raude (2004), Blanco (2010).
6. Stead also includes a section on experiments in photographing thought conducted by the French occultist Hippolyte Baraduc, as clarified by the British theosophist Annie Besant.
7. Laplanche and Pontalis identify a sense of projection "comparable to the cinematic one: The subject sends out into the external world an image of something that exists in him in an unconscious way" (1973, 354).

8. For more on the relationship of psychoanalysis to the supernatural, see Gay (1989, 105–30), Luckhurst (1999), Thurschwell (2001, esp. 115–50), Burdett (2014).
9. The same aesthetic can be applied to heavenly beings, including the apparitional Jesus at the climax of *The Birth of a Nation* (1915). See Maciak (2012).
10. See also Andersen (2014).

Worked Cited

Andersen, Nathan. *Shadow Philosophy: Plato's Cave and Cinema*. Abingdon: Routledge, 2014.

[Anon.] "Rontgen's Vindication of Reichenbach." *Borderland* 4:1 (January 1897): 35–6.

Baudry, Jean-Louis. "Ideological Effects of the Basic Cinematographic Apparatus." *Film Quarterly* 28.2 (Winter 1974–5): 39–47.

Blanco, María del Pilar. "The Haunting of the Everyday in the Thoughtographs of Ted Serios," in *Popular Ghosts: The Haunted Spaces of Everyday Culture*. Eds. María del Pilar Blanco and Esther Peeren. New York: Continuum, 2010. 253–67.

Borden, Amy E. "Corporeal Permeability and Shadow Pictures: Reconsidering *Uncle Josh at the Moving Picture Show* (1902)." *Beyond the Screen: Institutions, Networks and Publics of Early Cinema*. Eds. Maria Braun, Charlie Keil, Rob King, Paul Moore and Louis Pelletier. New Barnett, Herts: John Libbey, 2012. 168–75.

Burdett, Carolyn. "Modernity, the Occult, and Psychoanalysis." *A Concise Companion to Psychoanalysis, Literature, and Culture*. Eds. Laura Marcus and Ankhi Mukherjee. Chichester: John Wiley & Sons, 2014. 49–65.

Bulwer-Lytton, Edward. "The Haunted and the Haunters, or The House and the Brain." *The Caxtons; Zicci; The Haunted and the Haunters, or The House and the Brain*. Boston: Aldine Book Publishing, 1980.

Castle, Terry. *The Female Thermometer: Eighteenth-century Culture and the Invention of the Uncanny*. New York: Oxford University Press, 1995.

Cooper, Sarah. *The Soul of Film Theory*. Houndmills, Basingstoke, Hants: Palgrave McMillan, 2013.

Enns, Anthony. "The Horror of Media: Technology and Spirituality in the Ringu Films." *The Scary Screen: Media Anxiety in* The Ring. Ed. Kristen Lacefield. Farnham, Surrey: Ashgate, 2010. 29–44.

Freud, Sigmund. *The Psychopathology of Everyday Life*. New York: Norton, 1965.

Gay, Volney Patrick. *Understanding the Occult: Fragmentation and Repair of the Self*. Philadelphia: Fortress Press, 1989.

Goldstein, Alvin G. "Hallucinatory Experience: A Personal Account." *Journal of Abnormal Psychology* 85:4 (1976): 423–9.

Gorky, Maxim. "A review of the Lumière programme at the Nizhni-Novgorod Fair," as printed in the Nizhegorodski listok, newspaper, July 4, 1896, and signed "I.M. Pacatus." Appendix 3 to Jay Leyda, *A History of the Russian and Soviet Film*. London: Unwin House, 1960. 407–9.

Jordan, David Starr. *The Days of a Man: Being Memories of a Naturalist, Teacher and Minor Prophet of Democracy*. New York: World Book Company, 1922.

Jordan, David Starr. "The Sympsychograph: A Study in Expressionist Physics." *Appleton's Popular Science Monthly* 49 (Sept. 1896): 597–602.

Knight, Mark. "'The Haunted and the Haunters': Bulwer Lytton's Philosophical Ghost Story." *Nineteenth-Century Contexts* 28:3 (September 2006): 245–55.

Laplanche, Jean and Jean-Bertrand Pontalis, *The Language of Psychoanalysis*. New York: Norton, 1973.

Leeder, Murray. "Ghost-seeing and Detection in *Stir of Echoes*." *Clues: A Journal of Detection* 30.2 (2012): 81–2.

Leeder, Murray. "Victorian Science and Spiritualism in *The Legend of Hell House*." *Horror Studies* 5.3. (2014): 31–46.

Luckhurst, Roger. "'Something Tremendous, Something Elemental': On the Ghostly Origins of Psychoanalysis." *Ghosts: Deconstruction, Psychoanalysis, History*. Eds. Peter Buse and Andrew Stott. New York: St. Martin's Press, 1999. 50–71.

Maciak, Phillip. "Spectacular Realism: The Ghost of Jesus Christ in D.W. Griffith's Vision of History." *Adaptation* 5.2 (2012): 219–40.

Matheson, Richard. *A Stir of Echoes*. New York: Tor, 1958.

McCorristine, Shane. *Specters of the Self: Thinking about Ghosts and Ghost-seeing in England, 1750–1920*. Cambridge: Cambridge University Press, 2010.

Milbank, Alison. "The Victorian Gothic in English Novels and Stories, 1830–1880." *The Cambridge Companion to Gothic Fiction*. Ed. Jerrold E. Hogle. Cambridge: Cambridge University Press, 2002. 145–65.

Münsterberg, Hugo. *The Photoplay: A Psychological Study*. New York: D. Appleton and Company, 1916.

Natale, Simone. "Spiritualism Exposed: Scepticism, Credulity and Spectatorship in End-of-the-century America." *European Journal of American Culture* 29.2 (2010), 131–144.

Nead, Lynda. *The Haunted Gallery: Painting, Photography, Film c. 1900*. New Haven: Yale University Press, 2007.

Pliny the Younger. *Complete Letters*. Oxford: Oxford University Press, 2006.

Raude, Stephen. "The Thoughtographs of Ted Serios." *The Perfect Medium: Photography and the Occult*. Eds. Clément Chéroux, Andreas Fischer, Pierre

Apraxine, Denis Canguilhem and Sophie Schmit. New Haven: Yale University Press, 2004. 155–7.

Rayner, Alice. *Ghosts: Death's Double and the Phenomena of Theatre*. Minneapolis: University of Minnesota Press, 2006.

Stead, W.T. "Suggestions from Science for Psychic Students: Useful Analogies from Recent Discoveries and Inventions." *Borderland* 3.4 (October 1896): 400–11.

Thurschwell, Pamela. *Literature, Technology and Magical Thinking, 1880–1920*. Cambridge: Cambridge University Press, 2001.

van Schlun, Betsy. *Science and Imagination: Mesmerism, Media and the Mind in Nineteenth-Century English and American Literature*. Berlin: Galda + Wilch Verlag, 2007.

Wyse, Bruce. "Mesmeric Machinery, Textual Production and Simulacra in Bulwer-Lytton's 'The Haunted and the Haunters; or, The House and the Brain.'" *Victorian Review* 30.2 (2004): 32–57.

CHAPTER 8

Conclusion: Lost Worlds, Ghost Worlds

Peter Bradshaw began a 2014 review in *The Guardian* of a programme of century-old films (*A Night at the Cinema in 1914*, assembled by Bryony Dixon and released by the British Film Institute) by describing it as, "more like a séance than anything else: an eerie summoning of ghosts from the early days of cinema and the twentieth century" (Bradshaw 2014, n.p.). Bradshaw describes newsreel footage of Archduke Ferdinand's family, the Germans' invasion of Louvain and British feminist Emmeline Pankhurst, as well the Florence Turner comedy *Daisy Doodad's Dial* (1914) and an early Charlie Chaplin film where he lights a cigarette with a gun (characterized by Bradshaw as "the explosive birth of the modern" [2014, n.p.]). Like Gorky close to 120 years earlier, he is watching material devoid of supernatural subject matter, but draws upon supernatural analogies to characterize it all the same: the headline describes "Ghosts from the Early Days of Film." Another review in *The Guardian*, by Jonathan Romney, adopted similar language, describing "haunting glimpses of a long-lost world" (2014, n.p.).

Nonetheless, there is a distinction to be drawn between Gorky's reaction and Bradshaw's insofar as Bradshaw is responding to the pastness of these images (even the "birth of the modern" is a distantly removed concept in our postmodern epoch). Bradshaw draws on the séance metaphor for these century-old images because they are old, unfathomably old—seemingly older than films should be. In his 1946 *The Theory of Film*, Béla Balázs wondered "Why are old films funny?" (1970, 36), arguing that outdated modes of cinema have not yet aged into being considered the product of a bygone age, so they register as comically deficient rather than as a product of history. Times have changed, however, and now these images from early cinema (and hardly the earliest, it must be said) produce uncanny effects because they seem to be speaking to the viewer across a gulf of time. Like a ghost, they are both too departed and too present, something that ought to be lost but remains nonetheless. Bradshaw characterizes *A Night at the Cinema in 1914* as a "fascinating archival experience, though finally a little necrophiliac and claustrophobic" (2014, n.p.)—airless as a tomb (or an archive), and as lively as sex with a corpse.

One question this book has largely deferred is "Why now?" What is it about recent decades that has facilitated the rise of the spectral turn, and the public interest in the supernatural and its relationship to cinema and other media of projection? It could be said, following Laura Mulvey and others, that the commercialization of the internet and the accompanying rise of the digital have confronted us with a new spectral force that inspires reflection on the newness of media that are now old. Martin Jay argues that our times have seen the uncanny becoming paradoxically domesticated, and makes an example of the use of digital imagery of the famous dead "to sell soft drinks and shake the hand of Forrest Gump" (1998, 163).[1] It certainly appears that the cycle of magic-themed films of the twenty-first century, including *The Prestige* (2006), *The Illusionist* (2006) and *Hugo* (2011),[2] which play reflexively with a real or imagined version of early cinema's spectrality and its impact on its audience, are at least in part a response to the advent of the digital.

Also relevant, I would suggest, is a postmodern rethinking of the idea of the archive. We certainly need not select one exclusive explanation (indeed, Colin Williamson [2015] notes a profound "archivist's ethos" in the above-mentioned cycle). The idea of archives as neutral spaces that store the past indiscriminately has declined in favour of the interrogation of the power they wield over history, memory and identity.[3] One fact to which any scholar of silent cinema can attest is that film archives are maddeningly incomplete, haunted, as it were, by their gaps, like the bulk of George Albert Smith's trick films.[4] Further, the films we do have are often accessible only in reconstructed, altered, incomplete and inadequate forms; as Charles Musser has noted, "Often 'restorations' create synthetic texts that have no historical standing—mishmashes of variant prints that obscure as much as they illuminate" (2004, 102). And finally, as Bradshaw seems to observe of *A Night at the Cinema in 1914*, to experience such films is often to experience them as archival products, rather than as "living" texts. Early cinema is itself apparitional.

One example perfectly exemplifies how the ghostly character of early cinema manifests through the archive's gaps. The three-part 2006 BBC documentary *The Lost World of Mitchell & Kenyon* chronicles the rediscovery of 826 films made by Edwardian filmmakers Sagar Mitchell and James Kenyon, a near-miraculous event that has been estimated to have increased the British Film Institute's collection of silent films by somewhere between 20 and 25 % (Carroll 2006, 55).[5] Much of the documentary concerns modern English people watching films of their ancestors, footage of vanished locations, as well as long-forgotten parades, sports events and other public spectacles. There is almost a mediumistic quality to these mediatized communions with their long-departed forebears and the vanished Edwardian world. Frequently, we are shown how print records, family photos and other documents give names, identities and backstories to the persons recorded by Mitchell and Kenyon's camera, and understand that these tokens of history in turn become more meaningful when coupled with the cinematic records. The documentary thus emphasizes the restoration of lost continuities as the archive's project.

But one intriguing moment in the first episode shifts the focus onto noncontinuity and the archive's ghosts. We see presenter Dan Cruickshank sitting in an editing suite watching one of Mitchell and Kenyon's many street actualities, an image crowded with men leaving work. He notes the appearance of a smartly dressed young girl looking at the camera. She walks directly towards the camera: "Startling, eerie," says Cruickshank as the film slowly advances, and with it the girl. Her grey silent stare is indeed unnerving, even when the film is played back at the original speed, and her slow walk forward is of the ghost girl Sadako emerging from the television set in Hideo Nakata's *Ring* (1998). The image is full of the uncanny potential of the "Kingdom of Shadows" … all the more so for the knowledge that, whoever this girl is, she is long dead.[6] If the other cinematic subjects emphasized in the documentary seem more alive on account of their presence on celluloid, this girl somehow seems *more* dead. "Sadly," Cruickshank's narration tells us, "we weren't able to find anything out about the little girl" (Image 8.1).

The sombre moment hangs over the rest of the documentary, for it reminds us of the archive's limitations. The girl exists now, we understand, merely as a shadow on film, metonymically standing in for all that is lost to collective memory. Even as *The Lost World of Mitchell & Kenyon* focuses

Image 8.1 The face of loss: from *The Lost World of Mitchell and Kenyon* (BBC, Episode 1, 2005)

on continuity and restoration, its project is still haunted by its own gaps and absences, as any attempt at reconstructing cinema's own fragmentary early history is likely to be. As Nathan Carroll writes, "Maybe what we are archiving here is a narrative sum total of lost times: accumulations of differentiated film fragments digitally assembled into narrative wholes, whose coalesced remnants map resemblance to the memory of an ever-present 'lost world'" (2006, 62). Or "ghost world."

A recent project by Guy Maddin exists at the juncture of the internet's spectral potential and the archive's fragments. Maddin's modus operandi throughout his career has been to revive defunct cinematic styles from the silent and early sound eras, and he has proved perhaps the director most consistently obsessed with ghosts and the supernatural. Often these have been ghosts of a very personal kind, from the paternal revenant of *The Dead Father* (1985) to the phantasmagorial childhood city of *My Winnipeg* (2007), with many a spectre in between (see Wershler 2010, esp. 103–16; Beard 2010, esp. 331–3). This later phase of Maddin's career moves the theme of the ghost on to less personal terrain, refocusing on what was always an implicit theme of his work: the history of cinema as a ghostly world of loss. Maddin does not believe in ghosts, but regards them:

> as memories. Hamlet's father's ghost in the play is some sort of really extra-felt memory of the father ... so strongly felt that even guards are seeing him, not just the son. And so, when trying to put on the screen my own desires to see these lost films, it's a kind of a wishful thinking strong enough to not only see ghosts but to actually make them happen. Kind of like what a lot of mediums who ended up as charlatans but probably started out as strongly desirous of making contact with real spirits. (Leeder 2015, n.p.)

Thus Maddin sees the spirits of these lost films as bodiless memories waiting for new incarnations, and himself as the medium/charlatan to do it. Beginning as a set of gallery exhibits called *Hauntings*, Maddin has focused on the remaking (for lack of a better term) of lost films, and even unmade films—a response to the fragmentation of the archive that only reinforces its incompleteness. As Maddin told interviewer Craig Hubert:

> it occurred to me to make contact with the spirits of lost films, these films of no known final resting place, these unhappy souls doomed to wander the landscape of film history unable to project themselves. I thought I could put a bunch of actors into trances and invite the spirit of a lost film to possess, compel them to act out a long forgotten plot and shoot them as a spirit photographer and make my own versions of these lost movies. (Hubert 2015, n.p.)

These range from films by well-known directors like F.W. Murnau (the 1920 *Dr. Jekyll and Mr. Hyde* adaptation *Der Janus-Kopf*), Alfred Hitchcock (the abandoned *Psycho* [1960] follow-up *The Blind Man*), Erich von Stroheim, Ernst Lubitsch, Jean Vigo and Kenji Mizoguchi to far more obscure lost films (including the Hungarian film *Drakula halála* [1921], which predated *Nosferatu* as the first film featuring Count Dracula).[7] These were shot in public space at the Pompidou Centre in Paris and the PHI Centre in Montréal, with Maddin holding séances at the beginning of each workday, meant to half-sincerely conjure the spirits of lost films. Says Maddin:

> It was at a weird hour. It was never at midnight or when it was dark out. It was at the start of a workday. Sometimes as late as noon. We would lower the lights on the set and just calm the actors, try to put them all in the same state of mind just by listening to my voice ... I would just calm them, get them

ready for the day's performance, get them to open up, open to receive the will of the long lost narratives. They're also just opening themselves up to my will and also to just the possibility, all the sorts of possibilities that actors are always in contact with when they're at their most open … It's a matter of almost hypnotizing them verbally and then just getting them slowly massaged in the narrative footprints that they'd be following throughout the course of the day. (Leeder 2015, n.p.)

Of interest here is that the ghosts conjured were those of the films themselves, rather than of their makers. The original films remain lost; Maddin's films are copies, fakes, ersatzes, which simultaneously diminish and increase the lostness of their originals.

In cooperation with the National Film Board of Canada and Evan Johnston, this project evolved into the online film generator *Seances*, which debuted in April 2016. The previous year, speaking at the Banff Centre on 22 July 2015, Maddin showed segments of his then-forthcoming film *The Forbidden Room* (2015) and coined the term "ectoplasmovision"—refined to "ekoplasm-o-vision" in an interview a week later (Leeder 2015, n.p.)—to characterize its gauzy aesthetic, which uses digital techniques to suggest the ephemerality of a decaying film strip. While *The Forbidden Room* strings together these lost films into an absurdist, nesting-box like narrative, the online incarnation of *Seances* works differently. When one goes to http://seances.nfb.ca, an instruction reads:

> Touch and hold to conjure.
> Then sit back and relax.
> It's your one chance to see *this* film.

The roiling, shifting title screen that follows presents a series of floating words, changing every few seconds, while an instruction reads "Click and *hold* to watch your film." The virtual space suggests the decay of analogue film and the glitchy instability of digital images (see Olivier 2015). With each change of the protean title, the user is promised a different film. Built using the video rendering program Imposium, *Seances* spawns a unique set of segments, algorithmically programmed to flow logically from one to the next, built out of segments of the dozens of short films shot in Paris and Montréal. Still more complex, however, is Imposium's application of audio-visual effects like datamoshing, sound interruption, sound flowing, rotoscoping and motion tracking to further destabilize every individual film (Pangburn 2016, n.p.). Akin to old TV ghosts, competing images bleed in and bleed out, pixellating and distributing digital noise—all part of the show.

Any individual film created by *Seances* is an unstable object: created, experienced (unpausable, unrewindable, unshareable) and then lost. As the dead are apt to, they manifest in fragmentary and only semi-coherent forms, and here the web interface substitutes for a human medium in this electronic séance. When I asked Maddin if he sees the internet as a haunted space, he replied,

> It seems to be a space no one quite understands. It reminds me a lot of some sort of afterlife: a space that doesn't really seem to exist in the three dimensions that we know, and so it does kind of remind me of that. It seems that we allow and encourage and need the visitations we spend our lifetimes now looking at. So it seems like the proper place. But it also seems like a place where it's promised data will last forever. But we're making films out of lost film material and then promising to lose them again. So we're trying to actually haunt the Internet a bit more than it already is … It's just the promise that the Internet has of storing things forever that almost promises the kind of immortality that an afterlife does, or that's impossible. And so introducing intentional data destruction online intrigues me. (Leeder 2015, n.p.)

Compare David Bordwell's observation that, "Louis Lumière's *La Petite fille et son chat*, a sort of home movie of his daughter teasing the family pet, was made on film in 1900. It is still around to charm us. The YouTube adventures of Maru, a LOLcat superstar, aren't likely to last so long" (2012, 189). If the internet is full of content, it is also full of loss, simultaneously forestalled and promised by the fragility and transience of the digital image.

So, like the internet itself, *Seances* is both endlessly productive and endlessly destructive, promising to be able to create billions of unique films which are then lost, as the bulk of all films have been. It conjures ghostly lost films from earlier eras of cinema only to produce new losses, new ghosts. Doing its own kind of double exposure, it superimposes the haunted spaces of vanished eras of the cinema and their vanished films over the internet, a space brimming with spectral potential of its own that in some ways parallels the ghost worlds of spiritualist rhetoric. In a sense, *Seances* constitutes an artistic exploration of many of the themes of this book, and testifies to the continued vitality of cinema's supernatural affinities as a subject of both scholarship and art.

Notes

1. Sarah Waters's essay "Ghosting the Interface: Cyberspace and Spiritualism" (1997) marks an early example of appealing to nineteenth-century supernatural metaphors to characterize contemporary technological hauntings (see also Batchen 1999, 2002; Sconce 2000; Edwards 2005; van Elferen 2009; Drury 2011, 257–73).
2. One could extend this list to include *Scoop* (2006), *Death Defying Acts* (2007), *Magicians* (2007), *Is Anybody There?* (2008), *The Great Buck Howard* (2008), *L'Illusionniste* (2010), *The Great Burt Wonderstone* (2013), *Now You See Me* (2013), *Magic in the Moonlight* (2014) and so on.
3. See Schwartz and Cook (2002), Freshwater (2003) and Manoff (2004). Note too that the art programme and accompanying book *Ghosting: The Role of the Archive within Contemporary Artists' Film and Video* (2006) takes its title both from "the appearance of an overlapping secondary image on a television or a display screen"—the video-age evolution of double exposures—but also from "'the ghost of acidification', the impact that the ravages of time have on nitrate film" (Lanyon 2006, 3). See also Ross (2013) on the Abraham Lincoln Presidential Library and Museum's use of the digital ghost of Lincoln to "resuscitate lifeless artefacts and [posit] history as a constructionist, adaptive pursuit" (2013, 825).
4. See Usai (2003) for a useful discussion of the archival issues around silent cinema.
5. For more on this collection, see Toulmin (2006) and the collection *The Lost World of Mitchell & Kenyon: Edwardian Britain on Film* (Toulmin et al. 2004).
6. In one of her essays on the collection, Vanessa Toulmin describes how "these dead souls are now forever captured in a celluloid tapestry of smiles, gestures, motion and poetic grace, ghosts of the past who beckon the modern viewer into the dawn of the twentieth century" (2010, n.p.).
7. See Rhodes (2010) for information on *Drakula halála*.

Works Cited

Balázs, Béla. *Theory of the Film: Character and Growth of a New Art*. New York: Dover, 1970.

Batchen, Geoffrey. "Ectoplasm: Photography in the Digital Age." *Over Exposed: Essays on Contemporary Photography*. Ed. Carol Squiers. New York: The New Press, 1999. 9–23.
Batchen, Geoffrey. "Spectres of Cyberspace." *The Visual Culture Reader*. Ed. Nicholas Mirzoefff London: Routledge, 2002. 237–42.
Beard, William. *Into the Past: The Cinema of Guy Maddin*. Toronto: University of Toronto Press, 2010.
Bordwell, David. *Pandora's Digital Box: Films, Files, and the Future of Movies*. Madison, WI: The Irvington Way Institute Press, 2012.
Bradshaw, Peter. "A Night at the Cinema in 1914 Review—Ghosts from the Early Days of Film," *The Guardian*, July 31, 2014 http://www.theguardian.com/film/2014/jul/31/a-night-at-the-cinema-in-1914-review-bfi. Accessed August 18, 2014.
Carroll, Nathan. "Mitchell and Kenyon, Archival Contingency, and the Cultural Production of Historical License." *The Moving Image* 6.2 (2006): 52–76.
Drury, Nevill. *Stealing Fire from Heaven: The Rise of Modern Western Magic*. Oxford: Oxford University Press, 2011.
Edwards, Emily D. *Metaphysical Media: The Occult Experience in Popular Culture*. Carbondale: Southern Illinois University Press, 2005.
Freshwater, Helen. "The Allure of the Archive." *Poetics Today* 24.4 (Winter 2003): 729–758.
Hubert, Craig. "Guy Maddin Hypnotizes Audiences with 'The Forbidden Room.'" *Bloutin Artinfo*. September 22, 2015. http://www.blouinartinfo.com/news/story/1242569/guy-maddin-hypnotizes-audiences-with-the-forbidden-room#. Accessed June 5, 2016.
Jay, Martin. *Cultural Semantics: Keywords of Our Time*. Amherst, University of Massachusetts Press, 1998.
Lanyon, Josephine. "Foreword." *Ghosting: The Role of the Archive within Contemporary Artists' Film and Video*. Eds. Jane Connarty and Josephine Lanyon. Bristol: Picture This, 2006. 3–11.
Leeder, Murray. "Ektoplasm-o-vision! with Guy Maddin." *Luma—Film & Media Art Quarterly* 1.1 (2015): n.p.
Lundemo, Trond. "In the Kingdom of Shadows: Cinematic Movement and Its Digital Ghost." *The YouTube Reader*. Eds. Pelle Snickars and Patrick Vonderau. Stockholm: National Library of Sweden, 2009. 314–29.
Manoff, Marlene. "Theories of the Archive from Across the Disciplines." *portral: Libraries and the Academy* 4.1 (2004): 9–25.
Mulvey, Laura. *Death 24× a Second: Stillness and the Moving Image*. London: Reaktion, 2006.
Musser, Charles. "Historiographic Method and the Study of Early Cinema." *Cinema Journal* 44.1 (Fall 2004): 101–7.

Olivier, Marc. "Glitch Gothic." *Cinematic Ghosts: Haunting and Spectrality from Silent Cinema to the Digital Era.* Ed. Murray Leeder. New York: Bloomsbury, 2015. 253–70.

Pangburn, DJ. "Guy Maddin's 'Seances' Film Gets an Algorithmic Remix." *The Creators Project.* Apr. 19, 2016. thecreatorsproject. vice.com/blog/guy-maddin-seances-film-remix. Accessed June 5, 2016.

Rhodes, Gary D. "*Drakula halála* (1921): The Cinema's First Dracula." *Horror Studies* 1.1 (2010): 25–47.

Romney, Jonathan. "A Night at the Cinema in 1914 Review—haunting glimpses of a long-lost world." *The Guardian.* August 3, 2014 https://www.theguardian.com/film/2014/aug/03/night-at-cinema-1914-review-haunting-glimpses-long-lost-world. Accessed August 18, 2014.

Ross, Ivan. "Digital Ghosts in the History Museum: The Haunting of Today's Mediascape." *Continuum: Journal of Media & Cultural Studies.* 27.6 (2013): 825–36.

Schwartz, Joan M and Terry Cook. "Archives, Records, and Power: The Making of Modern Memory." *Archival Science* 2:1–2 (2002): 1–19.

Sconce, Jeffrey. *Haunted Media: Electronic Presence from Telegraphy to Television.* Durham: Duke University Press, 2000.

Toulmin, Vanessa. *Electric Edwardians: The Story of the Mitchell & Kenyon Collection.* London: British Film Institute, 2006.

Toulmin, Vanessa. "'This is a local film': The Cultural and Social Impact of the Mitchell & Kenyon Film Collection." *The Public Value of the Humanities.* Ed. Jonathan Bate. London: Bloomsbury Academic, 2010. n.p.

Toulmin, Vanessa, Simon Popple and Patrick Russell, eds. *The Lost World of Mitchell & Kenyon: Edwardian Britain on Film.* London: British Film Institute, 2004.

Usai, Paolo Cherchi. *Silent Cinema: An Introduction.* London: BFI, 2003.

van Elferen, Isabella. "Dances with Spectres: Theorising the Cybergothic." *Gothic Studies* 11.1 (2009): 99–112.

Waters, Sarah. "Ghosting the Interface: Cyberspace and Spiritualism." *Science as Culture* 6.33 (1997): 414–43.

Werschler, Darren. *Guy Maddin's My Winnipeg.* Toronto: University of Toronto Press, 2010.

Index

A

Abbott, Stacey, 88, 118
The Abyss (1989), 13n11
Adorno, Theodor, 57
After the Ball (1897), 158, 159
airport scanners, 162
Aladdin and his Wonderful Lamp (1899), 85
Alice (1990), 98
American Society for Psychical Research, 90n14
"apparatus theory", 47, 57–9, 61n17
L'armoires des frères Davenport (1902), 91n20
Army of Darkness (1992), 161
Arnheim, Rudolf, 25
L'arrivée d'un train en gare de La Ciotat (1895), 52
Artaud, Antonin, 10, 23
The Ashpyx (1973), 125n3
The Avenging Conscience (1914), 161, 184

B

Badreux, Jean, 12n3
Balázs, Béla, 10, 24, 191
Baldwin, Samri, 80, 88, 91n17
Barnouw, Erik, 58, 59, 84, 100, 146
Barrett, William, 75, 76
Baudry, Jean-Louis, 57, 61n17, 185
Bazin, André, 98, 125n2, 184
Beckman, Karen, 85, 140, 150, 165n6
Becquerel, Henri, 105
Beloff, John, 68, 76, 89n1
Benjamin, Walter, 57, 61n16
Bergson, Henri, 10
Berman, Marshall, 7–9, 60n5
Berthin, Christine, 26, 27
The Bewitched Inn (1897), 165n12
The Birth of a Nation (1915), 188n9
Bishop, Washington Irving, 72, 73, 76, 78
Blackburn, Douglas, 68, 72–8, 87, 90–1n16, 90n15, 91n24
Blackstone, Gay, 159

Page number followed by 'n' denote footnotes

Blavatsky, Helena, 174
Blow, Mark, 119
Booth, Walter R., 137, 144
Borderland, 1, 71, 100, 101, 126n14, 180
Bordwell, David, 14n14, 89n3, 197
Bourget, Paul, 119
Bradshaw, Peter, 191, 192
Braid, James, 70
Bram Stoker's Dracula (1992), 117, 118
Brewster, David, 49, 50, 53, 57, 58, 60n7, 89n3, 103
Brighton, 11, 67–70, 72–6, 78–80, 123
Broad, C.D., 68
Buguet, Édouard, 216n10
Bulwer-Lytton, Edward
   Paul Clifford (1830), 187n1
   "The Haunted and the Haunters" (1859), 12, 174, 175, 177

C

Cabaret du Néant, 111, 113–18, 120, 127n20, 127n21, 148, 153, 154
The Cabinet of Dr. Caligari (1920), 24
The Camera Fiend (1903), 123
Cameron, James, 13n11
Cameron, Julia Margaret, 102
Campbell, Ramsay
   Ancient Images (1989), 186
The Canal (2014), 187
The Canterville Ghost (1944), 98
Canudo, Ricciotto, 10, 21–3, 36n1, 37n4, 37n6, 85
Carroll, Noël, 14n14, 61n19, 148
Castle, Terry, 5, 51, 52, 60n8, 146, 173
Castle, William, 161, 162
Celebrity Ghost Hunt (2012-present), 90n8
Chaplin, Charlie, 191

Charles of Saxony, Prince, 50
Cholodenko, Alan, 25, 35
Cinderella and the Fairy Godmother (1898), 85
Clair, René, 67
Clarke, Arthur C., 6, 13n11, 104
Coates, James, 105, 107
Cohl, Émile, 120, 137
Commoli, Jean-Louis, 57
Cook, Florence, 150–2
Coppa, Francesca, 159
Coppola, Francis Ford, 117
Corman, Roger, 108
The Corsican Brothers (1900), 86, 91n22, 124
Cousteau, Jacques-Yves, 25
Creery sisters, 75, 76
Crookes, William, 106, 107, 150–3, 155, 166n17
Crosthwaite, C.H.T.
   "Rontgen's Curse", 108
Cruickshank, Dan, 193
Cumberland, Stuart, 73
Curie, Marie and Pierre, 105

D

Daisy Doodad's Dial (1914), 191
D'Alcy, Jehanne, 135, 158–60
D'Alton, Emelie, 159
danse macabre, 11, 53, 135–67
Darnell, Nani, 159
The Dead Father (1985), 194
Dead of Night (1945), 58
Death Defying Acts (2007), 198n2
de Balzac, Honoré, 102
de Chomón, Segundo, 137, 165n12
de Kolta, Buatier, 142, 159
della Porta, Giambattista, 48
de Manasseine, Marie, 182, 184
de Philipstal, Paul, 50
Derrida, Jacques, 3, 26–31, 37n11–13

de Sica, Vittorio, 67
Desperately Seeking Susan (1985), 166n24
Devil, the, 46
Dickens, Charles, 53, 99
Dickson, Antonia, 69
Dickson, W.K.L., 2, 12n5
digital, the, 34, 192, 197, 198n3
Dijkstra, Bram, 154, 155
Dingwall, E.J., 78
Dircks, Henry, 52–5
Dixon, Bryony, 191
The Doctor and the Monkey (1900), 144
Dolar, Mladen, 8
Doyle, Sir Arthur Conan, 60n15, 123, 128n27
Drakula halála (1921), 195, 198n7
Duchamp, Marcel, 10
During, Simon, 7, 8, 48, 59, 72, 87, 88, 91n24

E
Earthbound (1920), 22
Edison Manufacturing Company, 1
Edison, Thomas, 12–13n5, 56, 91n19, 100, 136, 143, 181
Eglinton, William, 90n12
Einosuke, Yokota, 119
Eisenstein, Sergei, 91n18
EIZO, 163, 164
Eliot, T.S., 10
Elliotson, John, 70
Engledue, W.C., 70
Epperson, Gordon, 68
Epstein, Jean, 10, 23
Ernst, Max, 10
The Execution of Mary, Queen of Scots (1895), 136, 143, 144
Ezra, Elizabeth, 138, 141, 165n3

F
Faust and Mephistopheles (1898), 85
Fay, Anna Eva, 72
Files, Gemma
  Experimental Film, 33, 186
Fischer, Lucy, 138, 139
Flammarion, Camille, 21–3, 37n4, 37n5, 51, 54, 106, 107, 184
Ford, John, 67
Freer, Ada Goodrich, 180
Freud, Sigmund, 10, 37n10, 173, 183
Friedberg, Anne, 14n14, 49
Friese-Greene, William, 119
Fukurai, Tomokichi, 179

G
The Gambler's Wife (1899), 85
Gauld, Alan, 68, 79
Ghost Dad (1990), 35, 98
Ghost Dance (1983), 30
Ghost Hunters (2002-present), 90n8
Ghosts (1997), 161
ghost show, 11, 45, 55–7
The Ghost Train (1901), 117
Gillman, Charlotte Perkins
  "The Yellow Wallpaper", 174
Goldstein, Alvin G., 184
Gorky, Maxim, 2, 10, 22, 31–6, 37n14, 38n14, 38n15, 39n18, 153, 174, 175, 191
Gray, Frank, 83, 86–8, 89n1, 89n2, 89n5, 90n11
The Great Buck Howard (2008), 198n2
The Great Burt Wonderstone (2013), 198n2
Green, Tom (Brighton comedian), 123, 124
Griffith, D.W., 35, 161, 184
Griffith, George, 156–8
  "A Photograph of the Invisible", 156

Gunning, Tom, 8, 9, 13n8, 14n14, 29, 33, 35, 46, 58, 59n1–3, 60n8, 61n18, 107, 125n1, 126n8, 126n9
Gurney, Edmund, 46, 68, 74–80, 87, 89n7, 90n7

H
Haggard, H. Rider, 5
Hall, Trevor H., 69, 72, 78, 87, 89n5, 90n7, 152
  The Strange Case of Edmund Gurney (1964), 68, 89n6
The Haunted Castle (1896), 82, 85, 144
The Haunted Hotel (1907), 165n12
The Haunted Picture Gallery (1899), 85
hauntology, 26, 29–31, 36, 37n13
Hawthorne, Nathaniel
  The House with Seven Gables (1851), 99
Heard, Mervyn, 50, 54, 60n8, 86, 146
Heaven Can Wait (1978), 36
Here Comes Mr. Jordan (1941), 98
Herrmann, Adelaide, 159
Herrmann, Alexander, 146
Hertz, Carl, 159
Hitchcock, Alfred, 195
Hope, William, 103, 128n27, 153
Hornung, Ernest, 123
Houdini, Bess, 159
The House of Ghosts (1908), 165n12
House on Haunted Hill (1959), 161, 162
The House that Jack Built (1900), 82
The House Where Evil Dwells (1982), 98
Hugo (2011), 192
Huxley, T.H., 5
hypnotism, 70, 71, 79, 90n10, 186

I
The Illusionist (2006), 192
L'Illusionniste (2010), 198n2
Illustrated Polytechnic Review, 53
The Invisible Woman (1940), 128n26
Is Anybody There? (2008), 198n2
Is Spiritualism a Fraud? (1906), 91n20

J
Jackson, Michael, 161
James, Henry, 5
  The Turn of the Screw (1898), 99, 174
James, William, 75, 79
Der Janus-Kopf (1920), 195
Jason and the Argonauts (1963), 161
Jenkins, Charles Francis, 2, 56
John Carpenter's Cigarette Burns (2005), 187
Johnson, Alice, 78
Johnson, V.E., 5, 6, 10, 119
Johnston, Evan, 196
Jordan, David Starr, 12, 178–80
Jordanova, Ludmilla, 155, 156
Joyce, James, 10

K
Kamuf, Peggy, 26, 37n12
Kardec, Allen, 23
Kellar, Harry, 146
Kenyon, James, 193
kinetoscope, 1, 2, 55, 119, 181
King, Katie (ghost), 150–2, 155
Kircher, Athanasius, 47–50, 57–9, 60n4, 146
A Kiss in the Tunnel (1899), 89n2
Kittler, Friedrich, 145
Klass, Morton, 4

*Körkarlen. See Phantom Chariot, The/
    The Phantom Carriage/Körkarlen
    (1921)*
Kurosawa, Akira, 67

L
Landon, Perceval
  "Thurnley Abbey", 149
Lawrence, D.H., 10
Leadbeater, C.W., 82
Legend of Hell House, The (1973), 187n2
Le Prince, Louis, 34
Leroux, Gaston, 148, 149
  The Phantom of the Opera
    (1909/10), 36, 148, 149, 166n15
Let Me Dream Again (1900), 82
Light, 71, 73, 74, 76
Lightfoot, Gordon, 184, 186
  "If You Could Read My Mind", 184, 185
Limon, John, 13n9
Lodge, Oliver, 75
Lollabrigida, Gina, 67
The Lost World of Mitchell & Kenyon (2006), 193, 198n5
Low, Rachael, 67
Loy, Mina, 10
Lubitsch, Ernst, 195
Luckhurst, Roger, 12n2, 13n10, 26, 28, 33, 70, 73, 75, 165n10, 188n8
Lumière brothers, 2, 12n3, 147

M
MacIntyre, F. Gwynplaine, 158
Mackey, David A., 167n24
Maddin, Guy, 194–7
Magicians (2007), 166n22

Magician's Cavern, The (1901), 144
Magicians: Edmund Gurney and the Brighton Mesmerist, The (1967), 89n6
Magic in the Moonlight (2014), 198n2
magic lantern, 11, 35, 47–50, 52, 59, 60n4, 81, 99, 103, 138, 146
Mangan, Michael, 144
Mannoni, Laurent, 47, 60n8, 146
Mann, Thomas, 107, 108, 126n16, 166n19
  The Magic Mountain (1924), 107
Marey, Étienne-Jules, 97
Margaret, Princess, 67
Marx, Karl, 26, 57, 58
Mary Jane's Mishap (1903), 84, 124
Maskelyne, John Nevil, 72, 73, 166n18
Matheson, Richard
  Hell House (1973), 187n2
  A Stir of Echoes (1958), 186
McCorristine, Shane, 46, 82, 180
McGrath, Roberta, 60n13, 137, 147, 150
Méliès, Georges, 3, 11, 33, 59, 61n18, 82, 87, 88, 91n20, 109, 120, 125n1, 135–67
Merck, Mandy, 36
Merry Frolics of Satan, The (1906), 146
Mesmer, Franz Anton, 69, 90n9
mesmerism, 11, 67–91, 174
Mesmerist and the Country Couple, The (1899), 91n19
Mesmerist, or, Body and Soul, The (1898), 83
Metz, Christian, 57, 61n17
Michelet, Jules, 102
Mitchell, Sagar, 193
Mizoguchi, Kenji, 195
modernity, 7–9, 14n13, 23, 28, 45, 46, 59n2, 117, 143

Monroe, John Warne, 23, 102, 106, 126n8, 126n10
Monster, The (1903), 144
Moore, Alan,
  League of Extraordinary Gentlemen, 127n26
Most Haunted (2002–10), 90n8
Mulvey, Laura, 34, 45, 192
Mumler, William, 103, 126n10, 157
Münsterberg, Hugo, 183, 184
Murnau, F.W., 39, 127n23, 195
Musser, Charles, 47–9, 51, 58, 119, 192
Muybridge, Eadweard, 97, 119
Myers, F.W.H., 46, 74–9, 180
Mystic Swing, The (1900), 164n2
My Winnipeg (2007), 194

N
Narboni, Paul, 57
natural magic, 11, 45–61
Nead, Lynda, 33, 85, 86, 140, 158, 181
nensha, 125n7, 179
Nicol, Fraser, 68, 79, 80, 90n16
Nightmare Before Christmas, The (1993), 161
Niven, Larry, 6
Nosferatu (1922), 24, 39n12, 88, 127n23, 195
Now You. See Me (2013), 198n2

O
occultism, 4, 10, 105
Ogier, Pascale, 30, 31
Olivier, Laurence, 67, 196
Oppenheim, Janet, 68, 76

P
Paley, William, 119, 127n24
Pankhurst, Christabel, 160
Pankhurst, Emmeline, 191
Pankhurst, Sylvia, 160
Partie de Cartes (1895), 32
Paul, R.W., 91n20, 119, 136
Peeping Tom (1960), 123
Peirce, Charles Sanders, 75, 90n13
Pepper, John Henry, 53–6, 58, 91n22, 116, 117, 125n4, 147
Pepper's Ghost, 11, 45, 53–6, 58, 91n22, 116, 117, 125n4, 147
Perez, Gilberto, 25
Persona (1966), 161
phantasmagoria, 11, 45, 49–53, 57, 58, 60n8, 100, 111, 146, 173, 186, 194
Phantom Chariot, The/The Phantom Carriage/Körkarlen (1921), 22, 37n3
phantoscope (projector), 2, 56–9
philosophical toys, 52, 56
photogénie, 21, 23, 24
Photographing a Ghost (1898), 84
Piper, Leonora, 79, 88
Plait, Phil, 164
Playback (2012), 187
Pliny the Younger, 185
Porter, Edwin S., 137, 164n2, 165n12
Le portrait spirituel (1903), 91n20
Pound, Ezra, 10
Prestige, The (2006), 192
Prolific Magical Egg, The (1902), 165n9, 165n11
Psycho (1960), 195
Pushkin, Alexander, 34

Q
Quiet Ones, The (2014), 187

R
Raia-Grean, Courtenay, 107, 152
Raven, The (1915), 161

Rayner, Alice, 187
Les Rayons Röntgen/A Novice at X-Rays (1898), 109, 112, 120, 165n11
Redfern, Jasper, 119
Rêve et Réalité (1901), 82
Ring/Ringu (1998), 187n4, 193
Ring, The (2002), 187n4
Ring Virus, The (1999), 187n4
Robert, Étienne-Gaspard, 50
Robert-Houdin, Jean-Eugène, 73, 109, 136, 141–3, 159, 165n7
Roderick, King, 6
Romney, Jonathan, 191
Röntgen, William Conrad, 99, 100, 103–6, 108, 117–20, 122, 127n18, 148, 153, 156, 178–80
Roszak, Theodore
 Flicker (1991), 186
Royal Polytechnic Institution, 53

S
Sadoul, Georges, 67, 84, 89n3
Santa Claus (1898), 83
Schivelbusch, Wolfgang, 8
Schröpfer, Johann, 50
Schwartz, Louis-Georges, 30, 31
Sconce, Jeffrey, 6, 7, 12n1, 198n1
Scoop (2006), 198
Seances (2016), 196, 197
Selbit, P.T., 160
Serios, Ted, 179
Shaviro, Steven, 29
Sherlock Jr. (1924), 184
Showalter, Elaine, 150
Shutter (2004), 125n3
Singer, Ben, 9, 14n14, 23, 143, 185
Sinister (2012), 187
Sjöström, Victor, 37n3
Skeleton Dance, The (1929), 161
skeletons, 11, 12, 51, 53, 100, 107–9, 114, 115, 117, 118, 120, 121, 123, 124, 135–67
Smith, George Albert, 3, 11, 67–91, 97, 121, 192
Smith, Laura Eugenia, 81
Society for Psychical Research (SPR), 11, 46, 67, 68, 73–83, 87–9, 90n11, 90n12, 90n14, 91n16, 107, 147
Solomon, Matthew, 12n5, 14n12, 69, 88, 125n1, 141, 142, 164n1, 164n3, 165n6
spectral turn, 3, 10, 11, 21, 25–9, 35, 192
spiritism, 21–3, 37n4
spirit photography, 11, 68, 69, 82, 84, 97–128
spiritualism, 4, 5, 10, 12n1, 12n5, 24, 27, 54, 55, 69, 72, 75, 84, 88, 101, 109, 125n1, 125n6, 147, 166n18, 174, 180, 198n1
Le Squelette joyeux (1897), 147
Startled Lover, The (1899), 165n4
Star Trek (1966-9), 13n11
Stead, W.T., 1, 2, 10, 12, 12n2, 106, 107, 180–3, 187n6
Stevenson, Robert Louis, 5
Stewart, Balfour, 75
Stewart, Garrett, 127n22, 160
Stir of Echoes (1999), 185
Stoker, Bram, 5, 117, 118
 Dracula, 117, 118
supernatural, 1–12, 12n5, 13n8, 21–9, 31, 33–6, 37n2, 38n12, 45, 46, 48–52, 55, 56, 58, 59n3, 60n8, 67–70, 73, 75, 79–82, 84–8, 97–108, 118, 122–4, 144, 148, 173, 174, 176–8, 182–7, 191, 192, 194, 197, 198n1
 definition, 4
Swingewood, Alan, 7
Sword, Helen, 10, 27

T

Ten Ladies in One Umbrella (1903), 166n23
Testament of Dr. Mabuse, The (1933), 83–4
These Amazing Shadows (2011), 175
13 Ghosts (1960), 161, 162
This Way Out (2008), 161
Thompson, Silvanus, 99
Thor (2011), 13n11
Thornton, E.H., 98–9
Thriller (1983), 161
Thurschwell, Pamela, 3, 28, 76, 90n10, 90n12, 188n8
Tingler, The (1959), 162
Todorov, Tzvetan, 59n3, 174
Topper (1937), 128n26
Tsivian, Yuri, 33–5, 104, 109, 125n5, 153, 165n9
Turvey, Malcolm, 14n14, 24
Tyler, Parker, 24–5
Tyndall, John, 5

U

Uncle Boonmee Who Can Recall His Past Lives (2010), 98
Uncle Josh at the Moving Picture Show (1902), 33
Uncle Josh in a Spooky Hotel (1900), 165n12
Undressing Extraordinary (1901), 144–5
Un ragno nel cervello (1912), 120

V

Vampyr (1932), 161
Vanishing Lady/Escamotage d'une dame chez théâtre Robert Houdin, The (1896), 11, 136–44, 147, 149, 150, 155, 156, 158–60, 163, 164, 164n2
A Victorian Lady in Her Boudoir (1896), 158
Vigo, Jean, 195
A Visit to the Spiritualist (1899), 91n20
von Keller, Albert, 155
von Reichenbach, Karl, 106, 179
von Stroheim, Erich, 195
von Uchatius, Franz, 181

W

Warner, Marina, 8, 46
Warning Shadows (1923), 52, 60n9
Waters, Sarah, 198n1
Weber, Max, 8, 30, 48, 60n5
Wells, Fred (Brighton baker), 71, 79
Wells, H.G., 5, 127n26
 Invisible Man. The (1897), 85, 122
Whissel, Kristen, 143
Wilde, Oscar, 5
Williams, Linda, 139–40
Williams, Randall, 55
Winter, Alison, 70
Wizard of Gore, The (1970), 166n24
Wizard, the Prince and the Fairy, The (1900), 144
Wollen, Peter, 25
Wood, Gaby, 142–3
Woolf, Virginia, 10
World Without Sun (1964), 25

X

X-Ray Fiend, The (1897), 83, 89, 119–24, 144, 153, 158, 163
X-Ray Glasses/Les lunettes féerique, The (1909), 120
X-Ray Mirror, The (1899), 120

X-rays, 1, 7, 11, 12, 97–128, 137, 138, 142, 144, 148, 150, 153, 155–8, 160, 162–4, 166n19, 167n26, 175, 178–80
X: The Man with X-Ray Eyes (1963), 108

Z
Zecca, Ferdinand, 82
Zevon, Warren, 167n24
Zola, Émile, 120

The manufacturer's authorised representative in the EU is Springer Nature Customer Service Centre GmbH, Europaplatz 3, 69115 Heidelberg, Germany. If you have any concerns regarding our products, please contact ProductSafety@springernature.com

Printed and bound by CPI Group (UK) Ltd, Croydon, CR0 4YY
23/03/2026
02076734-0001